TUMBLEWEED

Tumbleweed

Rites and Wrongs of Passage in a Texas Town

Jeff Mudd

Published in 2000 by Southpaw Books.
Reissued, November 2012

Reissued April, 2026.

ISBN 978-0967918402

Muddbooks.com

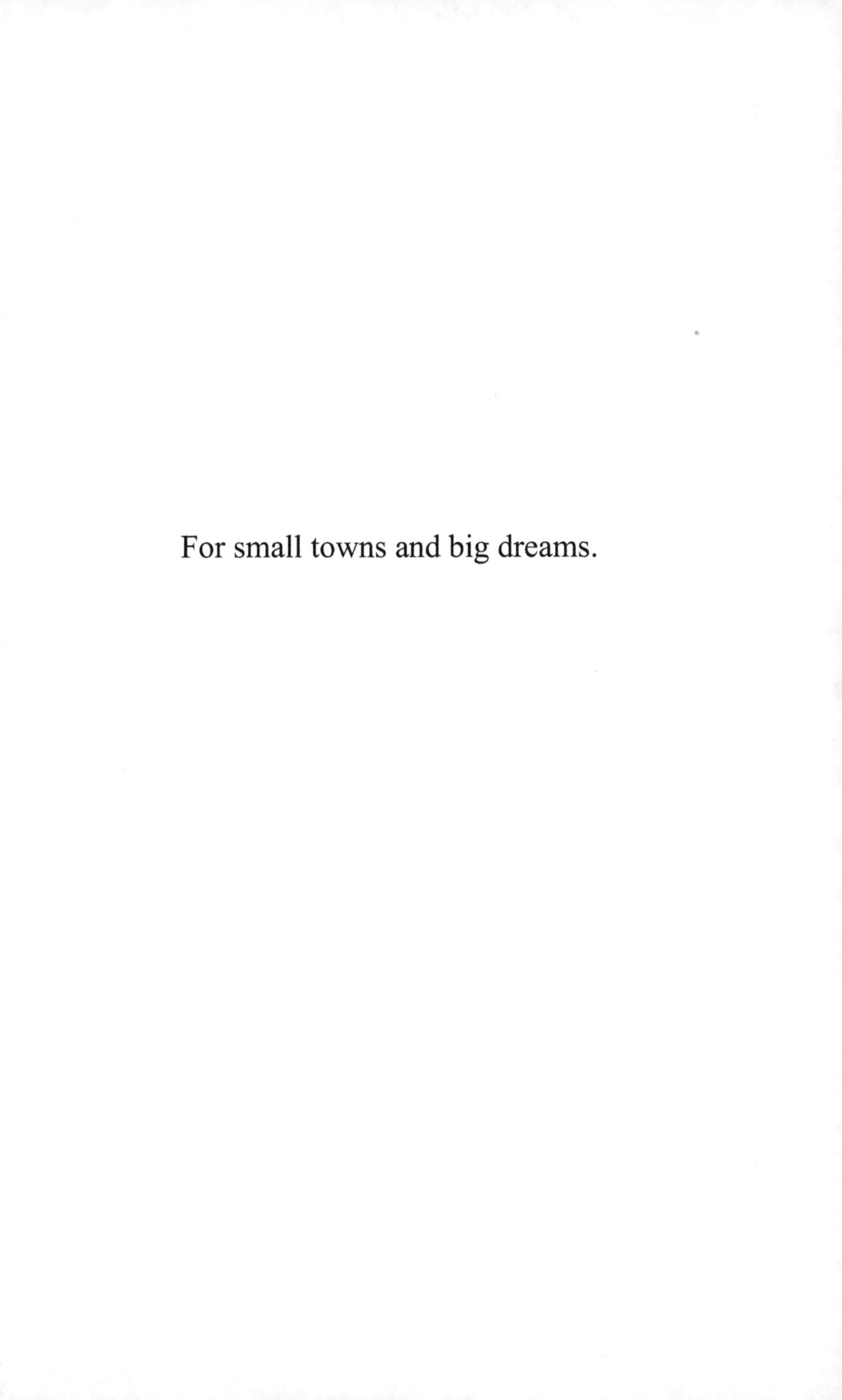

For small towns and big dreams.

Foreword

I remember sitting down to write *Tumbleweed* in 1998. I was twenty-nine, engaged to be married, living in a duplex, working as a sports editor at a small newspaper, staring at a blueberry iMac and a blinking cursor that felt like it knew more about my future than I did.

I was confident in my writing. Confident in my bride-to-be. Less so about everything else.

I wrote in spurts, pulling from memories—people, places, moments from growing up in Odessa. I changed the town's name to Midtex, adjusted a few details, protected the guilty. Some chapters stretched into two. Memories came flooding back, Others showed up out of nowhere. I worked around game coverage, deadlines, and a new puppy that had no regard for the creative process or new carpeting..

Somewhere along the way, it became a book.

A few months later, a small publishing company picked it up, and I waited for my first shipment. When the boxes finally arrived, I was out of town. They sat in my driveway in the middle of a rainstorm—my debut novel, soaked before I ever held a copy.

Life moved the way it does. The iMac didn't last. The marriage didn't either. But a lot did. I've got three great kids—McKenzie, McCoy, and Mitch—and a writing life that found its way back to me after some time away.

Since then, I've written a dozen books set across Texas. Some are funny. Others lean nostalgic. A few carry a little more weight. I've revisited Odessa along the way with *McCoy's Diner* and *Yearbook*, and I still find myself back there once or twice a year, in the same house I grew up in, sleeping in the same bed. Despite a few tweaks around the edges, not much in Odessa has changed—and there's something comforting in that. Home has a way of staying put, even when the rest of life doesn't.

I came back to *Tumbleweed* as my fortieth reunion at Permian High approached. It holds up better than I expected. Sure, it's wordy as hell and pretty corny in spots. I clearly had a lot to say, a lazy editor, a shitload of coffee, and a puppy scratching to go pee.

I don't know. I mentioned I was young.

I did my best.

But it's honest. It's tries like hell. Has some wit and heart. It's working to figure things out.

I'd like to think, all these years later, I am too.

Midtex

They laughed. Then again, they usually did.

It was my first day of school at Bubba T. Downing Elementary, but it took just one sentence to convince me that this was no place to be, no place at all. Mrs. Burnett, my fifth-grade teacher, had just introduced me to twenty-five or so strange faces, all of them as confusing and cruel as the gigantic state of Texas that had just become my new home. Their heads shook like weeds in the wind once she finished, and the group cackle brought a sharp pain to my ears. A few of the boys lunged across the aisle to tap their buds, as if to amp up the joke. It was funny stuff.

As Mrs. Burnett hushed the class, I ducked under the shadow of her bony finger and beehive hairdo, which smelled like a combination of one of my mom's homemade frizz jobs and spoiled cole slaw.

"Now class, we're going to try that again," she said. "I said I'd like you to give a big 'ol, Texas-sized welcome to our newest Downing Tiger. Say hello to Jasper Schitt."

Yep, the name's Schitt. Yep, rhymes with you know what. Go ahead, get it on out. They did. There were a few mumbled greetings, but standing at the front of the class in a Cleveland Browns T-shirt and brown Toughskins, I could only pick out the laughter. I hadn't really minded when my friends back home teased me, but these weren't my friends. This was the enemy. And plus, the enemy was wearing short-sleeved shirts in November, for Pete's sake.

It wasn't fair, not one bit. I had turned into a solid citizen at Saybrook Prep and made bunches of friends back in Ashland, a little harbor town on the shores of Lake Erie in Ohio. Then my dad had to go and shake up everything. I was playing in the backyard, minding my own business, when he came out of the screen door of our two-story house. Glasses resting on his wide nose, pipe dangling from his mouth, he circled around and gave me a giant push. The momentum rocketed me from his cloud of cherry smoke and toward the top of the nearby pine tree, a truly amazing feat reserved for king-sized pushes from my dad. I was on top of the world.

"Son, we're moving to Texas next week," he said as I blurred by him in the opposite direction. I wasn't sure which brought me back down, the gravity stuff or the news.

I tossed my winter jacket off the globe in our living room and started spinning. I found the United States, in which my dad promised me Texas sat, and looked super hard. It wasn't on either side of Ohio, or even in the Great Lakes region, which I figured pretty much made up the entire world. After all, I'd really only been to Cleveland, about 30 miles away, and Niagara Falls, the site of my seventh birthday party. Mikey Anders had plowed down too much cake and puked on the log ride, but that was a whole other story.

It took me forever to find Texas, and this place called Midtex especially. There was no water at all, just three fingers of nothing in every direction. I'd heard of Texas, of course, because that was where Roger Staubach and the Dallas Cowboys and J.R. Ewing and cowboys lived, but Midtex was a new one to me. But there it was, right there on the far left side of Texas, scribbled next to a spider's web and hiding under a wad of dust. Midtex, with the thing on the Houston Oilers' helmets drawn next to it. The dust, as I later found out, was fitting.

I shoved the hair from my eyes and realized that Texas was as big as 10, maybe 20 Ohios. But there could never be another Ohio. Ashland had hills and trees and snow, plus a place called Funsville down the street that had a go-cart track, six pinball machines and a long row of trampolines. It was pretty much all a kid needed in life. I still told Mom there was nothing to do all the time, but that's the job of a kid.

My thoughts drifted to Bart Crumbie, my best friend since, well, since we'd decided it was so and swapped blood just to prove it. His dad was a dentist, but when Bart wasn't being ordered to brush or floss or rinse, we would pedal like crazy through the neighborhood or head down to

Chesnut Beach to skip rocks or dig up shells. We were Butch and Sundance, only on Big Wheels and, now, Schwinns, and whatever we did, we did it together.

I looked through the front window to the Logans, where Nicky lived. We often shared a bath, Nicky and I, just splashing and carrying on and having a big time. Her mother would come to dry us off, covering Nicky's naked body and always smelling like one of my parent's parties. Ashland being dry, my folks were the presidents of the booze club in town.

My three older brothers—John, Matt and Simon—seemed to like that. All already in their teens by the time I was born, they weren't around the house much, having already moved out and moved on to whatever being young in 1978 meant. To me, it meant sports and school and more sports. To them, I think, it meant wide collars and tall shoes and long hair and lots and lots of celebrating life.

But when they did come around, they were like party clowns to me, all packing their own type of entertainment. John had "The Claw," which was really just a stiff hand to my stomach. It hurt like heck, but it was a good pain. Matt always brought "The Whoopee," a sky-high toss in the air followed by a high-pitched 'Whoopee!' And Simon, the youngest besides me but still fifteen years older, was in my opinion the world's best tickler. I didn't want to ever grow too old for hooks and whoopees and tickles, but I knew that day was probably coming fast.

They usually came separately, though Matt and Simon sometimes traveled in a pack, and never stayed too long. When one would bolt, he would mess up my hair or slug me and promise to return soon, then sneak a bottle of Canadian Club out of the garage and take off. I wondered which they would miss most when we moved, me or that stash.

John was the oldest and smallest of my brothers, but he was big on fun. Almost every Saturday, we would drive down to Ashland River together to fish and to monkey around with his sheepdog Alpo. Oh, and to jump off the free frunk. The free frunk was really this huge tree truck that had a rope swing attached to it. Made for a scary ride, but a good scary. Well, used to be, when I only had nine teeth or so, I couldn't pronounce my tees so good, so I called it the free frunk. Anyway, I would miss John and our Saturdays together, but I didn't miss sounding like a dope.

In the garage as we were packing up, Dad gave Mr. Dixon (the booze club vice-president) the club bottles, tucking one under his arm and grunting something under his breath as he passed our neighbor his president's card. The last few days had been a blur, a rush of stuffing boxes, signing school transfer forms and wiping away tears. I hadn't taken the news well, but mom told me that dad's new job offer was one he couldn't turn down. He was the boss of the local Republic Tire factory, and the manufacturing plant in this Midtex place, Mom swore, was bigger and better. I didn't see how any rubber could be better than Ohio rubber, or any house better than our three-bedroom spread on Carpenter Road. I also didn't have much say in the matter.

Early on our last day, I made my final tour. For old time's sake, I pulled out my Big Wheel, the fancy kind with the lunch box and the side brake, and peddled knees to chest up Beacon's Hill to the Crumbie house. Bart answered the door, curly white hair standing like springs on his head, and together we took one last ride. We stopped at Murphy's Stable, where a couple of white horses munched away without a care in the world. The air was sharp and dry and smelled like a snowstorm, and little was said. My Aunt Alice once told me that three white horses in one spot was good luck, but I couldn't find a third on that day.

"So when ya comin' back?" he asked, flipping one of those chewy orange Circus Peanuts into his mouth. When away from the fluoride police, the kid was a sugar fiend. "I dunno," I answered. "I'll come as much as I can." Texas seemed like a darn long pedal away.

"Ya better," he returned, picking a sticky glob from his teeth.

"So ya really like those things?" I asked.

He shrugged. "Aw, better than beets."

I understood. If you asked me, they were nasty, but anything beat beets. Besides, Bart's dad made him floss after every single meal, even made him lug home his used, mangled, bloody string from school as evidence, so I figured the kid deserved a break.

He punched me in the arm, friendly like. I did the same. We sat there on the fence and threw rocks at the barn until the horse hair made my allergies kick in and my eyes swell shut. Anyhow, it was how guys said goodbye.

For the first time in my life, I then left a woman behind. Or a girl, anyway. Nicky and I dangled our feet in her pool, the not-so-fancy kind that sat above ground level, as my parents packed the U-Haul. A fuzzy man who smelled like smoke came outside and touched Nicky's shoulders and let out a hack, then disappeared in a rush. Men were always appearing and disappearing from the Logan house. Poof. I thought that maybe Miss Logan would make a better magician than a secretary.

As we sat in silence, tracing the icy water with our frozen feet, Nicky started to cry. I figured it was how girls said goodbye.

"I still wanna marry you," she said quietly.

"Oh, I still wanna, too," I answered quickly.

Don't tell, but I wasn't so sure about that. I mean, we'd said some things a couple years before in the tub, but we were practically babies then. Girls were starting to freak me out, especially naked ones in the tub. Plus, Mom said there was someone for everyone, and I didn't much expect to meet my "someone" in the tub.

Here was my thing with girls. A few weeks before Dad dropped the bomb, I was watching the tube and eating Coco Nuggets before school. This white-haired guy named Phil had his very own show, and he was sprinting all over the room sticking a microphone in guy's faces and asking them what they looked for in a girl. They said different stuff— personality, looks, sense of humor, smile, junk like that. I just rolled my eyes and spooned the last few flakes of cereal outta the way, because with Coco Nuggets it was all about the milk.

See, I didn't care if a girl had all of that put together. If she couldn't play some ball or at least make a scary face or a weird noise with her body, preferably from her armpit, I didn't see any use for her. So I was probably too young to start looking at all.

There was one last goodbye to say. While Dad latched the trailer to our green sedan, I slipped to the back of the house, where a smelly wire crate rested on a square of crushed grass. I unhooked the latch and pulled out Bingo, my pet rabbit. I raked my fingers through his white fur and stared straight into his pink eyes. He would be happier, I promised him, because there was a whole new world out there to see. Judging from his fast getaway into the woods behind our house, he agreed.

I just wished I felt the same way.

I was usually a big fan of road trips, because they meant lots of junk food and sports magazines. And peanut brittle from Stuckey's, too. The stuff stuck in your teeth for like three states, but that was a small price to pay. Plus, we got to stay in Howard Johnsons along the way. The rooms there were only 20 or 25 degrees, but they gave kids free candy, which was worth a little frostbite.

From inside the house, I heard Dad leaning on the horn, but I had one last thing to do. I got a good push and slid down the banister, all the way to the stump at the bottom. It was one of my best all-time rides, actually. We were moving into a stupid one-story house, so my banister sliding days were over. Plus, I knew there would come a day when a boy couldn't go around straddling things without hurting himself, so I had to get it while the getting was good.

A few minutes later, we backed away from 847 Carpenter Road, from the only home I'd ever known.

***

The drive to Texas was horrible, awful, the pits. We crossed through states I had barely even heard of and just kept on going and going and going and going. My folks sat there and stared straight ahead like it was no big deal. But it was a big deal. And not a case of soda, nine sports magazines or two freezing hotels could change that. I tried to pull the blubbering bit, but we weren't stopping. Three days, 1,373 miles, three video games, seven batteries and a couple dozen "I gotta go's" later, I was a Texan. Didn't even ask when we were going to get there. Not once.

We checked into the Inn of the Golden Rooster, a 10-story hotel that appeared to have lived through that whole Reconstruction thing, as our new house was being finished.

I was granted a three-day delay from starting school, a deal that I'd cut from a tantrum somewhere in Oklahoma, and my mom and I planned a sightseeing trip while Dad got settled at work. He'd slipped out in the early morning light, leaving behind his trademark cherry fog while heading to his bigger and better rubber plant.

"Bye Kathy," I heard him whisper.

"Bye hon. Good luck."

Dad was headed off to the pickle factory. Don't ask me why, but that was what he called the office. Sometimes I wondered if Dad really did work at a pickle factory, if he would say he was going off to the rubber plant. Anyway. Mom and Dad had known each other for their whole lives and had been married for almost as long.

They grew up in some teensy town in Missouri, the same one Mark Twain and Huck Finn came from, and went to grade school together. Dad was a couple of years older, but their school only had about 15 kids, so I figured their choices were pretty squeezed. Anyway, they seemed to like each other all right.

"Hurry up, sweetie," my mom said through the door. I was in the bathroom getting primed for our big stinking day.

"Okay, okay, okay."

I found my face in the steam circle in the mirror. Oh, if I'm going to be talking to you and all, I might as well describe myself. Long mug. Longer nose. Blonde hair. No shoulders. Bird legs. I hoped to grow some more, especially in certain places. I figured I looked like a mix between that gee-whiz kid from "Lassie," only probably not that good, and a doghouse with a head, but maybe not that bad.

Mom was right about one thing. Everything was bigger in Texas. The roads were wider, the cars were longer, the toast was fatter. Texas Toast, the menu in the hotel cafe we were in called it. I couldn't remember what Ohio toast had looked like, only that it hadn't hogged half my plate. Just for kicks, I ordered up a Shirley Temple with my eggs, but our waitress laughed and pinched my face and brought me a Roy Rogers. Pretty much the same concoction, 7-Up and a splash of cherry juice, but with a Texas twist. I was all for that. There was no slick way to ask for a drink named after a chick.

After breakfast, we came from The Rooster's shadow. I slipped off my baseball jacket, the fancy kind with the patches from all the American League clubs lined down both sides, and handed it to my mom. Some guys in suits scooted in and out of the tall buildings that surrounded us. I had no idea what those suit guys did. The clock on the bank across the street said it was already 84 degrees. I bet Texas doesn't have bigger winters, I thought to myself.

"Honey, what would you like to see first?" Mom asked, digging for a brochure that the front-desk clerk had given her.

I didn't care what I saw first or second or even third. "I dunno. Doesn't matter to me."

But Kathy, as her friends and my dad called her, or Mom, as I liked to call her, rallied quickly. "How 'bout the World's Biggest Jackrabbit? Would you like to see that?"

My thoughts turned to Bingo. He had been a good rabbit, not the kind that left you with pebbles for change after picking him up. I wanted to be with him, bouncing through the forest and racing to gather food before snow carpeted the Ohio ground until March. Bart had an igloo-making kit, and I was one of the better ice architects on the block. I could have managed. But as a convertible blazed past, I admitted to myself that even Bingo wasn't the biggest rabbit in the world.

I shrugged. "Okay."

The cab driver was smelly but smart. The World's Biggest Jackrabbit, as he warned us on our way to the thing, was an attraction ripe for the World's Biggest Suckers. It wasn't a rabbit at all, just a statue of a creature that barely resembled one. It was covered in cracked gold paint and stood three feet above me, watching my every move. He was plain ugly and not even the least bit cuddly, with an evil smile stretched across his crumbling face. It was what dad called false advertising.

The World's Biggest Meteor Crater was next. We took a different cab to that hot spot, turning the buildings to toys in my rear view as the driver babbled away in a foreign language. My mom called it a Texas drawl, but the guy sounded more like Deputy Dawg to me.

"Where y'all from?" he blurted out between spits into a red plastic cup.

"Ohio, near Cleveland," Mom answered politely. "Ah, Yankees, huh? Long way from home, ain't y'all?"

"Yeah," I shot back quickly, though not as politely.

"Yes, yes we are," Mom said all proper and parent like.

"A very, very long way from home."

She didn't say so, but I don't think my mom wanted to leave Ashland either. After all, she was leaving behind three of her four kids, all of her friends and her beloved garden. She was just wild about that garden, and it was a dandy, too. Since the cab had just passed a city limits sign of a place called No Trees, I didn't figure that her thumb would be so green in Texas. Anyhow, I caught her crying on the morning we left. I figured crying was how ladies said goodbye, too.

An odor drifted to the back seat of the cab. It wasn't dad's brand. I knew that much for sure, having given him a new jug of Old Velvet the Christmas before and sampled it at Shankle's Drugs myself. I think it was Miss Logan's brand. We drove on, slicing through rows of those pumping oil derricks and leaving any trace of familiarity behind. I knew the feeling.

The World's Biggest Meteor Crater, as we discovered after a 20-minute trip through an empty patch of nothing, was really just the World's Biggest Hole in the Ground. The pit stretched for miles, surrounded only by a few wandering dots in the far distance, suckers like us. They disappeared after a few moments, peeling away in a van and leaving the three of us alone with what the brochure called "one of the world's great wonders." In a way, it wasn't false advertising. I wondered where in the heck we were, and what in the heck we were doing there.

A thorny bush skipped past as we climbed back in the cab, almost taking out my legs on its way to the hole. My mother did a Heisman Trophy pose to avoid it and screeched and snapped me into her arms, while our cabby coughed out a deep, thick laugh. Tumbleweed, he called it as we pulled away. They must have traveled in packs, because three more somersaulted by as I pressed my nose against the hot window. Tumbleweeds, shoot; those things were flying trees.

***

Our new house reeked of fresh paint. It was in the pretty fancy part of town and stood next to a row of other new homes, most with "For Sale" or "Sold" signs jammed in the ground and all cut from the same mold. The yards were just rectangular patches of dark, brown dirt, and the backyards all had tall, wooden fences around them. There had been no fences in Ohio, only open spaces with room to roam. I didn't know how a kid was supposed to clown around with fences plastered all over the place.

There were two boys near my age having a catch down the street. One had a good arm, but the other threw like a girl. Mom said I should go join them, but I was in no mood to play. Judging from their quick glance in my direction and quicker return to their game, they were in no mood to ask.

Later, as I sat in my bedroom, a couple of movers with bunches of tattoos unloaded our Ohio home. The men tossed furniture and boxes around me, swallowing me in a pile of wood and cardboard and plastic. Except for my Slinkee, everything seemed to have survived the move. (Once those Slinkees got twisted, they were toast.) I tore through a box marked 'SPORTS STUFF' and dug out a photo of Archie Griffin, the terrific former Ohio State running back, and tried to hang it up with a wad of gum. It fell and rolled back up. I leaned against the bare wall and started to bawl. Shaking and everything, like a big, fat baby. Figured it was how I said hello to Texas.

***

So I thought it was a sharp enough outfit. Mom had laid out a white turtleneck and blue jeans for my first day of school, but I decided to go with brown on brown, the basic Slowpoke candy bar look. We were starting to have daily battles over the clothes thing. I mean, she was a girl and all, but I had the hang of it, no sweat. I mean, a kid couldn't go wrong with brown on brown, right?

I dragged a brush through my hair, which mom had sculpted with scissors and a ruler a couple weeks back. If she was going to break out the toolbox to give me a haircut, she needed to grab one of those level things with the bubbles, too. Man, was this thing crooked.

I wiggled my toes through the carpet. It was thin and smelled new, and I realized that it was probably the very best thing about my new home. Back in Ohio, we had that thick, shaggy stuff, and it was almost impossible to play with my Army men without them toppling over. Plus, you couldn't nail a bazooka guy or a walkie-talkie sucker with a rubber band when he was hiding in that thick gunk. With the skinny carpet, they would be sitting ducks. Anyway, it wasn't much, but it was something.

After putting Snoopy back on his toothpaste house, I laced up my black tennies, the lame kind with the three white stripes, and headed out to the unknown.

Except for my sick stomach, everything seemed in order as we rolled across the Texas-wide roads and toward Downing Elementary. I had the green-handled scissors made special just for lefties, along with a bunch of different colored spirals, two Big Chief notebooks and a 64-color box of crayons with the built-in sharpener. On my lap sat a shiny new Addams Family lunch box, a late replacement for my Pele pail, which had also taken a pounding in the move. Over the phone, Simon had promised me that Pele was about washed up anyhow.

So I was ready for fifth grade, in supply if not in spirit.

Mom mouthed something to herself about being late for the water guy as I clutched her hand and climbed the front steps to the school. There weren't many reasons left to squeeze your mommy's hand in public, but being terrified was one of them. We entered the main office, where a bunch of grown-ups were running around like ants. It looked like one of those hills that Dad used to dump gasoline on. That was always a weekend bonus, bouncing around with him on the riding mower and making a few pit stops to wipe out some insect civilizations.

A guy with square glasses finally noticed us. He was also the hairiest human being I'd ever seen, with one of those beards that started right under the eyes and ended down by the chest. He flashed a fake smile and extended a huge, hairy hand to my mom. "Well, hello there! I'm Jimmy Edmondson, the Downing Elementary principal. And you must be?"

He started pumping my mom's hand, making her answer sound like she'd had a jackhammer for breakfast.

"I'm......Ka...the....rine.....Sch..hii...hitt.

And...this...is...Jasp....er...er...er."

He stopped and then brought three fingers to his mouth. Except for his eyes, it was pretty much the only part of his face not carpeted with fuzz.

"Didn't quite catch that last name. What was it again, please?"

"Schitt."

He didn't hide it very well. His lips curled up at the edges, making the same quick, sneaky, clever grin that often snuck onto the faces of strangers after hearing our last name. He must have caught himself, though, because his recovery was pretty slick.

"Yes, of course, of course," he said, ruffling my hair and shooting me a wink. "We were expecting young Jasper here. From up north, right son?"

"Ohio."

"Ohio, why of course." He returned his attention to Mom. "Well, we're certainly proud to have him, ma'am. He'll be in Mrs. Burnett's class. A fine teacher, just an excellent, dedicated educator. She should have everything ready for him."

At least she was ready. The walk to Room 29 was the longest of my short life. Mr. Edmondson had recruited Mr. Greer, a worker ant I figured, to escort me to class. As we made our way down the thin, pale hallway, I looked out the long stretch of windows and saw a green Continental parked along the street with a familiar face poking through the open driver's window. The water guy could wait.

I suppose Mom was pretty, in a mom sort of way. Her hair was red, but not red like a fireplug, and curly, or at least made that way by the noisy contraption she was always camping under. She wasn't tall or short or skinny or fat, but she smelled kind of nice and her teeth were good and straight. I don't know what else to say. I think she was too busy worrying about us to worry about checking herself out all that much.

The guy dropped me off at the classroom, then patted me on the back and said something that I didn't listen to.

He handed me off to this Mrs. Burnett, who herded me to the front of the room and arranged my shoulders just perfect so I could hear every laugh from every mouth in the room when she introduced me. Only a chubby kid in the back kept quiet, mostly because he was trying to inhale a Clark Bar in one swallow.

Schitt. I didn't really mind it that much. It wasn't a birth defect or anything, just a tough break. Later on in life, I hoped that maybe it would lose some of its humor. Plus, nobody ever remembered a Smith or a Brown, but a Schitt, now that stuck with you. But standing there in front of a bunch of jokers in Mrs. Burnett's class, waiting it out and wanting to run, I cursed my parents, my name and the whole stinking mess.

Plus, my first name didn't exactly make me an ordinary Joe. I mean, Jasper? Dad said that after Matt and Simon and John, they'd wanted to pick a more original name. Because Schitt didn't set me apart enough already. I figured they'd run out of saints and switched over to cartoon characters. I guess it could have been worse; I could have been a Boo Boo or a Jughead. I always thought Jack was a good, solid name, the kind of kid you could borrow lunch money from, but, tossed together with my last name, it would have given the amateur comedians even more material. Anyway, my folks always said I wasn't an accident, but I knew I was probably either a last stab at a Jessica or, probably, just a good time for dad after a block party.

In my 10 years, I'd already heard every name and joke and riddle in the book. Trust me, don't even try to think of another. Schitthead. Schitt for brains. Dumb Schitt. Eat Schitt. The list went on and on and on. Heck, I knew how to use it in a sentence before I even knew not to step in the stuff. And nobody cared that it wasn't even spelled the same, because proper spelling didn't count on the playground. It was a German name, kind of like Schmidt, except funnier. I hated it when new teachers couldn't pronounce it, like it was a real tongue twister, because that meant I had to start out the day by saying something that sent most kids to confession.

"Schitt," some teacher call out, like it rhymed with kite.

I always wanted to let it slide and tell her later. But for some reason, they always just had to know right then, like it was a spelling bee or something. They would give up in a second on Jimmy Rianazantioski, an Ohio classmate who had six syllables on me, but they never let mine slide.

"Schitt," I'd finally say correctly.

Then the place would erupt, and I would sink into my chair and turn red and feel small and stupid. It was the usual deal. But what could I do? It was the name they'd given me, period. If I could have paid off the doctor and been a Johnson or a Jones or even a Rianazantioski, I would have probably cut a deal. And not that it was a big thing, but I wondered if any girl would ever want the thing.

"Now that is not nice, not nice at all." Mrs. Burnett shook her head and squinted at the class, then led me by the arm to a seat near the front of the room.

I'd gotten used to the heckles back in Ohio, but they were already dying out by the fourth grade. I was an honor student, even placing second in my class spelling bee, and a terror in the schoolyard. Tetherball, kickball, clod fights, you name it. Plus, a road had been paved by the athletic heroics of my brothers and the community visibility of my parents. Ashland was used to Schitt; Midtex and Bubby T. Downing Elementary wasn't.

My family tried to prepare me. Dad said that Schitts were lovers, not fighters. Simon told me to take a shot at the first sucker to say anything. Matt told me to skip out. And Mom told me to make them laugh. Well, I could think funny, but I couldn't be funny, at least around strangers.

Thinking funny things was about as useful as a salad fork.

Besides, if a new kid bombed early, it was all over. Once, a transfer student back at Saybrook tried out a bad knock-knock joke on his first day, and he ended up finger painting with the girls for a good year. Unless you could make up for it by having a swimming pool or a pinball machine or something neat like that, you were a goner. So an attempt at humor was way too risky.

Anyway, that's pretty much all I will say about the name thing. Still, I had promised myself not to cry, and I didn't.

At least not out loud.

***

I tried to pay attention during class, to do the good student bit. But my ears rung long after the howling stopping, drowning out Mrs. Burnett and her lecture on the Texas state flower, the bluebonnet. I heard only a scattering of her words, instead tuning in to the whispers behind my back. I felt a burning inside my chest, a sudden need to jump on my wobbly desk and to lash back at the unfairness of it all. Or at least to chunk something at someone.

"Jasper, what was the state flower of Ohio?" Mrs.

Burnett was in my face, her fangs sparkling.

A quick panic replaced my anger. The entire class turned to me, waiting to see if the new kid with the funny name could deliver in the clutch. It was my first, maybe only, chance. I felt my left eye start to twitch. Always happened when I got real nervous, always the left one.

Of course I knew. It was the carnation, the same flower that I'd picked and carefully arranged in an empty pickle jar just the spring before. It was illegal and all, but crimes like that were allowed on Mother's Day. All I had to do was spit it out. Carnation. Carnation. Carnation.

I shrugged and disappeared into my arms, wishing the whole scene was made from an Etch-A-Sketch. A quick shake, and, poof, gone.

Looked like a sure six months of finger painting for me.

The horn for recess saved me. Like one of those fake snakes from a can of nuts, everyone exploded from their desks and headed for the door. I had to admit, recess was a favorite subject of mine, too, but I was in no big hurry.

Mrs. Burnett's voice stopped everyone in their tracks. "Now kids, don't forget to get your permission slips signed for the field trip to the slaughterhouse. If you don't have it in by tomorrow morning, you'll have to stay behind with Miss Abercrombie's class."

Yep, that about summed it up. Ohio had Funsville; Texas had slaughterhouses. I promised myself to remember to forget about the slip.

As I made my way to the playground, I thought about walking right by the monkey bars and straight back to Ashland. I could hide away on the moving van and be back in no time. But those drivers were pretty scary and almost, but not quite, as hairy as the Edmondson guy. I settled for an empty swing on the far end of the yard.

The cool kids headed straight for the brick wall, where a couple of dodgeball teams were quickly divided up. You could tell they were the cool kids because the other ones wandered off to play in the dirt. Dirt kids ended up being dirt eaters and scab chewers, and there was no future in that. I watched them alone, dangling my legs and tugging lightly at the chains but feeling no urge to swing. Besides, there wasn't even anything to shoot for, not a pine tree in sight. There were hardly any trees in Texas. No good ones, anyhow.

They were pretty decent players, especially the fast kid in the "Keep on Truckin'" T-shirt, but not of my caliber. Not to brag, but it was the plain truth. Though small for my age, I was a marksman with the enemy in my sights and an escape artist when being chunked at. I wasn't always picked first in the other sports, but dodgeball was my game, maybe even my future career. I could have wowed them, if only they asked.

They didn't.

My eyes shifted to the opposite side of the yard, where a group of girls were playing that crazy Red Rover game. One by one, they would sprint into the neighboring chain, usually springing back toward their team without making a dent. The teams remained locked until the one they called Alice, by far the biggest kid in our class, maybe the biggest kid I'd ever seen, took down an entire line. They tumbled down together, stared at each another and busted out laughing. Big girls had it tough much of the time, but they owned Red Rover.

Mr. Edmondson wandered onto the grounds, joining Mrs. Burnett near the merry-go-round. His head glistened under the hot sun, and I couldn't help but wonder why his face could sprout all that hair and his poor head couldn't.

One of life's cruel jokes, I figured. But Mrs. Burnett seemed to like him. Each word he directed at our teacher made her about double over. After a minute, he glanced at his watch and strolled away, brushing his hand quickly and lightly across her back. The glare from his ring flashed in my eyes.

"I think they're boyfriend and girlfriend."

I hadn't seen him sit down next to me. It was the Clark Bar kid, the wide load from the rear of my class. He had stuffed himself into the swing and was slowly rocking back and forth, dragging his toes along the crusty ground.

I twisted toward him. "Huh?"

"I said they're boyfriend and girlfriend, Mr. Edmondson and Mrs. Burnett. They're married to other people and all, but that don't stop 'em. Nobody is supposed to know, but I do."

"So how do you know?"

He grunted and pulled closer, chocolate still lining his lips. "'Cuz I watch things. I saw 'em holdin' pinkies the other day, right over by the monkey bars, so they must be boyfriend and girlfriend."

That sounded about right to me. I'd seen the older kids in school doing it lots of times, and the teenagers back at

Cummings Lake Park back in Ohio would sometimes even grab each other's belt loops. Plus, my parents held entire hands, though not all that often, and they were way more than boyfriend and girlfriend. I figured it was a law or something, like the one that said dads mowed and moms mopped.

"Does anyone else know?"

"Nope, nobody. Just you and me and the tree."

I laughed at that one. I liked rhymes, always had, and it felt good to smile. Seconds later, Mrs. Burnett blew her whistle, and the games broke up. Red balls were left bouncing in place, and the Red Rover chains unlocked. I started back, too, but a hand stopped me in my tracks.

"Secret?" asked candy face.

I shrugged and nodded. "Sure, secret."

He unfolded from the swing, lifting himself with a squished face. The whistling of his breath was the only sound as we retreated to room 29, looking like the numbers 1 and 0 shuffling side by side.

***

That night was a little better. Mom had tacked up some of my favorite posters - a signed Meadowlark Lemon, Brian Sipe, Pete Rose - and cooked her world-famous meatloaf. At least it was world famous to me. Except for a ride on the back of Simon's motorcycle or maybe a licorice rope from Thorton's Drugs, I couldn't think of anything much better than a slab of mom's meatloaf swimming in ketchup.

She was a great cook. Fat hamburgers, skinny spaghetti, short sausages, long French fries. You name it, Mom could pull it off. That was a bonus, because I really, really loved to eat. To me, the best restaurant was the closest one. Her meals were always good, but, most of all, always hot. Not McDonald's apple pie hot, but hot enough that even Sam, our poodle that dropped land mines all over the place, would blow on the scraps that I snuck him.

Anyway, I had a good set-up. Mom cooked, dad cleaned up and I just ate and ate. Mom thought I had a worm.

Dad came home just in time for dinner, just like always, and asked how our day had been, just like always. He looked tired but pretty happy as he sat down and said the same prayer that I'd heard before almost every dinner of my whole life. Dad did and said the same stuff over and over and over, but at least it was usually good stuff. I figured it beat having a dad who did and said a lot of different stuff that mostly stunk. Plus, he could yank out his false teeth on command, which was a plus and a hit at parties.

He shoveled a bite into his mouth, taking little time to chew before throwing in another. "So how was school today, son?" he asked as a lump tumbled to the plate below.

I shrugged. "Okay I guess."

Mom dangled a bite before her mouth. "Did you make any new friends?"

The meatloaf was going fast, so there was little time for small talk.

"I dunno. Maybe one."

"Really, that's great, son," Dad said, a chunk anchored on his chin. Seriously, I sometimes wondered if he could even feel his face. "So what's her name?"

"John!" She yelled, then looked at him and ran her fingers quickly across her chin. It was the mom signal to wipe off your face.

Dad did because, well, he almost always did what mom said. Then he winked at me and returned to his plate. He was a pretty funny guy. I think he got his humor from his dad, my grandpa. Grandpa had this hilarious bit where he would tell someone that he'd just bought the best kind of hearing aid you could buy. When the guy asked him what kind it was, Grandpa would look at his watch and say what time it was. It was an old-fashioned joke, but I think the guy was born back when Abe Lincoln was still around, so that made him a pretty old-fashioned guy. Anyhow, it was still almost enough to want to need a hearing aid.

"Now honey, what's his name?" Mom asked.

"I dunno," I said. And I didn't.

Not until the next day, anyhow. Standing at the podium in a green dress that reminded me of sherbet, Mrs. Burnett cleared her throat and opened her attendance book. Though I'd had to pretend not to see a few finger points on my way to class, I still felt a little better. Dad let me beat him twice in checkers the night before, and I found a new football sitting on my bed after dinner. And Mom made a monster batch of chocolate chip cookies and went heavy on the chips. With cookies, the chip-to-dough ratio meant everything.

Oh, and I told myself to stop being such a whiny, annoying tit. That helped some.

***

"Mandy Albertson," Mrs. Burnett began.

"Here."

"Andrea Arnold."

"Here."

"Raymond Brooks." "Here."

"Bubby Buttowski."

I waited for the laughter. Except from me, it never came.

"Hwrr."

I whirled around. There in the very back, his mouth packed with a Moonpie, slouched my new best friend, a chubby kid named Buttowski who liked to watch things.

One new friend and one decent secret.

Oh, and skinny carpet. Okay, so it wasn't Funsville, this strange, new land.

But I figured it was better than beets.

Shunkin'

Miss Anderson was at it again. She'd just whipped across three lanes and slammed the school bus into a grassy bank next to Wickersham Paints. From the next-to-last row, I ducked behind the freakishly oversized head of Alice Lowenstein.

"I said no shunkin'!" Miss Anderson barked from the captain's chair. "Who in Sam Hill is doin' all that shunkin'?!?"

I couldn't remember any Sam Hill at our school, but shunkin' was actually chunking, or at least shunking, and Miss Anderson was the helpless, daily victim of it. It involved many weapons. Paper airplanes, candy wrappers, even gum sometimes. But spitwads were by far the ammunition of choice.

I wasn't sure why we did it, the 10 or so of us who were active launching pads. Maybe because her wild, sticky hairdo was such an easy, inviting target. It was more like a flypaper wig, really, and should have had circles and point values drawn on it. Maybe because our daily thirty-minute bus ride to school was so darn boring. Or maybe because we were 11 years old.

Probably that.

Billy Teakwood was our leader. Billy lived around the corner in a cul-de-sac, and his mom was once a centerfold in "Playboy," back when they wore bikinis and those huge, goofy sunglasses. (That didn't make him the top marksman on the block, but you can't leave information like that out.) Anyhow, he could nail anything from almost anywhere on request. Billy would have done well on "Wild Kingdom," shooting those poison darts at cheetahs with the gray-haired guy. You didn't want to end up across the firing line from him during neighborhood BB gun battles.

"I've told ya a hundred times, there ain't going to be no shunkin,' not on my bus. Now who did it?" Miss Anderson was shaking her finger at us. Her head bobbed in tune, and a few pellets of Mead fluttered to the floor. On a good day of shunking, her hair resembled a decorated Christmas tree by the time we pulled into the Downing parking lot. I thought she should have at least worn a hair net for protection. That way, she could have shaken it out like a doormat at the end of the day.

It wasn't like anybody was going to confess. She had to catch us; those were the clear and simple rules. And she had a few times, using that big billboard of a mirror above her seat to nab a shunker. She busted Billy once and pulled him clean off the bus by the ear. Made him walk the last six football fields or so to school in the pouring rain.

Swear to God.

I guess that was it - the thrill, the danger. It wasn't like we could get into any real trouble yet. Running with scissors, stuffing a third-grader into a locker, throwing things at your bus driver. Those were the felonies of a preteen in our neighborhood.

I was so ready to be older. Older kids, they had all the fun. At the Picadilly High football games, you could see them across the field in the junior high and high school sections, wandering all over the place with no supervision at all and trying to hook up or at least getting room to roam. We elementary kids had a special area, a little playpen thing right next to the parents on the home side. It was no different than sitting at the kid's table at Thanksgiving dinner. Ridiculousness.

"Pshhhhhhhhhhttt." The bus was on its way again, pushing off, slicing into morning traffic and leaving behind a thick trail of muck. Even though it was only the middle of March, the air was already sticky and hot. I tried to slide down my window, but those things were impossible. Texas, I'd learned, was either one of two things: hot or hotter. I didn't figure to see my breath again anytime soon.

***

But all in all, Midtex hadn't ended up being such a horrible place after all. Over my sixteen-month stay, I'd slowly stopped thinking so much about the past and starting peeking toward the future. I missed the sledding and the snow ice cream and the canceled classes and all, but not the shivering in April or the icy sidewalks or the runny noses.

There was no such thing as a cold nose in Texas.

About three weeks before, I even said "y'all." Didn't mean to, it just slipped out. The guys at the corner bus stop were playing keepaway with my thermos and, outta nowhere, it spilled out in a heap.

"Hey, y'all stop goofing around!" I yelled. And there it was. I wasn't yet a Texan, but I was on my way. Probably just a matter of time before "fixin' to" worked its way into my vocabulary.

I wasn't much of a morning person. My daily routine was three snooze bars, two "time to get up, sons" from my dad and one "okay!!" from me. I hated that my first thoughts of every day were wicked ones, but until I got some breakfast, that's just the way it went. So on the bus, I usually rode along in silence. I noticed the incredible amount of pick-up trucks on the road. Some were shiny and new, but most were beaten up like old Tonka toys. Almost all of them had one thing in common - bumper stickers. "It's Hard to be Humble When You're From Texas," said one. "Midtex Bull Riding Association," read another.

And finally, my favorite: 'Eat Shit, Pardner.' That would have worked in any state, except someone had gone and given it a local flavor.

Again, that Texas pride thing and all.

I studied the people in the cars that whizzed by. The men all seemed to have mustaches, big fuzzy ones like Yosemite Sam. One was actually talking on a phone. Right there in his truck. It was so big that the man and the phone and the mustache barely fit together in the cab. Looked like he was yapping into a toaster oven, and I knew they'd never replace CB's.

Driving wasn't really that important to the women. Most of them were looking into their rear-view mirrors and just sort of glancing at the road every now and again. One lady caught me staring at her at a stop light. She had big hair and big fingernails and a big wad of gum in her mouth. She smiled and popped her gum. I looked away quickly. To be honest, I still wasn't so sure about the whole girl thing.

***

Still, Texas folks seemed like a pretty friendly bunch. Always smiling and winking and having no idea what 15 below felt like. Miss Anderson was an exception. I'd been her twice-a-day passenger for months and never once seen her smile. Not once. Come to think of it, I didn't even know if she had teeth. Maybe that was what was holding her back. No, I decided, she was just a crab.

From the sixth row, Tad Galbreath launched a wad from a straw. Tad was one of those kids who challenged everyone to do crazy things but usually never really did them himself. Let's jump off this ledge, he'd challenge, then tiptoe down after everyone jumped. Anyway, his shunk didn't have much oomph behind it and landed two rows short. Good aim, lousy lungs.

"No sir, ain't going to be no shunkin,' not on this day," Miss Anderson howled, never taking her hands off the 10 and two position. She was a much better driver than the lady to our direct right, who was pecking at her hair with a pick and weaving side to side like a top losing speed.

I didn't know why Miss Anderson even bothered. She always screamed there wasn't going to be any shunking, yelled it like six times each way, and there was always going to be at least a little shunking. It was as sure as bean burritos on Wednesdays at Downing Elementary.

The trick was just not to get caught. Sometimes that was no small feat. Even though I wasn't a very serious shunker - to me, it was strictly a hobby - even I'd almost been nabbed once. It happened on a Friday, candy day at Downing, and I was high on Nerds and Gobstoppers. We'd gone across to the Fill 'Er Up convenience store at lunch and loaded up on anything with sugar as its primary (or only) ingredient. Plus, Tad had come to school with a huge batch of homemade cinnamon toothpicks. He was hocking them five for a dime, and I'd spent at least a buck on them.

Anyway, I was kind of in a shunking mood on that trip home. So I wadded up half a science test into a Big Gulp straw, which made for an excellent bazooka, and scouted her. See, Miss Anderson always rotated her stare between the road, the side mirror and the rear-view mirror. Like a floor fan, only with eyes. Plus, I had to watch out for Alice, who would tattle in a second. She had her fat head in a book. To the left, a third-grade boy with billions of freckles stared at me and twisted his gum. He knew exactly what was going on but knew better than to rat. See, I was a sixthgrader standing tall on the top step of the elementary school ladder; he was still eating paste.

It was all clear as we bumped along Roy Rogers Road. I loaded up the ammunition, waited for Miss Anderson to check the road and started to let it rip. Only she crossed me up, giving the road just a brief glance before moving her eyes back to our reflections, and mainly to mine. Our eyes locked. Luckily, I was able to reverse the direction of my breath from a vicious exhale to a quick inhale. Big gulp.

"Jasper, what cha doin' back there?" she asked, her eyes narrowing.

"Um, just gnawin' on a straw, Miss Anderson."

"Yer not thinkin' of doin' any of that shunkin', are ya?"
"Oh no, no ma'am." It felt like I'd swallowed a shrub.
"Mmm, hmm," she croaked suspiciously.

It wasn't like we were going to get expelled, anyway. I don't think Miss Anderson had too much pull with the folks at school. She was always threatening to write us up a bus report, but as far as we knew those reports were about as real as the licks we would supposedly get for cheating in class. Billy shunked and cheated all the time, and the worst he'd gotten was a three-block hike and a desk in the corner of Mr. Edmondson's office. Still, I was always extra careful, because I wasn't the kind of kid who strutted around thinking it could never happen to him. Heck, I usually expected it to happen to me.

We pulled into the parking lot at, as always, ten 'til eight. It was a drizzly day and had been a slow, sleepy ride. As we piled off the bus, Miss Anderson looked straight ahead as the students unloaded. A few people, girls, said goodbye to her. Nothing was returned.

Nope, the lady wasn't exactly a burst of sunshine to start the day. I wondered if we'd made her that way or were just the final part of a bigger, lousier puzzle. As I passed her, a flick of something fell outta her hair and fluttered to the worn blanket that covered her shoulders.

"Psssshhhhhttttt." The bus door slammed behind me, and a blast of hot air whacked me from behind. As Miss Anderson wheeled away, I looked back just in time to get a faceful of coal black exhaust. Even her bus was evil.

We made our way past the kiddie halls, where students were buzzing around like Electric Football players. One kid steamed past me on a skateboard, then made a fancy turn into Room 141, just missing his teacher and pinning her against the door. I should have told her that a few rocks on the ground at the entrance would put a quick end to that.

Know the 'ol stick-in-the-bike-spokes trick? Well, same theory.

I felt kind of bad when teachers got grief from us. At least they were trying. But most of the material was easy breezy, and we all knew that it was pretty pointless, too. C'mon, we weren't stupid. I knew for a fact that Dad didn't need to know squat about the Sioux Indians to run a rubber plant. He should have just gone to rubber school and skipped the whole history business.

Plus, I heard they did it all for chicken feed. The teachers at Downing seemed nice enough, but there was always a tired, ragged look about them. And I don't mean just their clothes. Their faces were all faded, like an old photo. I'd personally already scratched 'be a teacher' off my list of things to do or to be in life. I figured that if being a teacher was so great, somebody would bring one to Career Day sometime. Never happened.

A day in elementary school was like a row of dominos, a carefully lined row of six subjects with two breaks. Social studies came first, followed by writing and science. After a recess of 20 minutes, which was barely enough time to work up a decent sweat, we had Arts and Crafts. They really should have called it 'ruining your new shirt' hour, because there was nothing artsey or crafty about my creations.

***

At lunch, we broke off into our gangs. The seating changed by the day, of course, depending on who was who's new best friend or who hated who during that given week. There was only one rule - boys ate with boys, and girls ate with girls. Oh, and dirt eaters with dirt eaters. A few guys in my class had girlfriends - and even I thought Darcy Winkle wasn't completely disgusting - but you didn't talk about that at lunch. There were more important things to do, like slinging butter tabs on to the ceiling or using corny sticks as pretend daggers.

After lunch, it was time for Music class, and we were herded off to D-wing. For two reasons, this was actually nap time. One, because we were full of steak fingers or corn dogs or pizza, and two, because Mrs. Maddux was our music teacher.

Mrs. Maddux had been at Downing forever, maybe longer. And she took her job and music really, really seriously. Every year, she supposedly introduced herself to the class in the same way, though I'd only been lucky enough to hear it once. It went something like this.

"Hello, class, and welcome to the magical world of music," she'd say behind these tear-shaped glasses that had those little chains dangling off each side. "For those of you who are new or who don't remember, I'm..."

Then she'd start scribbling her name on the chalkboard, one stinking syllable at a time.

"Mrs., because I'm a very happily married woman...." Like we were already farkling for first dibs at her. Farkling, as in rock, paper, scissors. No dynamites.

"Mad...., 'cuz I do get that way sometimes," she'd continue, twisting her mug back toward us. "Especially when I don't see four on the floor."

Oh, Mrs. Maddux was a maniac about four on the floor, as in four legs of our chairs on the slick tile floor. If she saw anyone tilting back in their chairs - we didn't have desks in music class, just two long rows of metal folding chairs - then she went ape. Her pasty face would change from an onion into a tomato in a heartbeat.

"Aaaand Dux....," she'd finish, plopping the chalk in the tray and turning to us. Then, the grand finale. "As in ducks, as in quack, quack, quack, quack, quack, quack!"

All the while, she'd be doing this loony duck imitation, flapping her hand over her mouth and waddling and squatting around the room. As I remember, we'd all frozen like popsicles, even the ones who'd survived the bit before.

You didn't catch a 60-year-old lady doing farm animal impressions every day, especially when you were just expecting to pop in and learn a few bars of something obscure while your corn dog settled.

But Mrs. Maddux started with a bang and faded fast. For the rest of the year, music class was an endless collection of songs we'd usually never heard of and would never remember. She called them the oldies but goodies. We called them the oldies.

In Music class, I learned to sleep with my eyes open, like a snake.

Our last hour of school was spent on English. This was my favorite, probably because I spoke it fluently. Besides, after mouthing "Rocka My Soul" for the 93rd time, even those infinitive phrases were a gas.

So that was the school day. Basically, it was just a never-ending string of different colored books. You pulled one out, flipped through it for 45 minutes or so, doodled or tugged on Crystal Kennedy's hair while Miss Gerren snuck a cigarette in the storage room, then yanked out another book. There really hadn't been much important stuff since the alphabet.

A few minutes before class, I made the right-hand turn into G-wing, having no idea what March 21, 1979 would bring.

***

I was struggling with the word 'omission.' We were taking our daily spelling test, and I'd breezed through the meat of it. 'Banister.' Piece of cake. 'Catsup.' Tricky, but I could picture the crusty bottle in our fridge. 'Melodic.' Easy. I quickly jotted it down. Mrs. Maddux would have been proud.

But I was stuck on the omission thing. One 'm' or two? I gnawed on my pencil. I was no genius, but this was my specialty. In social studies or math, red marks were no big deal. In spelling, the stuff looked like blood to me.

Chuck Wentworth was a major suck-up, the king of the hand raisers, but he'd at least filled in the blank next to omission or ommission or whatever. I could see it, barely. Miss Gerren was staring out the window dreaming of her next drag. The lady would have preferred a carton of cigs over an apple. Anyhow, it wouldn't hurt to sneak a peek.

But Chuck, like most brainiacs, was one of those coverer-uppers. His left arm was shadowing most of the answers, including the one I needed, and his body hung low to the desk. You would have thought he was protecting the secret recipe to Coca-Cola or something.

I wrapped my legs around the chair and leaned out.

Farther, just a little farther. Almost there.

"Mister Schitt, just what do you think you're doing?" Her words stung me from my ears to my toes. Busted.

"Um, just stretchin,' Miss Gerren," I said. In a way, it was the truth. She didn't buy it, and I didn't blame her. After a quick swipe of my paper, she pointed me to the corner of the room. On the way, the class let loose with a round of 'oooohs,' and Miss Gerren gave me an 'F' on the quiz. I scrunched into the undersized desk, my back facing the class, and reached for the red dictionary on the shelf.

The word that cornered me, by the way, only has one 'm.' Omission. I would have missed it. I had a few beefs with the English language. For one, I thought 'grammar' would be a lot easier to spell if it were 'grammer.' And why did 'mortgage' have to go and have a 't' in it? And what was a mortgage anyway? I also didn't know why dictionaries had to be a foot thick. Most of the people I knew, even the grown-ups, only used a couple pages worth of words, tops.

The zero would hardly ruin me. It was pretty much impossible to fail a grade in elementary school. I'd only known one kid to get left back. Jo Jo Marx, who rode the short bus and ate dead batteries and live bugs on double dares, had been in fourth grade for like three years. People were starting to lap him.

But the bummer was that Miss Gerren would be on the lookout. A teacher's pet who found his way into the doghouse was history. You got a teacher huffing over your shoulder all the time and your rubber-necking days were pretty much over.

Recess was, as always, too short. I mean, c'mon, 20 minutes was hardly enough time to divide up sides. We were playing kickball that week, and Casey Chandler and I were captains. I picked Chuck first. He wasn't very athletic and didn't even play organized sports, but I noticed that his brown suede shoes were like two bricks. He'd be able to wail on that red rubber ball.

"Chuck?" whispered Casey, who'd already made Wayne Emms his top draft choice.

"Seen his shoes?" I shot back.

He panned down. "Oh. Dang." Casey knew he'd blown one. In kickball, see, it was all about the shoes.

Still, his team was beating mine, 3-2, in the bottom of the last inning when I strutted up to the plate. I checked the outfield positioning. In the distance, Miss Gerren was heading back to the room, and the girls' card game was starting to break up. Some girls jumped rope or did Mad Libs at recess, but most of them were serious Uno! addicts.

On the other diamond, Coach Fred was rounding up the balls. He was a stocky guy who kept us in line on the schoolyard and lived right across the alley from school. He had this bristly haircut, and Kent Stanton said the guy had been a hot shot back in Vietnam. Anyway, Coach Fred didn't really coach anything, but he tossed the ball around a little and let us rub his prickly hair, which was nice of a war hero.

So I was our last chance, and we had runners on second and third. I pointed my toe toward center field. I didn't have a bat, but they knew what I meant.

"Woohoo!" hollered the other side. "Bring it on!"

Casey rolled the ball - the captain was always all-time pitcher - and it dribbled my way. He was probably the best pitcher in our class. Kept it bouncing and spinning all the way, making it tough to take a good whack. In real

baseball, you would have called him "crafty."

"Whoooooshhhh!"

I didn't mind that we didn't win the game. But a big patch of mud covering the seat of my pants wasn't exactly what I'd had in mind, either. The pitch was there, then it wasn't. Looking straight into the sky, Tad stepped over me and flicked dirt in my eyes. It was turning into that kind of day.

***

"Now class, all together now, with feeling!" Mrs. Maddux was trying to teach us a song from "Grease." I liked the movie and all, plus that Olivia Newton-John was a peach. But Mrs. Maddux was no Olivia Newton-John, and there was no way I was going to sing "Summer Lovin'" with any kind of feeling at all.

"Met a girl, cravin' for me!" It was the boys' part, but only Alex Kerns was singing. There was something funny about Alex. I mean, the kid drank Creme soda, wore sandals and called his dad "father."

"Met a boy, cute as can be!" It was the girls' part, and the room was shaking.

It went on, our mumbles, their high-pitched shrills. Jenna Shinn was practically blowing out a vocal cord. And let me tell you, Jenna Shinn was no Olivia Newton-John, either.

I was wondering what could happen next. I'd gotten busted by Miss Gerren, boinked my butt in front of the guys and dripped a good part of a Nutty Buddy down my shirt at lunch. (I swear, the bottom of those Nutty Buddies were booby traps.) So I tilted back, half-listened to Mrs. Maddux skip the needle over the dirty words in "Greased

Lightning" and counted the cracks in the ceiling. Seventy-three, seventy-four...

"Okay, mister, that's it." From the tone on her voice, Mrs. Maddux should have been flapping her hand over her trap. The lady was mad.

She rushed my way, her chins following. "For years, I've told you all four on the floor or out the door, and this time I really mean it!" And she did mean it. In no time, I had two on the floor, as in two legs heading for the office.

I was Mrs. Maddux's last straw. She clomped behind me on the way. I wasn't too worried. Not keeping four on the floor wasn't exactly worth a call to the folks. I'd probably be jailed next to a kid who hadn't picked up his feet while walking. Shuffling, that was another big crime at Downing.

Giving flat tires to the backs of shoes, too.

"Just what happened to your hind end, mister?" The very thought of her eyes on my caboose gave me the chills.

Still, it didn't exactly feel like a death march. The office wasn't so bad. It was the coldest room in the whole school, and sometimes there were little cups of punch lined out for the sick kids. More than once, I'd seen Mr. Edmondson roaming the halls with a Kool-Aid mustache on top of his real mustache.

Mrs. Maddux disappeared into a back room in the office. From around her shoulder, I could see Mr. Gorman, the assistant principal, nodding like a robot. He was trying to pay attention, but I could tell he just heard vibrations flying out of her head hole.

Finally, she came out and stood over me.

"Now, you stay here for the rest of the hour. You're not to move an inch, understand?" I nodded, and she stormed out. (Shuffled, if you have to know.)

No problem, I thought to myself. In fact, I was pretty darn comfortable right there. The air conditioner was blasting, and in the background the radio was playing a snappy tune. I picked up a Highlights magazine, flipped to the section where kids sent in their drawings and wondered if the six-year-old who'd sketched the cool tiger was really 16.

So everything was fine. That is, everything until Fast Eddie Kemp walked in.

***

Fast Eddie wasn't on the track team. In fact, the only running Fast Eddie ever did was from the police. He was riding on those laws that protected minors, probably dreading the day he turned 18. So far, depending on whose story you believed, he'd gotten away with robbery, assault, a whole lot of skipping out and maybe (or maybe not) even the murder of Melanie Maloney's cat. But no one ever saw him doing any of that. He was kind of like Paul Bunyon, a tall tale. The stories just kept getting bigger and bigger. Still, just in case, we all steered way, way clear of the guy.

He was supposed to be in the class two doors down from ours, but you could usually find Fast Eddie in one of two places - in the principal's office, or out by the long-jump pits smoking Camels. Or, on that afternoon, naturally, right next to me on the bench.

I couldn't help but look, although I did it secretly, like a pitcher checking a runner at first base. Eddie was still in that disco mode. He was wearing a half-buttoned silk shirt covered with little drawings of the Alamo, and a sunshaped medallion dangled across his chest. His pants flared out at the bottom, ending right at a scuffed pair of square black shoes with two-inch heels. Would have made a good kickball pick, I noted to myself.

"So, whatta ya in for, Jasper?" he asked, his droopy eyes tuned straight ahead. It took me by surprise, because I knew he didn't know my name. I wasn't sure he knew his own.

"Um, well, Mrs. Maddux, um…" I struggled. It was the first time I'd been asked that one. I felt like a bit character in a prison movie, the kind that got killed before the good parts.

"Tiltin,' huh?" he said, unimpressed. Then he rolled his head in the opposite direction along the wall. I had to admit, it wasn't a very impressive offense. "Gotta keep four on the floor in there, dude."

For some reason, I didn't just sit back, enjoy the padded seat cushion and the Arctic breeze and leave it at that. It seemed only polite to ask.

"So what about you?"

Fast Eddie tossed his head back toward me. His eyes were bloodshot, and a few blonde whiskers hung from his chin. We were probably about the same age, but he'd lived much longer.

"Killin' a tilter," he said blankly. His eyes narrowed under his stringy hair, and he dragged his tongue across his bottom lip. "Maddux pays me five bucks to snuff out tilters."

Then he looked me over from head to toe, slowly. "But I'd do this one for nothin.'" His eyes were fixed on mine, at least until I started messing with the dried ice cream on my shirt. Finally, the bell rang. It was probably only minutes, but they felt like dog minutes.

I knew he was kidding. I mean, the guy was dressed to boogie, not butcher. But it was my first death threat, so I took it seriously, like those people working at the X-ray machines in airports.

"No, William, they weren't screwed, as you so delicately put it. The important thing is that they were both willing to make a huge sacrifice for one another."

That was Miss Gerren's voice drifting from the classroom as I approached. She was explaining the moral thing to *The Gift of the Magi*, that short story we'd been reading where the guy sold his watch to give his wife a hair thingee, and the lady hacked and hocked her hair to give her husband a watch thingee. It was called irony, and the guy who wrote it had gotten rich off the stuff. I couldn't quite remember his name.

I wasn't that wild about the chalkboard part of English class, the verb usage and sentence diagrams and all, but I kind of enjoyed the literature part. I really, really liked to read. I especially leaned toward sports biographies, like the one I was reading about George Brett, the baseball slugger for the Kansas City Royals. If there was a job where a guy could just read all day long, I thought I'd like to look into it. Either that or play pro ball and goof off the rest of the time, like George. Or maybe be a game-show host.

I tried to be invisible as I drifted into the room. It didn't work.

"Well, thank you for joinin' us, Jasper," Miss Gerren said. I was late, the result of too many cups of grape punch and about a 10-minute wait outside the office bathroom. Mrs. Salmon, the school secretary, was in there forever. I don't even want to talk about that.

"Sorry, Miss Gerren." I started to slide into my desk.

"No sir, you're still in the back," she said, snapping her fingers and pointing toward Dunceland in the corner. My sentence wasn't up yet.

"Yes, ma'am."

I grabbed my book and headed off. Along the way, I heard Billy whisper, "Get back in that doghouse."

He was right on; it had been a dog of a day. The cheating, the kickball whiff, the chair. Oh, and the nice chat with spooky Fast Eddie and the discovery that Mrs. Salmon must have went with the chili for lunch.

I knew there were kids with pictures on those UNICEF cans at convenience stores who really knew what a lousy day was, but, as I squashed back into the desk, I didn't feel all that bad for them.

***

The last bell finally rang, and we were waiting for Miss Anderson - girls cluttered on the right of the bus stop sign, boys on the left. Everyone except for Danny Butler and Candy Kessler. They were, as usual, drooling all over each other behind the school sign. They made that kissing stuff look messier than barbecue ribs. Then again, I was a pretty big fan of barbecue ribs.

"Yeeeehaaawwwww!!!!" I felt the pull, but it was too late. From the force of the tug, there must have been at least three of them. Before I could even flinch, my underwear was stretched clear up to my collar. It was a full-on, first- rate, black belt of an atomic wedgie.

I turned to see Tad, Billy and Casey rolling around on the ground, laughing like monkeys and holding their bellies. I struggled to hurry my shorts back into my jeans, but they were too mangled to fit. Instead, I untucked my shirt, trying to hide them and to ignore the laughter that surrounded me. I wanted to give the whole day a big doover.

"Pssshhhhttt." The bus door opened, and I slugged Billy in the shoulder as he cut past me in line.

"Aw, just havin' some fun," he laughed, pushing Andrea

Woodsworth out of his way. "Don't be mad."

Tad ruffled my hair and blew past. "Wedged!"

I didn't mind the wedgie all that much. At some point, most of the guys in the class had gotten one, including the three wedgers in this case. It was actually a good sign. Nobody ever bothered to give the goobers wedgies. But to kick a guy when he was down, well, that was just wrong.

I settled into a seat near the middle of the bus, the one that made you scrunch all up because the tire was sticking out. Perfect. Nobody joined me. I think I had a 'Do Not Disturb' look hanging on my face.

I tried to do some homework, but it was like trying to write on a roller coaster. I made an 'm', and it wound end up halfway down the page. I tossed the spiral aside and opened up "How to Eat Fried Worms," a book I'd checked out of the library. But reading was out, too. After two paragraphs, my stomach started turning like I'd eaten, well, fried worms. I stared straight ahead.

"Don't ya even think about it, mister!" Miss Anderson was scowling into the mirror, her eyes wide and scary. And they were directed right at me.

"What, I'm just chewin' on it," I said, a straw dangling from my mouth. And I was, too. I'd gotten it at the cafeteria during lunch and tucked it in my pocket. Plus, it was one of skinny, red, stir straws that couldn't do any damage at all.

Shunking was the last thing on my mind. Honest.

"Uh, huh, surrre ya are," she smirked, returning her stare to Bunker Avenue. Tad, who was sitting directly behind her, covered a laugh.

"But really I...."

I felt something hit my lap. It rolled down my shirt, bounced at the third button and stopped right by my privates. I turned around to find Billy sporting a sinister smile that was usually reserved for mad scientists during the late, late, late show.

"Made it just for ya," he whispered. "Paybacks for the wedge."

I examined his gift. It was probably the most perfectly packed spitwad in spitwad history. Must have been half a sheet of paper. A real Billy Teakwood special. I turned back to him.

"Do it," he said, sliding me a straw. It was a McDonald's one, a grenade launcher as straws went. "Do it. Get Tad. Get that sucker."

Inside, I felt a rush of revenge, a feeling of rebellion. The world had been pounding on me all day, ever since the plastic bear whistled at me before school, telling me that my morning biscuits would go without honey. I owed the world, or at least bratty Tad Galbreath, one swing back.

I looked to Miss Anderson, who was back to her routine.

Road. Side mirror. Rear-view mirror. Road. Side. Rear view. Beating her was like getting away with a booger pick-and-flick in public: timing was everything.

I tossed my mangled straw aside, replaced it with the Howitzer and loaded the wad. It fit perfectly, with just enough room to spare. See, if you packed a straw too full, your missile got clogged. Small wads didn't have enough weight to complete their mission. Size mattered.

As Miss Anderson slowly turned on to Apricot Avenue, throwing her hands across each other like she was steering a battleship, I noticed Tad was nodding off. His head would fall, jerk up in a rush and repeat. Then and there, I decided to revive him with a nice, juicy surprise.

Side view.

I ducked low, propping the straw against the seat in front of me.

Rear view.

Luckily, I was again parked right behind Alice, the girl whose forehead was so big it was actually a fivehead. It was no different than hiding behind a boulder. I huddled near her but kept the straw zeroed in on Tad.

Road.

I let it rip, spun around and stashed the straw in the seat. Then I hit the dirt.

From the jerk that followed, I thought it was all over for us. The bus pulled quickly to the right, then weaved hard to the left. Everyone on the right side, including myself, was tossed into the middle aisle. The girls screamed at once, just like in music class. Finally, the bus stopped in a heap, slamming me into a steel chair leg.

Without a sound, Miss Anderson got up and started down the row. My face was planted against the sticky, black floor matting, and all I could see was her worn house shoes. (Terrible kickball shoes.) They worked past the kids on the floor and, step by step, headed my way. I'd never even thought of her having legs. They were short and stumpy, and I prayed they would pass over me.

Not a chance, not on this day.

"Young man, you git up this instant." Her tone was harsh, like a stove burner that you obeyed without hesitation.

I pulled myself up, still a little out of it, and stood before her. I avoided her eyes, instead staring at her mouth, which hung open a little. I wondered if the tooth was real gold. Finally, after a moment of nothing, I lifted my stare.

There'd been no accident. It was more like a disaster. The spitwad was sticking right to her forehead. Good velocity, bad aim.

My left eye, always the left, started to twitch.

"Just what do ya have to say for yourself, young man?" Miss Anderson asked. I looked to Billy. He shook his head slightly, as if to tell me that playing dumb wouldn't fly.

"Um, well, I, I didn't mean to," I stuttered, hypnotized on her forehead. The wad was practically welded on. I could feel a busload of eyes surrounding me. Tad was wide awake now and giving Miss Anderson rabbit ears from behind.

"You will never, ever ride this bus again," she said coldly. "Do ya hear me? Never!"

My stomach did a nosedive. For a bunch of reasons, that just couldn't happen. More than anything, it meant my folks would have to lug me to school every morning and then leave work early to pick me up. And the fact that I'd been banned from public transportation wouldn't be a good dinner topic, either.

"Please, Miss Anderson," I pleaded. "Please, I'll do anything. Anything."

She crossed her arms and bit her lip, as if she was thinking pretty hard. Finally, like the breaking of chains, the wad fell off. Together, we watched it catch a groove in the mat and roll back toward the emergency exit door. I wanted to follow.

For the second time in four hours, I was some lady's last nerve.

***

Her sentence was a little harsh, I thought while jogging across College Drive to reach Bushwood Trail. I mean, I didn't mind hoofing it home. It was only a mile or so, and I'd just gotten some new tennies that needed breaking in. Nope, taking the 'ol Kaepa Express didn't bother me one bit.

But a whole Saturday of work at Miss Anderson's house? First of all, I never pictured the lady even having a house. I guess I always figured she lived on that bus. But worst of all, her place was clear across town, meaning I'd have to get a ride, meaning I'd have to tell my parents why I needed to spend a Saturday on the south side. Or at least come up with a good story. Probably that.

I started working on my plan while cutting through Mr. Dickey's yard and knifing between Mr. Rawley's hedges. I finished it while hustling through the Steele's lawn, which was guarded by one of those plastic monkeys holding a lantern.

"I need a ride to the Boys Club in the mornin,'" I said to Dad, who was kicked back in the recliner, his face buried in the sports page.

He turned the upper-right corner of the paper down, just enough for his voice to buzz around the boxscores. "Oh yeah? What for?"

"Um, there's a big garage sale goin' on up there, and they need people to help out. You know, settin' up tables and stuff."

"A garage sale?"

"Um, yeah, to help raise money for new basketball goals and stuff."

"Oh, I see. Well, okay, sure." The paper returned to its original state. "What time?"

"Um, I need to be there around 7:30." Yep, 7:30. Miss Anderson had said to be at her front door no later than 8:00, and, judging from her directions, I figured that she lived at least 15 walking minutes from the Boys Club.

"Oh, okay, son." He wiggled his toe, and it stuck straight through the hole in his ragged, blue socks. Dad either needed smaller toes or bigger socks. They were all growing older together.

I felt a twinge of guilt while walking away, and it hung with me during a dinner of individual pizzas and garlic bread. I still felt pretty crappy about the whole day during *The Dukes of Hazzard*, but by the time "The Incredible Hulk" was over and the theme of *Dallas* started up, I was starting to come around. Compared to the Hulk, my problems were scratch.

For most Texans, Dallas was serious stuff. That was the big question of the day - "Who shot J.R.?" It was plastered on like every other bumper in town, and the show was especially huge in Midtex because they were always coming here to do business on the show. I had to admit, it was kind of cool hearing Bobby say, "Pamela, I'm fixin' to fly down to Midtex to close a deal." Anyway, Dad really got sucked in by it all, coming home a couple weeks back with a huge "Who Shot J.R.?" button dangling from his dress shirt. He bet me a buck that it was Ray. I said Sue Ellen. Mom pretended she didn't care, but I thought she was leaning toward Lucy.

Mostly, though, *Dallas* meant nine 'o clock, which meant ice-cream time. I spooned out a monster bowl of Tin Roof, bending back the spoon and dragging my hand along the side of the box, and drowned it in chocolate syrup. Dad went with the Rocky Road and then plopped down a hunk of orange sherbet in a cup for Mom. I figured that was part of marriage and love and all, being willing to get sticky for someone.

Our dog Sam hung close to our feet, waiting for a spill. Sam acted like a beggar on the street, always grunting for something or another. We didn't have much to do with each other, mostly because Mom was always getting his hair all puffed up and hanging ribbons from his ears. A kid couldn't run around the block with a dolled-up poodle with painted fingernails. Sam would get down and dirty for ice cream, though, and he made for a good dishwasher.

"Jasper's going to help out with an event at the Boys Club tomorrow morning," Dad blurted out during a commercial.

"Oh really?" Mom said, carefully spooning out some sherbet. She handled the stuff like it was an explosive.

I buried my head in the bowl and sunk low in my bean-bag chair, hoping it would all go away. Not only had my fib become common knowledge, but it was being plugged as a good deed.

The 'ol double whammy.

"So what kind of sale? Tell us about it." Moms never let stuff slide. I wanted to tell the truth, really I did. I mean, I was the fourth boy in the family, so they'd dealt with much worse. Plus, I was shooting at Tad, really I was. They didn't like him, anyhow. Too much like that Eddie Haskell on *Leave it to Beaver*, Dad always said. But I knew they'd be disappointed anyway, which came a pretty close second to a slow and hideous death in my book.

"Oh, it's just a thing to help buy some things for sports stuff." It wasn't much, but it was probably all they'd come to expect out of me. Anyway, I guess it was enough.

"Well, I think that's very nice of you, honey," Mom said, clinking her bowl. Sam trotted over for the kill.

"Takin' time out of your weekend and all."

I disappeared deeper into the bag. Inside, I felt even lower.

"Rrriiinnnggg!"

Ah, saved by the bell. It was Billy, calling to invite me over for some video games and his mom's strawberry cheesecake. True, he was the reason I was in the whole mess in the first place, but grudges played second fiddle to Intellivision every time.

"So can I?" Dad was glued to Bobby and Pam by then, so only Mom heard me.

"Oh, I don't think so, honey," she said. "You have to get up too early tomorrow. Is Billy going to help, too?"

Somewhere, I could picture Miss Anderson smiling away, her gold tooth sparkling, her forehead dry and clean.

I decided to call it a night and play some Nerf hoops in my room. It was the Lakers versus the Sixers, and I swapped between imitating Kareem Abdul-Jabbar and Dr. J, with a little help from "Silk" Wilkes and Maurice Cheeks. But it was pretty much sky hook, dunk, sky hook, dunk. The Lakers were in the hole, 128-127, with four seconds left when a hook from Kareem rolled in and out. But I figured he'd gotten fouled, and he drained the two free shots, nothing but string, to ice the game.

In Midtex, a kid had to have an imagination.

I wasn't a strong sleeper, having picked up a touch of the insomnia thing from my mom, who hadn't gotten much shut-eye since having four sons. Anyhow, that night I kept imagining what Miss Anderson was going to have me do. She'd decided that she and I could spend a day working around her house instead of my getting reported to the suits at school. I could have maybe talked my way out of the spitwad deal, but the flying bodies part would have probably landed me in detention with Fast Eddie. A day with the bus driver beat a week with a lunatic.

Still, as I drifted off around two o'clock, I dreamed that she was going to make me eat a spitwad bigger than Cleveland.

***

I could set a clock by my dad. Every morning when I got up, he'd be there, sitting at the dinner table in his baby blue pajamas, sipping on a cup of coffee. It was a given. The fiery end of his pipe burned like a lantern as I stumbled toward the kitchen in a ball cap, gym shorts and a Downing Tiger T-shirt. It was 7:12.

"Bout ready, Jasp?" he asked, pulling up from his chair.

"Uh huh," I mumbled. But I wasn't, not at all.

Dad could also get ready faster than anyone I knew. He would drag toward his bedroom, picking out the seat of his pants, and then appear in like 40 seconds ready to go to church. I think it was the coffee. People were like dust storms on that stuff.

The drive to the Boys Club was quiet. There was hardly anyone on the road, just a few work trucks with things like "Ed's Electrical Service" and "Del's Rigging" plastered on the sides. If it meant getting up at seven in the morning on a weekend, I didn't want to ever drive anything with my name on it.

Like I said before, trucks were a big deal in Midtex.

About everyone drove one. Old people and young people. Men, ladies, boys, girls. There were tall trucks and short trucks, wide trucks and wider trucks. Some people carted around stuff in them, but mostly they were just for show. I didn't quite get the point of an empty truck. To me, it seemed like having a Pez dispenser without any candy.

We pulled up to the Midtex Westside Boys Club. It was an old building with blue, chipped trim and a metal roof. Had been there for years and was a safe haven for the kids from the rough areas to hang out. I'd been a few times for league basketball games and once for a picnic, and the place was always busy with activity.

Well, not on this morning.

"So where is everyone?" Dad asked. Except for a red Jeep on cinder blocks, we were the only car in sight.

"Um, we must be early." I hadn't thought that far ahead. "Thought you said 7:30?"

I looked at the clock on the dash. It was 7:29.

"Um, yeah, well, the thing is inside, so I guess maybe everyone was early, and, uh, their parents left already." It was at least possible.

"Okay," he said, sounding satisfied. "What time do ya need me to come get ya?"

I didn't know when my sentence would be lifted. "Um,

I'll call you."

"Okay, well, happy sellin,' son!"

"Yeah, okay." I shut the door and walked slowly, very slowly, toward the entrance.

I wasn't sure if he bought it or not. Dad always pretended to believe but sometimes really knew. Mom, she hardly ever believed and always knew. And she heard everything, too. If you mentioned a toy or a game in February, you were sure to find it under the tree on the next Christmas morning. So you had to watch yourself around her because she didn't understand that the idea of some toys and games was only good for awhile, like milk.

But Dad gave me the benefit of the doubt, pulling out of the parking lot and turning right down Lone Star Lane. I guess he figured whatever I was up to couldn't be too fun, not way over in what a lot of people called "darkland."

I'd never felt more alone, or different. It wasn't that I bought into all that racial stuff. I never understood why we were always separated, blacks from whites, whites from most everybody, like we didn't know how to act if we crossed over a set of railroad tracks or passed a certain street. I left all that hating to old people who didn't have homework and ball practice to worry about. I mean, I usually felt a little out of place no matter where I was.

Still, I didn't know much about black kids. There were only a few at Downing, and they hung out in their own little pack. All I really knew was that the boys were fast and that the girls sprayed stuff in their hair that smelled like a beauty parlor. Midtex wasn't exactly a melting pot; it was more of a TV dinner with all the stuff still separated by aluminum walls.

Walking down Dixie Drive, I quickly found out that porches were the place to be. Every house had one, and they all already seemed to be full of people and music. I tried to stand tall and to walk tough, but my Ocean Pacific shorts weren't fooling anyone. I imagined myself a miniature Clint Eastwood, a mysterious wanderer. It made me feel a little safer, but not much. I know what you're thinking. Poor, spoiled, white kid. Well, I was thinking the same thing.

Still, it couldn't be as bad as the day before.

I walked along, eyes straight ahead, feeling like a duck in the shooting range at the carnival. In the distance, a couple of older kids were chunking around a taped-up ball. I remembered that a big neighborhood football game was supposed to get started around 9:00 in the pasture behind Monty Allen's house. Monty was a little weird, sometimes disappearing for days to go play that Dungeons and Dragons game, but he had the best football yard on the block, hands down.

***

Miss Anderson's house was much like every other one on the block. Old. Square. White. Small. Very small. Everything except for the yard, which was blanketed with grass that reached my waist and was every bit as big as

Monty's. As I made my way up to the sidewalk, passing a faded blue car in front that couldn't possibly run, I had a pretty good idea of what one of my chores would be.

I stepped to the front door and checked my watch. I didn't really need a watch, by the way, not having many places to be, but it felt a little adult to wear one. 7:58. Right on time with two minutes to spare, I thought as I tapped lightly. Nothing. I waited for a good minute before knocking again. More nothing. I squinted through the window. All was quiet and dark.

I was off the hook.

"'Round here." I was back on the hook. Miss Anderson was wearing blue jean overalls and leaning against a shovel. A red bandanna covered her hair, and her forehead was already drenched with sweat.

"Follow me," she mumbled, turning and disappearing around the corner.

I hopped off the porch and followed. She stomped through the grass in work boots, pulling an empty wagon, and I traced her steps. We reached the backyard, a spread that was every bit a jungle as the front. The yellow grass tickled my thighs as I caught up.

She stood there, wiping her forehead and scanning the yard. I stood a few feet behind and waited, then felt a stare and turned just in time to see the curtains in the back window fall back.

The yard was a disaster. Along with the high grass, there was stuff everywhere. Lots and lots of stuff. Toys.

An old car. A swing-set frame with no swings. A little plastic pool with no water. A shed with no doors. I kind of expected that Fred Sanford guy to pop outta it and say he was having the big one.

"We're goin' to clean up this here yard today," Miss Anderson stated, throwing the shovel over her shoulder. It wasn't a question. "You start mowin,' and I'll clean up ahead of ya."

She pointed to her left, where the mower was propped against the back porch. It wasn't a gas-powered one, like the one we had at home, or even an electric one, like the strange one with the orange cord that our neighbor Mr. Doogan was always getting tangled up in. It had a handle and a blade and ran on one thing. Me.

It might be worse than the day before, I thought as I grabbed the thing and started bumping along.

The blade was just a little sharper than a rock and was really no match for the grass. I squinted at the rising sun and leaned hard on the handle, slowly working it through the weeds and trying to stay straight. One wheel was shot, so the thing pulled hard to the left. After about 30 minutes, six strips and a few pounds, I was pretty wobbly, too.

Miss Anderson plugged away in front of me, loading what seemed like a toy store into the wagon. There were GI Joes with Kung-Fu grips, Barbies, Luke Skywalkers, Evil Knievels, all the good stuff. But they were all worn - Evil didn't even have a head - and looked about shot. Kind of like Miss Anderson, who said nothing but grumbled to herself a bunch.

She was pretty much what I'd expected her to be. She moved slowly, like it hurt, and her expression never changed a lick. It was like I didn't even exist, like the grass was just disappearing from behind her. It was only one day, I promised myself after finishing a long line and picking a sticker patch out of my sock. I looked around. The yard looked like it was in the no-turning-back stages of a crewcut.

***

After a couple of hours, the toys' owners started filing out of the house. First there was a skinny kid, probably about eight or nine and wearing a Dallas Cowboys #88 jersey. Next came a short, stubby one, I'd guess about two years younger, who was sucking on a giant-sized jawbreaker. Finally, out snuck a little girl who had bright, pink streamers in her hair and a Smurfs T-shirt that covered her from head to knee. The Andersons came in all shapes and sizes.

I felt them staring at me, this sweaty white kid pushing around the dinosaur. I was probably almost halfway done, but it seemed like I'd been hacking for days. They didn't offer to help, though the oldest boy did look sort of interested. I thought about maybe dancing around a little, making it look like a blast, an honor, like Tom

Sawyer painting his fence. Miss Anderson brushed past me and shot me a scowl. Or maybe not.

"Ya'll get on in an' get dressed," Miss Anderson barked. "There's work to do, ya hear?"

They must have known it was coming, because they started toward the door before she even spoke. They disappeared in a blur, leaving the thing hanging wide open. Miss Anderson had a lot more pull with her kids than with her passengers.

"An' get yer daddy up while yer in there!"

For the first time all day, I locked eyes with Miss Anderson. They were dark, just like always, but looked more tired than anything. It was like she'd had a long string of long days and had a lot on her mind. Another thing I was noticing about grown-ups; the older they got, the heavier their heads. More full of stuff and all, I guess.

"You a'right?" she asked.

I nodded.

She nodded back.

With that, she returned to her business. I did the same. Carving around a patch of tree roots, I pictured the guys back on the block, dividing up teams. Running, laughing, arguing, fighting. Ten or 15 guys could make a whole lot of noise and kick up a whole lot of dust. But Miss Anderson and me, well, we were just going to play the quiet game here.

Fifteen minutes later, her kids joined us. They looked the same as before, only with pants, and were each pretending to do something. The oldest kid pretended to pick up stuff. Invisible stuff. The younger boy pretended to pull weeds. Invisible weeds. And the little girl, who was half of nothing, was standing around and pretending to watch my every move. Well, she wasn't really pretending.

The kid was all over me.

"You boys helpin' any?" Miss Anderson cried out.

"Yes, ma'am," they said together.

At least they knew the game. Whenever their mom looked, they acted like they just couldn't wait to get to another weed or root or toy. When she looked away, they made faces at each other and giggled. It was no different than their mom's side mirror, rear view, road bit, and they had it down. Miss Anderson was pretty predictable, except for the time I'd let loose with the mother of all spitwads, of course.

Rolling toward the house, I noticed a newcomer on the rickety back porch. A man was leaning forward in his chair and sliding on his shoes. He was wearing a blue shirt with no sleeves, and his arms were bigger than my waist.

Finally, some real help.

Only he didn't help. After his shoes were good and tied, the guy just leaned back in the chair, fixed his black sunglasses on his nose and started rocking. And rocking. And rocking. It wasn't a rocking chair, just one of those metal jobs, but he had the balance bit down. I couldn't help but think that Mrs. Maddux would have nailed him in a second. (Four on the floor or out the door, you know.)

He propped his hands behind his head and threw his face toward the sun. A little grin stretched across his mug. Soon, the little girl climbed the three porch steps, crawled into his lap and threw her arms around his neck. He was going nowhere fast.

I reached the house and stopped for a breather. The sun hung directly above now and was starting to get serious. I wiped my face and reviewed my work. There was a hairy patch here and there, but it didn't look too bad, at least for having little more than a butter knife to work with.

Along the back fence, Miss Anderson had the boys down on their knees. Only they weren't pretending, not anymore. She was holding a bag and, very, very, very slowly, they were filling it with weeds and rocks and whatever else their bare hands could find. Under the Texas sun, nobody was fast, not even black kids.

I felt a little twinge in my stomach while looking at the yard. It might have been from hunger, but I wanted to believe it was more from, well, pride. It looked like the before and after of one of those makeover shows that ladies liked to watch. And best of all, I was way over halfway done. Well, not counting the front yard.

"I reckon this is for you."

I turned. It was the man, still rocking away. The little girl was still blanketed across his lap, but she was holding out a jar full of water.

"Go 'head, give it to the man, baby."

She offered it, and I climbed the stairs and took it.

"Thanks," I said to her. She hurried back into the man's lap and buried her head into his chest.

Taking a long drink, I snuck a look at him through the glass. He was staring right back at me, wearing those big sunglasses that looked 10 times as big through the funhouse effect of the jar. The little girl was staring again, too. Like father, like daughter, I figured.

For a bunch of reasons, I finished the water all in one tilt. One, I was really thirsty. Two, I didn't want to have to stand there and make conversation.

"Thanks again," I said, stretching out the empty glass. The girl hopped up and took it with both hands. The guy didn't even budge. Man, what a deadbeat, I grunted to myself as I returned to the grind.

I started to pick up the pace. Plus, with the path cleared,

I was able to tear from fence to fence at a decent clip. I did get a little out of control at one point, though, mauling over a miniature GI Joe and slicing his arm off. I tossed it in the wagon, real secret like, and continued on. His Kung Fu grip days were over.

Plowing through the last few strips, I got to wondering what made someone want to be a bus driver. They had to get paid by the hour, and since they only worked before and after school, the checks had to be peanuts. By the way, I knew a kid who worked at the concession stand for the Midtex Bears, the town's semi-pro baseball club, and that was his bonus at the end of the summer. Peanuts, a whole year's supply. His pockets were always loaded with them at school.

We called him Squirrel.

I could see being a truck driver, rolling across the country while sitting tall and having that loud and proud horn to blow, but a bus driver? I'd once been out to the bus barn on the far side of town, having left an Earth Science book under my seat, kind of on purpose, and everyone was dragging around and cussing and smoking. Seemed like not even the bus drivers liked being bus drivers. Maybe the man on the porch had a good job, but I couldn't see it. Not the human statue. I didn't know how they got by.

Thing was, they really didn't. They lived a life that I couldn't imagine, one full of hand-me-down toys and patched-up windows and folding chairs. And the inside of the house, well, I didn't even want to imagine it. With my mom, cleaning house was a never-ending deal. You picked up a cup, she wiped the ring under it. You threw some underwear in the hamper, they were clean and folded almost before you could pull on some new ones. And she was so organized that she still had the receipt on Sam the dog. I'd even thought about bringing her along to college with me someday.

But the Andersons, they were amateur cleaner uppers.

***

I finished 15 minutes later. Relieved of their duties, the boys were tossing around a foam football with a chunk torn outta it. The older one dropped back and let one fly, but the spiral began to sputter as it died about five feet short of its target. I recognized the flutter; dogs could really let the air out of those Nerfs.

The yard looked good, not great. It was pretty similar to the job I did at home. A patch here, a crooked line there. I was definitely no Mr. Sanderson, our neighbor who cut the yard perfectly and diagonally and wasn't satisfied until it looked better than Wrigley Field. But he was old. I was almost 12 and had bigger things going on. But anything was an improvement. At least it didn't look so "Hee Haw" anymore.

"C'mon, reckon we'd better get you somethin' to eat." It was Miss Anderson, hands on hips, sweating pouring off of her like she was a human glass of lemonade. I realized that mowing had probably been the easy part.

I shrugged. It was my way of saying yes. I was starving.

"Dinner!" she hollered, limping away. To me, dinner was what you ate after *Family Feud,* and lunch came after fourth hour at school. But I had a few friends who called lunch dinner and dinner supper. Anyhow, it was time to eat.

The younger kid spiked the football and did a quick dance, then raced his older brother to the front door. On the porch, the little girl snapped her book shut and slid off the man's lap. He leaned forward in his chair, still smiling that same goofy smile and going nowhere fast. Miss Anderson might have had the kids trained, but her husband, or whoever he was, owned her. No wonder she was always such a sour puss, I thought as I tried to find my legs under the dirt and scratches.

But it was pretty ridiculous. As I started toward the house, I saw Miss Anderson pull the guy out of his chair and practically roll out the red carpet for him until he got inside. As she leaned against the door frame and waited on me, I decided that even though I'd never really had a real girlfriend, I wanted that kind of deal when I found one.

I stumbled on the bottom step, and it hit me harder than an Indian knuckle torture in the middle of my chest. Miss Anderson wasn't just a lady who drove a bus or the wife of a deadbeat in a rusty chair. Nope, she was a Mrs. Anderson, the mother of three small children, the keeper of a house that was falling apart and the eyes for a husband that couldn't see a lick.

He wasn't the only blind one.

"C'mon up now, before it's all gone," she said to me through the screen door.

I hurried inside to find, well, another mess. Clothes hung everywhere, some clean, some not, and the sink was full of dishes, none of them clean. The kitchen was small and gray and grimy. Besides Mrs. Anderson and me, everyone was packed around the table. The laundry made the whole room smell like an old sock. I noticed some different-shaped bowls of food on the table. At least I hoped it was the laundry I smelled.

"Um, may I go the bathroom?" I asked. I was about to blow.

"Sure, son," said the man, looking straight ahead. "But ya best make it on back reaaaal quick, because food don't last long 'round here." I nodded.

"We'll wait," Mrs. Anderson said, dragging the chair in from the porch. "Bathroom's down the hall and on the left."

I made my way, wondering if the rest of them knew what I was even doing there. I figured they did, at least the man, and wondered what they thought of me. It had been disrespectful, but, more than that, just plain mean. Strangers did mean things to other strangers all the time, but they didn't usually end up cramped at a dinner (or supper or whatever) table with them.

I took care of my business, watching out for the split spray and the shake and taking extra careful aim. Bad shooting, after all, had started the whole thing. Returning to the kitchen, I saw that the rest of the house was also in a sad state. The furniture was old, but not good, expensive old, and the television was tiny, with a wire hanger dangling out of its back. Clothes, mostly little clothes, were scattered all over the room, and a box of Fruit Snaps was turned on its side on the floor. And on the coffee table sat a scattered pile of stamps. Green ones. I wasn't exactly sure what they were for, but I knew that you didn't want to have to need them.

I ducked under a shirt hanging in the hallway. It was red and blue with a little patch across the heart that said "Dixie's Diner." Dixie's was an all-night grease pit out on Highway 118 that had a reputation for great burgers and terrible customers. I hoped they at least didn't shunk things.

"Good Lord, bless this food that you have given us this day," the man said, his clenched hands resting against his shades. "An' thank ya for the many blessings you have given to this here family. We accept your gifts with humble, happy hearts an' hope that you'll continue to shine your light over this home, now and forever after."

I thought he was done, but I stayed tucked, just in case. Even if he had been, it was one of the best prayers I'd ever heard. Not one on those that you memorized in Sunday School, but the kind you sort of felt.

"An' thank ya for bringin' our young friend here with us today." I opened my eyes. I was the only one. "Amen," he said.

"Amen," chimed in the rest of them, as if it was rehearsed.

"Amen," I said too late.

***

For the next 30 minutes or so, we had probably about the most normal meal that any six people at a table made for four had ever had. After a few minutes of dish clanking and plate filling, the boys started talking and never really stopped. But it was about pretty good stuff, like sports and toys and baseball cards. I found out that Raymond, the oldest and just two grades behind me, was the quarterback of his flag football team, liked science class best and had two Hank Aaron rookie cards (!).

And Kevin, a kid who ate first and chewed later, wanted to get a paper route so he could save up for a Dallas Cowboys #56 jersey. That was the number of Hollywood Henderson, a flashy linebacker for the Dallas Cowboys with gold stars in his teeth. It figured. The kid was going to be a tank, and he was already a ham.

I didn't say much and spoke only when spoken to, but I listened a whole lot. Over at Monty's, I imagined that my friends were talking about the same kind of things. Except for the food, which I didn't really understand but ate most of anyway, it was like any meal on any side of any tracks.

The little girl was cute. Every time I looked over at her, she hid behind her dad. When she thought it was safe, she peeked back and snickered. She wanted to say something but couldn't. I felt the very same way with the girls at school.

But she also fed her pop his entire meal. I had the feeling that he didn't need the help, but he let her do it all the same. She spooned him each bite very carefully and always made sure that he was ready for another one.

"All gone, daddy?" she'd ask.

"All gone, baby," he'd say, smiling and opening wide. It was probably an old game to them, but I thought it was pretty neat. Tell you the truth, I sort of had to smile to keep from bawling.

Other than that, the guy didn't say much. He laughed a lot though, a deep one that reminded me of the guy from *Soul Train* on Saturday mornings. On his arm closest to me, I noticed a tattoo. It was a heart, with the words "My Arlene" scribbled in black, fancy letters within it.

It was weird how things could change. In half a day, 'ol Miss Anderson had become a Mrs. Anderson and grown legs and gotten a family, a house and a first name. (At least for his sake I hoped her name was Arlene.)

My bus driver didn't say much, either; she just sort of munched slowly and let all the noise bounce off her. Figured she was used to it. Every so often, she told the boys to chew their food once in a while or wiped off the girl's milk mustache, but mostly she just listened. My dad sometimes said that I was an observer, a watcher. Well, she was the same way.

Toward the end, I looked up at her. She was turned toward Raymond, who was explaining to Kevin why The Incredible Hulk could never whip Superman. Superman would just fly away, he said. (That was an easy one, but I didn't feel right about saying so.) Anyhow, Mrs. Anderson was smiling. It wasn't one of those wide, cartoon grins, just a little line stretched across her face, but it was more than I'd ever seen from her. Like Kevin with his money, maybe she just wanted to save them up for something nice.

"Son, we surely appreciate the work ya done here today," the man said while the boys were clearing the plates. "Did a good thing out there."

"Thanks. I mean, thank you, sir."

He looked at me, or whatever, and nodded his head slowly. I guess all was either forgiven or forgotten.

I was ready to tackle the front yard. It was a little past 1:00, but I could probably be done by four if I really hustled. I'd learned how to handle the little clipper, and, far as I could tell, there weren't as many action figures to watch out for. A few kids were running around in the street, and several more were hanging out on their porches. I was going to show them all what a kid could do running on a full belly and a whole bunch of want to.

But Mrs. Anderson never gave me the chance.

I saw them out of the corner of my eye, the four of them. She was in the lead, with Raymond and Kevin on either side. The little girl - unless it was 'pumpkin' or 'baby,' I still didn't know her name - was lagging a little behind. I propped the handle of the mower against my stomach and waited.

"You run along, we'll finish up from here," she said, shadowing over me. When she wasn't hunched over in her bus seat, thc lady was a load.

"Oh, no, I..." I said. I didn't want to leave, not really.

"Said we'll finish up from here," she repeated. And she meant it. I was free to go.

"Um, well, okay."

With that, she offered her hand. I took it, quickly, and squeezed it firmly, just like Dad always said to. It was soft and warm, different than I would have imagined. Different than her. And her eyes weren't quite the same as before. They had more life, and it didn't look like she wanted to smack me around so much anymore.

I pulled back my hand to find it filled with a $20 bill. It was faded and soggy, but twenty bucks all the same.

"Oh, nooo I...."

"Need some help gettin' home?" she interrupted. "I could drive ya if ya need it."

At first, it sounded like a good idea. It would save my folks a trip, and it might rescue me from another fairy tale. But Mrs. Anderson did plenty of driving as it was, and the folks might be a little suspicious about me piling out of a beat-up, blue tank.

"No, ma'am. I've gotta ride."

"A'right then. Again, we appreciate ya for what ya done."

For what I'd done? What I'd done was slap her upside the head and risk a bunch of kids' lives, including my own. But in the end, I guess the whole day had been more of a slap to my own face.

For some reason, standing there with eight eyes on me, I remembered that writer's name, the irony guy. O. Henry. By the way, how does someone get a letter for a first name?

They turned to go, all at the same time. The guy was on the front porch, tilted back in the same chair, rocking back and forth and sporting the same pasted-on smile. I had to hand it to Mister Anderson; he sure knew how to relax. "Maybe we could play some ball sometime." It was Raymond, who was standing halfway up the sidewalk.

"Maybe so," I shrugged, all the while knowing that we would likely never stand on the same sideline together.

Midtex still had too many different teams.

He smiled and caught up with Kevin. They all climbed together on to the porch. The boys vanished in a rush, laughing all the way, and the girl slid back into her dad's lap. Mrs. Anderson walked past, ran a hand across their heads and slowly stepped into the house.

I studied the bill. Except on birthdays and maybe from somebody old dying, I didn't run across them too often. It was twice what Dad paid me to do both our front and back, and it would have bought almost anything that I wanted. To me, it was good money.

I made sure nobody was watching, which wasn't easy around that block, and stuffed the bill into the rusted mailbox with 'An ers n' stenciled across it. To them, I had a feeling, it was great money.

I started down the road, hoping that Kevin picked up the mail on Mondays.

***

Darkland, or whatever, didn't seem as scary as before. Porches were still the place to be, and music drifted from each one. Conversation was everywhere, except for the few seconds that I passed by. On our block, cars just rolled into garages and vanished behind the electric doors. Poof, see you later, mister. Here, they parked on the porches and got to know each other. It was like a block party, except without that nasty, green, fluffy dessert stuff.

It must have been a slow day at the Boys Club. A purple Pinto had joined the busted Jeep, but besides that, the place was still a ghost town. If there really would have been a sale going on, they wouldn't have raised enough dough to buy a needle for an air pump.

I called Dad from a pay phone. I hadn't seen a phone at the Andersons, which seemed like a pretty good idea. Phones were boring. I didn't see why my friends' older brothers and sisters were always blabbing away on the things. If you didn't live within a bike ride of a kid, there really wasn't much point.

Dad pulled up about 20 minutes later, and I climbed in the car. His hair was matted, and his face was sunburned. I caught my crusty, baked reflection in the side mirror. It looked like we'd both spent the day in the yard. For me, I figured, the end was near.

"Hey there, son."

"Hey," I returned, securing my waist with the seat belt.

"So how was your day?"

I could have said that it was hot and hard, that I'd eaten some really weird food and seen some really strange and sad and sweet stuff.

But I didn't.

"Okay."

But he didn't say anything else, didn't ask me about the sale or wonder out loud why the parking lot was still deserted. He just coasted along, rolling past the porches and over the tracks and toward our neighborhood of neatly trimmed yards while some guy on the radio was singing about loving rainy nights.

"Dad, I need to tell ya somethin.'" It just sort of came out, and I didn't know where it was headed. But it felt like the right direction to go.

"You do? 'Bout what?" He was tapping his fingers on the steering wheel. Dad had really fallen for the country music thing, but I hadn't yet. Sounded like they were all stuffed up or something.

"Um, about what I've been doin,'" I said. It suddenly felt like the seat belt was putting a Vulcan death grip on me.

"Did ya work hard today, do your best?" he asked, never taking his eyes off the road.

"Yeah," I said. It was the truth.

"Do everything that you were asked?"

"Yes sir."

"Well, good for you then. Most of the time, that's all a fella can do." With that, he reached for the radio, turned it up a little and started to whistle.

I guess the Andersons had a phone after all.

I leaned my head back, closed my eyes and listened to some country guy sing about having four hundred children and a crop in the fields.

I think that's what he was saying, but four hundred children sounded like an awful lot, even for a Catholic.

Shanks, Dad

It was pretty big, at least to me.

I'd been to the golf course lots of times, tagging along with my dad while he played and mumbled under his breath. Seemed to be a better mumbler than a player. And I'd even learned most of the rules, though I'd never seen the guys on television kick the ball out from under a tree. I guess Dad knew something they didn't.

Anyway, he finally asked me to play the summer between seventh and eighth grade. I got up early that Tuesday morning and cleaned my shoes, just like Dad always did. I didn't really know why, because they were already clean, but it seemed like the golf thing to do. Dad did the same, mopping off the funny-looking tongue and propping the mammoth black bag against his company ride. The bag was almost as tall as me and filled with all sorts of clubs. Most of them looked they'd been used a lot. An awful lot.

Except for Dad, golf wasn't very big in my family, which was strange since we lived right next to a course back in Ohio. Once, when I was just a little kid, back in like first grade, a boy got plunked in the head with a shot and almost died right out on the green next to our backyard. He was so close that I could have thrown a rock at him.

Decided that was the last thing the kid needed, though.

Baseball and football and basketball, now those were the things to do in my family. I even had all the right stuff for them. My grandpa had given me a Rawlings mitt with a Luis

Tiant autograph scribbled right across the palm. He pitched for the Red Sox - the Tiant guy, not my grandpa - and I heard he could hardly speak English. That was okay with me, though, because I couldn't speak a lick of Mexican. I tried to copy his herky-jerky windup for a while, but after walking seven batters and nailing two more against the Moose Lodge Knights, I switched back to the Dodgers' Don Sutton delivery. I had Sutton's eight-track instructional tape called "How to Pitch," but it talked more about Don and how great he was than it did his pitching.

He did have a great afro for a white guy, though.

Matt and Simon put up a basketball goal for me the summer before. Basketball, or hoops, was their game. Back in high school, Matt once grabbed 38 rebounds, all inside of four quarters. Saw the newspaper clipping myself. Thirty-eight, that was more than I could jerk down in a whole life. Anyway, all day long they worked on it, digging a hole and pouring cement and stuff while my dad teetered on a paint-spladdered ladder and attached the hoop. Eight feet on the nose, just like the one down at the YMCA. Perfect. Then Matt said he was going to break it in by dunking, and he just plain broke it. I got a new red, white and blue basketball out of that one, and Matt received a lifetime suspension.

And football, well, football was the deal around Midtex. The Picadilly High squad had won like a zillion games over with its mascot, the Pumas. Anything with a nickname and a mascot, well, had to be doubly good. Dad said that Gojo was a voodoo hex or something like that, but it sure seemed more like a religion. People were sure nuts about that team, especially the old-timers. They would deck out in black from head to toe and drive to the Friday night games with their cars and faces all painted up. They always followed each other, honking and waving those puffy number-one fingers out of their shoe-polished windows. It looked like a funeral, all that black, but it sounded more like a party, like one of those crazy Irish burials you heard about. Something like 15,000 people went to their home the years and even had its own special chant - Gojo - along games. Fifteen thousand! That was like one out of every five folks in town. A few people followed the Midtex Mustangs, the town's other team and one that didn't even get puffy fingers, but the Pumas were the ones that everyone pushed and packed and pleaded into broken-down Barnett Stadium to see, even though their final scores were usually around a hundred to zilch. In school, we'd studied about the Romans scrunching into that joint to watch those lions munching on helpless folks in goofy sandals. Well, same kind of thing.

I had a football, a bright, orange, plastic one with the two stripes, but my hands were still too small to really hurl it that far. I hadn't even gone out for the school team like most of the kids on my block, because I was also still a bit too small to get killed. Flag was my game. I kind of wished it could always be flag.

My tennis shoes couldn't get any cleaner. "Um, ready to hit the links, Dad." See, I knew the right things to say on the course because I'd watched lots of it on television. Birdie. Bogie. Par. Slice. Fade. And oh yeah, the Golden Bear. He was Dad's favorite, this Jack Nicklaus guy. I remember seeing him interviewed after he won a tourney and being surprised at his voice. It was high and squeaky and almost hurt my ears. Though I'd never heard or seen one in person, the guy sure didn't sound like any bear.

I knew more about golf. I knew that you could snatch up your ball in the fairway and put it on a fluffy clump of grass. I knew that you were allowed to pick up all short putts or even kick them away while they were still rolling if they weren't going to drop. I knew there were plenty of second and third chances. Gimme. Mulligan. Foot wedge. Fore. I learned these not from the Golden Bear but from Dad, whose voice sounded much more convincing.

"Excited?" he asked, stretching one hand across the steering wheel. His hands were so much bigger than mine that I was sure I'd never be able to throw a decent spiral.

"Yep," I answered. And I kind of was, too. We drove on without saying much more, listening instead to some radio announcer talk about crops and rain and dirt. I wanted to tell my dad that I hoped to not disappoint him, but I didn't.

See, there were three things I never, ever wanted to happen. I didn't want them to ever find Gilligan, because then that would be that. I didn't want to ever have a job where I wore one of those shiny orange jerseys and tossed around orange cones all day. And I didn't want to disappoint my dad. I didn't want him to ever die, either, but Elvis and John Wayne had over the last few years, so I knew that was out of the question. Hey, if The King could bite the dust on the crapper, anyone could.

But it wasn't like I'd never played. I'd hit plenty of balls. Well, whiffle balls in the back yard. They would whistle through the air, or sometimes just crawl through the grass, and land about as far as I could kick one. The nine-iron was my favorite club, because with that one I could blast balls about as high as the oak tree that we planted when we moved to Texas. I liked the tall shots best for sure.

Heck, I'd even played for real before. Well, kind of. Sometimes, when I was driving the cart for him, Dad let me knock a shot or two when nobody was behind us. I would line up straight as an arrow, take a few practice cuts for luck and let it rip. Only my shots never seemed to rip. They sort of just rolled or swerved or sometimes did nothing at all. Once though, just as the sun was falling behind the trees, I hit a seven-iron shot, a real tall shot, and stuck the ball about 10 feet from the hole. It didn't spin backwards or anything, but it stayed put real nice.

Dad, heels kicked up on the cart's dash, scrambled up after that one.

"Hey! That's the one that'll keep ya comin' back!"

I'd heard him say that one to himself a thousand times on the course, usually down the stretch. I could understand a little, because I always heard the Little League parents yelling "it just takes one" to a batter when he was down to his last strike. So I figured golf was sort of like baseball, only with sweater vests.

***

We pulled into Sunshade Country Club, a place Dad had never taken me. I knew it was a country club because the sign said so, but it didn't look like the one back in Ohio, or even the one down the street at the Midtex Country Club. The clubhouses there looked like palaces, or at least really nice houses, but this one was on wheels. There were lots of places like that in Midtex, especially on the other side of town near the plants and factories, but none were parked on a golf course. Except for the numbered flags poking up all over, I would have never guessed it was the right place. I wasn't the only one fooled, either, because there were just three other cars and a tractor in the parking lot.

The man with the fat cigar and the terrible hack wasn't kidding - when he said a can of balls, he really meant it. He pulled a beat-up coffee can from under the counter and handed it to Dad, who gave the guy three bucks and dipped the rusty red can into an even bigger bucket of balls. The machine back at the course in Ohio spit balls out at you, but at Sunshade the guy with the fat cigar was the only one coughing.

He then reached under the counter, pulled out what looked like a soup can full of balls and offered it to me.

"What's that?" I asked.

"Kid's bucket," he smirked.

I took it, but not before giving him my best dirty look. I was getting a little tired of being a kid. I mean, the cheap movie tickets were fine and all, but the children's menus with the three runt chicken strips and the smaller buckets with nine balls was starting to get old. If I could look down on Goofy, meaning I was big enough to ride a real roller coaster, then I figured I could do about anything. I wanted to get old, fast.

We walked over the driving range, which looked like a cow pasture with balls instead of manure. Dad was just a bouncing bag with feet up ahead, but I could hear the clickety clack of his walk. Since I was a lefty, we'd had to rent some clubs for me, special clubs like everything else for southpaws. I wasn't completely sure, but I thought the woods were supposed to have grooves or at least lines in them. Mine looked like doorknobs on a stick. I wondered how the heck I could hit tall shots using doorknobs.

Pulling along my cart, which wiggled like the ones my mom always chose in the grocery store, I caught my double in the clubhouse window. My floppy hair bounced back at me, with the usual clump sticking up in the back. Time for some scissors and a ruler for sure. I had carefully selected a yellow shirt, the kind with three buttons, and some baby blue O.P. pants with the tie string. That morning, mom said I was turning into a handsome young man. Well, the goofball in the window wasn't so sure.

Watching Dad through a cloud of dust, I remembered something else mom once told me. She said that Dad, who grew up during the Great Depression, had been a man since he was about 12 years old. I wasn't really sure what it meant, but it sure sounded scary. All I knew was that I would be 13 in a few months, and sometimes I still sniffed on a marker every now and then. I would have to cut that out.

Golf. I knew it wasn't going to be easy, because Dad sure never made it look that way. The pros did, but you couldn't believe everything you saw on television. I mean, I knew Gilligan and those guys didn't really live on that island, no matter what I said earlier. I wasn't a dope or anything.

"Just keep your head on the ball and follow on through," said Dad. I nodded, plopped a ball down and drew a nine-iron. Maybe it wouldn't be so tough after all, because that was the same thing Dad said the first time he pitched to me. I was a pretty good hitter, and that ball was moving. This little ball was lazy.

And after about five swings, it still was. Every stinking time, I brought my club back, kept my head down and swung away. And every time, I checked the pasture to see what was happening. A whole lot of nothing, that's what. About three places away, there was a little girl, all of four or so, swinging pink plastic clubs with her Dad. And I was pretty sure she was laughing at me.

"Don't try and kill it, son. You have to let the club do the work. Here, watch."

He kicked a ball over to his side and pulled out a long club. The long clubs always made the whiffle balls just roll along for me, that's all I knew. But Dad was much better. He took a slow swing and, whack, hopped the ball all the way to the sign marked '100.'

"See, let the club do the work," he repeated.

He knocked a few more, some going past the sign, some stopping before it. He wrapped his tongue around his top lip on each backswing, just like when he hammered a nail or tightened a screw, then hitched up the back end of his pants after every hit. I noticed the man with the little girl was blasting balls into outer space. His clubs must have been doing more work.

A little car suddenly bumped into the pasture. It looked like some kind of space mobile and was surrounded by a big cage. The dented thing bounced along, and the kid with the straw cowboy hat bounced along inside it. Shots sprayed around him, but he kept smiling and singing along with a little radio propped on the dash. He turned toward the 200 sign, then the 250, more than safe from any dents by Dad or me. It looked pretty fun, and I decided to check into how a kid could become a ball picker upper.

It was my turn again. I had that nervous feeling in my stomach, like just before the first day of school each year. Actually, Downing hadn't turned out to be such a wicked place after all. I was an A-student and a hall monitor, just like before, and one of the fastest kids around. But I couldn't always outrun the same, stupid stuff. There'd been some new jackos at Northside - my junior high - and some new covered laughs and a few new enemies after the same 'ol corny jokes, but I made it through seventh grade without too much trouble. Besides, junior high was pretty much like elementary, only with longer words and bigger boobs. "Just keep your head down now, son." "I am," I whined.

"And follow through."

"I am," At that very moment, even I hated the sound of my voice. I tried hard to do both the next time, even curling my tongue around my top lip, and swung away. I felt the ball and heard the thwack. My hands stung a little, and I just knew it was headed for the 100, maybe even 150 sign.

"What in galdurn tarnation?!?"

At least my first real shot ended up on the green. Problem was, I was shooting for a space mobile, not a green. Away in the distance, a little man with about eight hairs was holding up a ball and shaking his finger at me. He was standing on the edge of the par-three course that shared our pasture, kind of, and a red, round lady next to him was yelling something at me. Somehow my shot had gone not toward the 150 or even 100 sign but instead sideways, almost backwards. I couldn't really hear the lady, but I was pretty sure she wasn't asking if I wanted my ball back.

"It's okay, son, it's not an easy game," Dad waved a hand and smiled at the couple. They shook their heads and waddled on. "You'll catch on."

He gently adjusted my shoulders toward a bare patch of land that had no signs or space mobiles and just a few balls. My new target looked just like I had described West Texas to a few friends back in Ohio. Flat, yellow and just plain ugly. There was no denying or defending the landscape of my new home.

It wasn't the first time that my dad and I had hung out together. We didn't go fishing or hunting together like some of my friends and their pops, probably because Dad wasn't much of a fisherman or hunter. He used one of those foldout pocket jobs when he fished, which kind of tattooed him as an amateur, and the biggest thing I'd ever seen him catch was my mom's arm on a lousy cast. And as for hunting, well, he was against the whole idea. I was with him on that one. Unless the ducks or deer or turkeys could pack some heat too, I figured it was all pretty unfair.

But we did have the Indian Guides.

***

Tell you the truth, there wasn't much cool about the Guides. We met every other Monday with a bunch of other fathers and sons wearing those feathered headbands and set about doing Indian stuff for a couple of hours. I always got a kick out of it, seeing these dads try to lace up a moccasin or bead a necklace while pretending to not watch Monday Night Football. That's mostly what we did, by the way. We made art and crafts. Goofy stuff, too. Beads. Ornaments. Baby totem poles. Didn't even learn how to scalp anyone.

Most of my friends were in the Cub Scouts, and, except for the goofy scarves, I'd always secretly wanted one of those sharp blue-and-yellow uniforms. But for whatever reason, our family had always hung out in tribes and worn feathers. Once a week, the Scouts all wore their get-ups to school and hung out in a big, proud pack in the cafeteria while we Guiders huddled over in the far corner. We didn't get uniforms but were encouraged by our tribe chief, Mr. Damron, or Big Sunset, to wear our headbands to school once a month. Yeah, like that was going to happen.

Then again, the Guides did have the soap-box derby.

Every year, a father-and-son team got to enter a car in the derby. Not the big cars that sped down the road in that little town in Ohio. The miniature cars carved out of wood blocks. Anyway, this one year our wood block looked especially fast. Dad made it down in his basement shop, then shaved it into a long triangle with the machine that had the steering wheel. I played a lot in the basement, usually by myself, at least until I got my tongue stuck on the freezer shelf for three hours. Anyway, I always pretended that machine was a race car or maybe a battleship, never knowing it was really a car cutter outter.

Dad did the tricky stuff, like putting on wheels and placing a weight near the hood or whatever. I was left with the fun parts, like painting it bright red and putting thin, black, racing stripes down both sides. I missed the lines a little, but I was always a weak colorer. We spent an entire Saturday doing it, and Mom brought us down bologna sandwiches cut into halves, so that was nice.

It was a double-elimination tournament. The Flying Cardinal, as we decided to name our racer, was scheduled to go first. Dad put the car into the slot and shot me a wink. It even looked fast, all shiny and red and ready to fly.

Turned out, it wasn't fast. In fact, it was pretty darn slow. After taking an early lead, the Cardinal started to shake and almost even stopped halfway down. The Black Bomber tracked it down and blazed by it as Big Wolf and Little Wolf, or Artie and Billy Goodwin, whooped it up and got all huggy and stuff. The Cardinal sputtered across, toppled onto its side and headed straight for the loser's bracket.

Little Eagle, or Marty Bradford, gave me a pat on the back, but it didn't help much.

"What's wrong with it, Dad? Huh? What's wrong with it?" I pouted as the crowd nudged me away and circled around the next race.

"I don't know, son," he said quietly. "You can't win every single time." But I could tell that inside his wheels were spinning fast.

Dad was the smartest guy I knew, and he could fix anything. He was always painting or hammering or trimming or sawing, and nobody got more excited about a new nut. Sometimes he would spend a whole day down in his shop, then pop up at dinner time all covered in sawdust and shavings. Often his pipe or a White Owl cigar hung from his mouth while he worked, and the curled-up tongue, well, that was a given.

But he couldn't fix the Cardinal, not even by tightening the wheels and adjusting the weight. It was born slow, and after getting creamed by the Marvelous Monster a few minutes later, it died slow. I tried to trash it, the Cardinal that couldn't fly, but Dad stopped me with one of his big paws.

"Hey, now don't do that."

"Well, why not? We're done with it anyway."

Dad took the car from my hands and then gave the front wheels a spin. One almost came off. I thought it was kind of funny, since he was the boss of making tires at the plant and all.

"Well, because we did it together," he said.

And I guess he was right. The Cardinal might have been the slowest, shakiest car in the whole competition, but it was our slow, shaky car. And besides, I bet no other Little Anything got to spend a whole Saturday in the wood shop with their Dad and bologna sandwiches.

***

My kid's bucket was empty. It had turned out to be plenty big enough. I could have had a truckload of balls, and I still would have stunk. I was sweaty and already tired, and my yellow shirt was covered in dirt and grass from the many missed cuts. But Mister Fat Cigar was hollering at us over a speaker that dangled from the trailer house, and the couple from the baby course was done and heading our way.

It was time.

"Now on the first tee, the Schitt twosome."

I kind of liked the ring of that. Growing up, people had always talked about the Schitt boys, meaning Matt, Simon and John. I came along later, too late to be one of the boys. But there we were, walking over to the big course, the Schitt twosome, the Schitt boys.

It was just my luck. While we were practicing, a few more cars had crept into the parking lot, and what seemed like 14 people had piled out of each one. They came in all shapes and sizes, wearing everything from tank tops to long beards, but they had one thing in common - they were all packed around the first tee box.

"Don't pay any attention to them, son," Dad whispered while washing his ball in the scrubber. He took off his glasses and wiped them with his shirt. I looked down to his sparkling spikes. Cleanliness was big in golf.

But it was hard to not pay attention. I took some practice rips and bent the club around my back, twisting around like everyone else scattered around the tee area. I had no idea what I was doing. All the while, no matter which way I spun, it seemed like all eyes were glued to me, especially those of the Barney Rubble body double staring right at me.

Dad went first. He'd looked so tall and powerful out on the driving range, but now he seemed tiny compared to the land stretched out before him. Drawing a club, a Hogan one-wood, he took a painfully slow practice cut just to size things up. Only it turned out to be the fast-forward version, because his real swing was even slower than the warm-up ones. Slow and easy, I figured that was just his style. Anyway, I thought it looked like a fine cut, but the ball wasn't as impressed. It trickled to a stop about 100 yards up and rested under one of Sunshade's few sunshade trees.

It was my turn. No, it wasn't. Before I could even move, Dad fished an orange ball out of his pocket and propped it on a tee.

"First hole mullie," he said hurriedly. Barney Rubble, who'd been joined by a bare-chested sidekick, spit in his red cup and tapped his cowboy-boot spikes on the cart trail. Red cups and spitting, that was big sport in Midtex.

Ah, of course, the mulligan. While the pros never seemed to bother with the things, Dad was a huge fan of them. On the tees, the fairways, the greens, where ever, whenever. Only sometimes they just didn't pan out, like in this case, when his second try disappeared into a briar patch.

"Awww, blew that one," Dad hissed. He tugged at his pants and motioned me forward. "I'll just play the first one."

Barney winced, but he hadn't seen anything yet. Standing on the tee, the feeling in my gut reminded me on my very first bike ride without training wheels. I'd known exactly what to do, understood the rules of gravity and all, seen the older kids do it. Pedal. Keep it straight. Steady. Smooth. Straighter. Smoother. But sometimes knowing what to do didn't keep a kid from chipping his pointy tooth.

I realized that knowing how to do it was what I really needed. And I didn't know how, I just didn't. And I was pretty certain that everyone in our greasy gallery was real sure of that.

"Now, just take an easy swing," Dad said, taking one of his own.

Easy for him to say. I took an easy swing, a real easy one. Then another. And another. The ball was still sitting on the tee. I tried a medium swing. Nothing. A super hard one. A cloud of dust. My stupid shadow wasn't helping matters, either. Thing was staring right back at me. I knew that was how shadows worked, but still.

And to make matters worse, it started getting harder and harder to see the ball through the stinking tears in my eyes. Plus, my left eye, always the left, started to twitch.

I looked back at Dad. He was wearing the exact expression as the time I whiffed with the bases loaded in the last inning against the B&D Grocery Gorillas. I could tell he'd felt even worse than me. At least I had a dugout to hide in and, later, a cherry-watermelon-raspberry-coconut snow cone to ease the sting. Suicide slushees could take the air out of most of life's problems.

Finally, I made contact. Well, when I say contact, I don't exactly mean contact. But I must have worked enough air pressure around my ball to at least budge it off the tee, because something happened. The ball tumbled about three feet ahead, then caught the ridge of the tee box and dribbled five feet further. The tee landed just ahead of it.

"Real nice, kid. Right in the middle of the fairway," Barney grunted, chuckling and rubbing his temples as he slouched deeper into his cart seat. The crooked smile on his face was about as real as mine during those family shots at Olan Mills. I stood there, panting, and tried to think of a comeback. It never came.

"Wanna take a mullie?" Dad already had a ball in his palm and a tee threaded between his fingers.

"Nuh uh."

I didn't want to give them the pleasure, at least not from up close. At least this way my back would be turned, blindfolded from the firing line. I huffed past him, nabbed my cart and yanked it and its wobbly wheel to the ball just ahead.

"Now son, don't forget to take your..."

I didn't take my time, not at all. Didn't keep my right arm straight. Didn't keep my head down. Didn't give a crap. I just hit it. Hit it far and straight, too far to see anymore and too straight to care. Found the sweet spot and felt nothing in my hands. But I felt awfully good inside.

I couldn't help but look. Barney was leaning forward, his eyebrows nearing the bill of his Pardee Gas cap. He worked his tongue around his mouth, preparing to let out what I expected to be another stream of chew. Instead, he looked straight at me and winked. "Pardner, that's the one that'll keep ya comin' back."

***

That was good, too, because I spent the rest of the day hitting shots that would have kept me away forever. Golf was one tough sport, and I understood why Dad always swore that he was giving it up for good. Putting wasn't so bad. I'd been to Putt Putt lots of times, splitting time between the Space Invaders machine, the carpet and the birthday cake. Birthday parties at Putt Putt were kind of lame, but they beat egg tosses and piñatas and lipsticky moms in some kid's backyard anyday.

The rest, the long-range stuff, well, was just plain unfair. For one, Dad was always preaching that there were three keys to success in anything - drive, determination and desire. It was maybe the favorite of his many Dad sayings. Well, I could think of another 'd.' A driver, a real one. Mine blew. Plus, golf was too long. One hole was 600 yards long! No joke. Now that was six football fields, and there was no running with the ball in golf. I did find that walking with it a tad, especially away from trees and sprinkler heads and bushes, didn't hurt anyone.

From what I saw between touring Sunshade's every last inch, Dad was having a pretty good day. He hit three browns - it really wouldn't be fair or accurate to call them greens - and even drained a long putt to save double bogey.

Only I guess it was really a bogey, because that's what went down on the scorecard. Like everyone in our family, Dad stunk in math.

Finally, we got to the ninth, and last, hole. I checked the scorecard sitting next to Dad's smoldering cigar. He had a 45, and I had a 9, 10, 11 and a bunch of blank squares. I stopped keeping score after sinking my drive into a swimming pool on the fourth, locating the only water hazard on the whole course.

It seemed only right, since I'd already nailed six trees, four beaches and, almost, a crazy lady. I also lost four balls and critically injured a few more. By the ninth, I was abusing something called the Flying Lady, which was bright pink and had a smiley face carved into it.

At least someone was smiling. Anyway, there was no sense pouring salt into my blisters by jotting it all down.

Dad looked tired folded over his ball. His shoulders were rounded, the same droopy shoulders that kept me from buying a backpack for school and required my presence in the scoliosis line when the doctors at school did backbone/hunchback checks. The docs always said they would "monitor" the situation, which was probably the same as telling a bow-legged kid that he had a minor case of the rickets.

Dad's schnozz was a different story. Unlike my long, skinny one, his was wide enough to support most anything, including the tinted glasses that hung from his sunburned ears. People always told him that he looked like Walter Matthau, that guy from *The Odd Couple*, but I had to go with the guy from *The Streets of San Francisco* and the American Express commercials.

He was older than most dads, over 50 already. A couple of times at baseball games my teammates asked why my grandparents always came to watch me. I shot back my standard answer, saying that they were my folks and that they'd saved the best for last. That, along with maybe a handful of seeds or a wad of Big League Chew, usually shut them up. Then I'd glance back at them, and there they'd always be, always in the very same spot. Mom and Dad had seen at least a million Little League games, but I guess they weren't sick of them just yet.

***

Thankfully, the ninth was a par three, a little less than two football fields long, and it would all be over soon. Dad took his tortoise swing and hit a burner that landed soon after contact but didn't call it quits until it was resting next to the brown.

"Handy," he said, scooping up his stogie. I'd figured out that the term 'handy' meant good for some, bad for others and pretty much outstanding for us.

I didn't waste any time. Rubble and his buddy had been tailing us all day, keeping Dad from many second or third tries and making my hunting trips into the pastures short ones. Dad tried to motion them through back on the fifth, but Barney smiled and waved, hit his tee shot three feet and pushed us on with his middle finger. I'd heard some TV commentator get all sappy about golf being "a gentleman's game." Well, not at Sunshade Country Club.

I hit my shot, an ugly one that made a quick detour into the rough, and cussed the fact that you had to play your foul balls in golf. I snatched my cart and started off. The wheel was barely hanging on, and so was I. It was hot, and the only relief to be found was under my Baltimore Orioles cap. I hated the Orioles, and especially that pitcher of theirs from the underwear ads, but sure did like the hat.

"Havin' fun?" asked Dad from a little ahead, peeling toward his ball and paying no attention to my Flying Lady that had crash landed into a groundhog hole. (Not the good kind of hole in one.)

"I dunno."

As you may have figured out, that was my answer for about everything, and I had it down just about perfect.

Whattaya want to watch, Jasper? I dunno. Anything new at school? I dunno. How's the 'ol team coming along? I dunno. Do you like the stuffed peppers? I du..well, that I knew. No, I actually didn't, and I didn't really care that half the kids in Asia would have hocked their left arm for it, either.

Tell you the truth, little had been said the entire round, or half round anyway. Dad was never far from his starting place, but he was usually straight. I was crooked. And when I lined up crooked, thinking I might maybe knock one straight, I ended up even more crooked. On the browns, I stood on the edge and watched Dad putt, or sometimes on a short one, scoot along his ball until it finally fell. Having already given up, I would then hurry on to the next hole for more adventures. That was the drill.

I didn't think golf was a talking game anyhow. Unlike baseball or basketball, golf seemed like a bunch of whispers interrupted by a hack now and again. There'd been a sign tacked up in the trailer's john that said, "The average round of golf takes four hours. About two minutes of that will be spent actually hitting the ball." Or something like that. Heck, I milked that off the third hole alone, easy. Besides, we Schitts weren't much on chit-chatting anyhow.

I pulled the cart along. With all the clubs, it had gotten heavier. For the first six holes, I didn't understand why there had to be so many. Didn't they all pretty much work the same? But on the seventh, I found out. I yanked an extra ball from my pants, pulled out a two-iron from 40 yards out and blistered a low screamer deep into the neighboring trailer park. Seemed the key to success was all about smart club selection and deep pockets.

I plucked my pink ball from the wrong hole and took a look around. I could see most of the spread, because only a few scrawny shrubs and an occasional lump separated the holes. I'd also heard that same TV announcer - some British guy with this perfect golf whisper - call this one course on TV a "cathedral." Well, Sunshade wasn't even a little chapel.

I noticed the crowd that had gathered. There were dots, mostly shirtless dots, scattered all around, usually surrounded by clouds of dust. They reminded me of Pig Pen from Charlie Brown, only I couldn't picture Pig Pen ever cussing for ten seconds straight without a breath. I could picture the Hawaiian shirt guy from a few groups back doing it, though, because he did after flinging his putter into a tree.

I could relate. It didn't bother me so much that I stunk, which I did. It just bothered me that Dad had to see me stink.

"Hey, would ya take a look at that!!!"

I checked the brown. No ball. I checked the other side of the brown. Nothing. He hurried toward the flag and stopped at the hole. After a tug of his trousers and a quick bend, the little sucker was between his fingers.

"Would ya look at that! Huh!?! Would ya look at that!" Then he did something really funny. He started to dance. Nothing as slick as the guy with the white suit, the Italian fellow from *Welcome Back Kotter*. It was more of a National Geographic move, a pygmy kind of thing. But it was a dance all right, and, using the putter as a cane and hopping on one leg, he kept it up all the way across the brown, down the bank and to his beat-up bag. Even guys who were men since 12 could act like they were 12 again sometimes.

He stopped and beamed back at me. "Did ya see that one, Jasper?!?

Huh?!? Did ya?!?"

Actually, I hadn't. Really, I was even kind of glad I hadn't been seen on the dance floor with him. But he had obviously chipped in from the *handy* area. And I hadn't seen him that happy since, well, since maybe ever.

"I sure did, Dad! Great one!" It was another one of those good fibs.

He brushed if off like it happened every day, then wiped his forehead with a hanky and pulled out the scorecard. (Hankies, by the way, had to be one of life's most disgusting inventions.) Anyway, the chip-in would go down as a '1' for sure. Maybe even a negative-1. All the while, he never stopped smiling or shaking his head or talking to his self.

There was no way to top that. I turned toward the driving range, blasted the longest, straightest, prettiest shot of my life and headed in. Dad threw his arm around me as we headed for the clubhouse restaurant, which was really a vending machine outside the crapper, and added up the damage while I bought a pack of stale crackers. He whispered his totals to himself, sometimes stopping to start again.

"Forty-three," he said, shoving the stubby pencil behind his ear. He swiped those things every time, turning them from a golf pencil into a shop pencil. Forty-nine, I thought, not counting his three lost balls or five mulligans or the gimme from eight feet on the fifth. I thought it not aloud. A forty-three, plus a dance shot, would keep him coming back for years.

That was fine by me, because golf gloves were cheap Christmas presents.

Dad bought a soda and looked past me toward the ninth hole, no doubt replaying the shot in his head. I fiddled with my tennies, which weren't clean at all anymore, and replayed a little of what had been about the most humbling two hours or so of my life.

"So, think ya might wanna play again sometime?" Dad tossed the bag over his shoulder. It slipped off. He shrugged, grabbed it by the handle and waited.

I made my way toward him. Just then, the wheel finally broke free from my cart. It rolled down the dirt path, bounced off the ball washer and settled under an old sign that said "My wife left me and took my golf clubs...and I sure do miss those clubs!" Seemed Dad was always hanging around when the wheels came off. Probably always would be, too.

I picked up my bag and tossed it over my shoulder. It slipped off, twice.

"I dunno," I mumbled.

But that time, I really did.

Last Lick

Our manhood was about to be challenged.

Or at least our teenagedom. We were only ninth graders, after all.

Coach Billy "Hurricane" Brooks didn't much care. It was a humid November afternoon in 1982, and the guy was steaming. Coach Max, our fearless field general/ceramics teacher at Bingham Junior High, had just interrupted our football practice during one-on-one tackling drills and ordered us over to the bleachers, where Coach Brooks was waiting on the bottom row.

I was all for a break, especially with Steve "The Mountain" Maloney licking his chops across from me in line, but this didn't feel like my kind of break. I had a swallow of icy water or maybe a little nap in mind.

We ran over to the rickety wooden bleachers, probably moving faster than at any point in the season. From far away, he looked like a monster, the Brooks character. Up close, he was much worse.

"Move it! Move it! Move it!" Coach Max yelped. He, of course, was trailing far behind. The guy was built like a slug and ran like one, too. A swell role model.

"You guys are flat out, piss poor pathetic!" Coach Brooks began once we were settled, after letting us silently marinate in the blistering heat for five minutes. "The biggest embarrassment in our entire feeder system, the biggest embarrassment in the history of this proud school!"

I stared straight ahead, right into his gut. He was wearing a black pullover with a blocked 'P' on the chest pocket, meaning that he was a Picadilly High coach. Meaning that he fell right under God in terms of importance around Midtex. Actually, it might have been a dead heat.

Avoiding anything close to eye contact, I eyed his black shorts. They were called coaching shorts, but they really should have been called too-short shorts. Most of his hairy thighs were exposed, but the lower portion of his leg was completely covered by white tube socks with two black stripes. I looked over to Coach Max. Blue coaching shorts, way too small and tight. Check. High tube socks with two blue stripes. Sure. Cheap, black plastic cleats. Yep. The basic coach get-up.

Anyway, I'd never seen the guy in my life, but rumor had it that he'd once coached at Bingham, way back when Coach Max still had hair. And he obviously wasn't too pumped about the state of football around his former school. We were 0-9 with three or four touchdowns to our credit all season, one by accident. The Bingham Buzzards might have had a history, but it wasn't a proud one, at least not anymore.

"A bunch of red-headed stepchildren!" he screamed. I wasn't too sure what that even meant, but it couldn't be good.

Myth had it that Bingham was once a football power, but long before the arrival of myself and my underachieving, uncaring, pretty much un-everything teammates. Northside Junior High was by then the unrivaled king of Midtex junior high football, and most of the Picadilly stars over the past decade had once sported the blue and gold of the Gators. Grayson, the high school's other feeder school, was usually pretty fair, or at least low in the red-headed stepchildren department. (But it was the hands-down champ when it came to girls, and you have to know that was a victory in itself.)

"Makes me sick to even see you in those uniforms! Puking, hands-on-my-knees-in-front-of-the-shitter sick!" Coach Brooks was frothing now. I could prove it, too, because from my front-row seat a piece of his shrapnel was glistening on my ragged practice jersey.

Anyhow, to tell you the truth, I was pretty puking sick of football, too. Not that I didn't enjoy the sport itself. I was crazy about watching people pound each other on television. I just wasn't that wild about getting pounded myself. And as a runt halfback with a puny line in front of me, I got pounded plenty. To me, it was mostly just an insane way to pass the time and to have at least an outside shot at the cute girls. The P.E. kids weren't even in the starting blocks in the race for chicks.

Looking down the line to avoid Brooks's stare, I figured that most of my teammates felt the same way. David Garcia, our quarterback, was picking out his ears. David was the nicest guy in the world, but he wasn't exactly the kind of guy you wanted to follow into battle. Many times, when he called a play in the huddle, he spoke so softly that we went to the line guessing what that play might be.

Turned out that it was usually the one that lost eight yards.

And he was one of the more fierce Buzzards.

Payton Alfred, one of our few black players, was almost asleep next to David. He'd been named after Walter Payton, the silky-smooth running back for the Chicago Bears, but the similarities stopped right there. He was a wide receiver, and a pretty fast one at that, who hadn't caught a pass all year. His dad had been an All-State something or other over at Midtex High, but history wouldn't repeat itself. Payton lacked the hands and the heart, but, on a bright note, he could do a spot-on Lionel Richie impersonation in the showers.

Anyhow, if you asked Coach Brooks, we were all lacking a little of something.

"You pissheads don't block, ya don't tackle and ya don't care!" he barked, stretching his neck out like a rooster just for show. "And not one of you sapsuckers is ever going to make the grade at Picadilly High School!"

In a way, he was probably right. Sure, some of the players slumping around me would someday play at the next level, but I couldn't think of anyone who could actually dent the starting lineup. Maybe big Mountain Maloney, who was at least a human landfill on the offensive front, or Mark Simms, a linebacker who actually played with a passion if not with much talent, but not many else. For the most part, our roster was packed with a bunch of future tackling dummies and scout-team zeroes.

"And that was the poorest friggin' excuse for an effort I've ever seen in my entire gaddam life against Northside!" Coach Brooks went on, pacing the line. He was going on 15 minutes and about 60 cuss words and showing no signs of tiring. "What the hell was that?!? Can anyone tell me?!?"

Silence, of course. Even Coach Max was hiding behind Jonathan Larrabee, our overworked punter.

"Anyone at all! C'mon, I dare one of you snifflin' nimrods to grab his gaddam sack and tell me what the hell happened!"

Last week had easily been our lowest moment. Who knows, it coulda been the darkest hour in school history. Northside, our supposed archrival, had whipped us 50-0. Yep, fifty for them, zippo for us. We'd grown up with some of those guys before being separated, and they'd left the field laughing at us. I mean busting up right in our faces while we did that lame be-a-swell-sport handshake line at the end and said "good game, good game, good game" like a bunch of stewardesses.

It was one thing getting pummeled by strangers, another weekly tradition, but getting humiliated by guys you'd wrapped houses in toilet paper with way-back-when was another story.

The final score was a little deceptive; it wasn't nearly that close. We didn't make even one first down, though I did fumble forward once for a seven-yard gain on third and 28, and the game ended with Northside kneeling on our one-yard line. The bus ride was the longest and quietest of my life. Coach Max, who was retiring at the end of the school year, couldn't even think of anything to say. Not one tired cliché.

I was supposed to be on the other bus, the loud, rocking, chanting one. A few of us were. After eighth grade, after two mostly decent years at Northside, the school district had taken one section of the country club - mine, the one obviously without much football talent - and imposed what they called the busing law, which took the supposedly rich and moved them to mingle with the supposedly poor. I couldn't see too much difference. None of us knew much about much; we Northside kids just got dropped off in nicer cars.

It didn't work anyway, this grand plan. The whites still hung with the whites, the blacks with the blacks, the Hispanics with the Hispanics. They could desegregate us in the classrooms, but we just resegregated ourselves everywhere else.

Anyhow, on the night of the massacre at least, I'd wanted to be on the Northside bus. I'd be seeing a lot of them during the summer baseball leagues, probably even hang out with a few, and it would be a constant source of ribbing. I spent my two seasons at Northside deep on the bench of undefeated teams, mostly playing only when we were up by, say, 70 points, but that night it would have felt much better than being a starter on a team headed nowhere fast.

It wasn't like Bingham was set up for football greatness. Not anymore. The facilities and equipment were ancient, and we shared a weight room with the girls teams. Putting a 14-year-old boy in a cramped room stocked with girls and a few plates of rusty iron made for a no-brainer. Not many strength gains going on; decent place to hook up a movie date, though.

But all in all, I liked it better at Bingham. Most of us *richies* did. The Bingham holdovers were icy to us at first, turning their backs to us at lunch, but thawed pretty quickly. Plus, you didn't have to worry about stupid things. People who were stinking loaded, I was figuring out, worried way too much about stupid things.

So Bingham Junior High was full of good people, just lousy football players.

***

The Northside loss stung for a few days, but it was over and done, at least to us. Heck, we even did our best to rebound, leading an out-of-our-league Travis Gorillas squad by a 7-6 halftime count the very next week. We lost 37-7, losing like six fumbles after the break, but that's really not the point.

For a while, we'd been so close. We'd played like champions.

"At no point this season have you jokers even been close to havin' a winnin' football team!" Coach Brooks continued. "Y'all have absolutely no idea what it takes to be a champion!!" His rant was going on 30 solid minutes, and the sun was setting fast. If Coach Max canceled the rest of practice, which was almost in the bag since our skinned-up field had no lights, I'd be home before *Family Ties*. I thought to myself that little Michael J. Fox would have made a nice fit for our squad, and it made me smile a little.

But a little was too much.

"So tell me, little funny man, what do you think it takes to be a champion?"

I just barely heard the words, having almost tuned out this maniac by then. But I felt them. They were directed right at me, right at the kid who was among the least likely to come up with the right answer.

I played dumb. Maybe, I figured, he would think I was deaf or blind or at least stupid. On our team, it wouldn't have been completely out of the question.

No such luck. "Are ya going to answer me, little funny man?" He was inches from me, hovering under the bill of his cap and huffing hard. He smelled of tomato soup.

As for me, I was numb. All I could do was look up and catch my image in his mirrored sunshades. My shoulder pads devoured my neck, and my eyebrows were starting to turn into an eyebrow. Man, was I a dork.

He moved closer and clutched me by the jersey. With one tug, I was on my feet and in front of the team.

I wasn't one for public speaking, especially when the public was a bunch of friends that I saw every day. I never asked to be a leader or a spokesman. Following was just fine by me.

"C'mon all-star, answer me!!!"

I turned to him, knees quivering and hands shaking uncontrollably, like one of those dancing dashboard dolls, and noticed for the first time that his teeth were as yellow as corn on the cob. I'm talking golden nuggets. Coach Brooks was a heck of a screamer, maybe even a great motivator and teacher of the game, but the guy wasn't much for hygiene.

Bad choppers or not, he wasn't going to go away. I cleared my throat and faced the team. Luckily, because of the sun, they were just specks with hair, though Coach Max's melon was shimmering like a strobe light. Still, I couldn't ever remember being more nervous, and that was saying something. My left eye, always the left, began to twitch.

"Um," I began. "Well, what I think it takes to be a champion is, um...well, what I think is..."

Good players maybe? I couldn't say that. Good coaches? Couldn't say that, either. I had no idea. I mean, I'd been on some good teams, mostly in baseball, but hadn't actually thought about what had made us good. And at Northside, I'd been too far from the action to notice, or care, why we were always 10-0.

"Um...well....see....the thing is.....well...." For a split second, something worth something came to me. But with the heat on, I lost my train of thought, and it was a pretty short train to begin with.

"Sit the hell down, kid."

I did so, and fast. If the Buzzards could have all been so nimble, Coach Brooks wouldn't have been so hot and bothered in the first place.

"Now lemme tell you somethin' before I go," he said, hands on hips. "I'm going to be at your next game against San Jack, sittin' right the hell behind your bench. And gentlemen, you'd better gaddam show me somethin,' or you can forget about ever, ever having the honor to wear this 'P' across your chest."

He pointed to his shirt, thumped it really, and turned his back. At a full sprint - people like Coach Hurricane Brooks didn't walk anywhere - he tore across the practice field and into the parking lot, finally stopping at a pick-up truck. With that, he hopped in and peeled away down Walnut Grove Lane. You had to give the guy a little credit - if it had all been an act, some spook tactic, he'd kept it up until the bitter end.

We sat there for a moment, speechless. Finally, Coach Max stepped slowly before us. He looked tired and defeated and ready to retire right then. I thought he was about to chew us out, too. "Go on home, boys." I was wrong.

It was a lonely walk in. A few guys jogged past me, elbowing me and laughing, but mostly the team was scattered about. Finally, I felt an arm fall around my shoulder. Ah, at last, a little comfort.

"Great freakin' answer," snapped Chad Jonessey, roaring with laughter. Chad, a starting defensive end who had decent size and ability but a pint-sized desire for contact, was one of those guys who just wouldn't let things go. If someone slipped in the showers, he'd talk about it for three years. The guy was a human rerun.

"Aw, piss off," I snorted. He shoved my head from behind and ran off. My choke would last him until 1994.

Joe "Loco" Robinson, a manchild who'd once sliced a bird in half with the radial arm saw during Wood Shop, was leading a rap chant up ahead.

"And boyyyyyy, the bells are going to toll, when 'ol Joe shows his pole, to that hot young thang toniiiiiighhtttt!"

It wasn't half bad, I admitted to myself. Maybe Joe had found his calling. I was pretty sure he'd never be a carpenter.

I wandered toward the locker room, feeling heavy and out of place in my pads. To my right, a couple of players were Indian wrestling. To my left, a few more were trading sniffs on a magic marker. Yep, the pep talk had really hit home.

"Hey Jasp, don't worry 'bout it, I woulda done the same thing." Kurt Hart, helmet pulled up and resting on his head, had joined me. He was one of our better players, a small-but-slippery linebacker, and we'd become fast friends. We met in Mr. Herrera's shop class and had tormented the poor teacher ever since. Anyway, he was one of the first to accept us transplants from Northside, and, being one of the more popular students, the rest had fallen in. Kurt would make good with a lamp post.

"Yeah, thanks," I sighed. I needed something, anything. I watched the team file into the locker room. Some players carried helmets that were too big; others wore pants that were too small. Anyway you sliced it, the Buzzards looked as mismatched as a beard without a mustache.

"You couldn't have won no matter what," Kurt continued. "That guy is a lunatic. Heard he knocked the shit out of Todd Gregory's big brother a few years ago for fumblin' against Abilene High."

"For real?" I asked. If it was true, Brooks would get tired of slugging people around Bingham. The football was like a wet bar of soap to us.

"Yeah, and he also flirts with some of the girls up there and drinks all the damn time. Damn, like he's one to talk."

Kurt always knew a little something about everyone. He had such an easy way about him that people just sort of told him things. A military brat during his early days, he'd learned to mingle with about any crowd. I thought he'd make a good politician someday, promising the world to everyone and having them all swallow it whole. The kind of kid who could convince you to buy a jar of air.

Still, nothing could make me feel too much better. I'd blown it, plain and simple. I'd given a good enough speech on the finer points of The War of 1812 a week earlier in American History but had folded like a map under Brooks's soupy breath.

***

Football wasn't always such a pain to me. Flag football at the YMCA was a blast. A running back for the Jaycee Hedgehogs, I'd been one of the quicker players in the league, my pipe-cleaner legs a threat to break the big one at any moment. The double reverse was our secret weapon. But the days of the double reverse were long gone, though my pipe-cleaner legs were not.

Back then, I ran for the pure fun of it, knowing the worst that could happen would be a painless yank of my flag. Now, though, fear was my fuel, and the enemy was after my health. And like I said, the Buzzards weren't running on a full tank.

I think Coach Max knew all of that. Once in a while he put up a good front, saying things like, "Okay boys, I really think this is going to be our week," but most of the time he appeared to be in a deep trance or nearing a coma. I suppose that way down he knew that no week was going to be our week.

I guess the years had caught up to him. He was probably about 60, meaning he'd blown his whistle at least a million times and lost half that many games, all at Bingham Junior High. It was no better than being a career French fry cook at a fast-food joint without ever getting moved up to the register. But the tip-off to his burnout was the fact that he could even bothered to get a name straight. Garcia was Garza. Robinson was Roberts. Hart was Harrison. Schitt was Schmidt. No kidding; he couldn't even nail mine. And we were his starters, his top guns. The poor guy either couldn't remember or was trying to forget.

A few weeks earlier, he called roll in the locker room before practice. As usual, his gray and blue 'B' cap was offcenter, his smudged glasses crooked on his peeling nose.

The guy was always torched.

"Davis." "Here."

"Donaldson."

"Here."

"Furman."

"Here."

"Halifax."

"Here."

And on it went, right down the row.

"Okay," Coach Max said, sliding the pen behind his ear.

"Did I miss anyone?"

"I don't think Heath Meals is here today, coach," piped up one player.

"Whose meals?" Coach tried to straighten his hat, moving it off-center to the other side.

"Heath. Heath Meals."

Coach Max took to scanning the list.

"Keith who?"

"No, Heath. Heath Meals!"

"Heath Meals?" It was no act. "Hmm, Meals, Keith." He grabbed the pen and jotted something at the bottom of the list.

It was the seventh week of the season.

So I guess it could have been worse. At least he knew we existed. To Coach Max, Heath Meals, a backup tight end, was every bit as real as Sasquatch. "Okay boys, let's get to work!" Our fearless leader.

The mood was light in the locker room. In the showers, Payton was leading a rendition of "Celebrate" by Kool and the Gang, while some guys were already bailing out of our stuffy quarters. The stench was almost too much to stomach.

And as luck would have it, my locker was right next to our gamiest player. Joel Schlichter had moved to Midtex at the beginning of the school year and quickly earned a reputation as someone to steer clear of. I'm not sure where he'd transferred from. Someplace that smelled like deviled eggs. Anyway, I had him in three classes and, because of our last names, he sat right behind me in all three. It was like having a shadow that feared Zest.

I slid past Joel and plopped on the bench. Already dressed, he was fiddling with a red knot on his forehead, the reward for three long months of bashing heads. He looked over at me, a small, dried river of blood branded on his brow.

"I really, really hate this crap," he said without even the smallest expression. And with a quick turn, he was gone.

Well, gone but not forgotten. His smell had sort of become a permanent resident of our row. Come to think of it, our wing was filled with characters. Jimmy McCullough had a steel plate in his head. Don't ask me why. Kevin Wilton could suck spaghetti through his nose. Danny Colantino had a Daffy Duck tattoo on his left shoulder and wore about 14 gold necklaces. So while we had definite personnel problems, the Buzzards didn't lack in personalities.

It was getting late, but I didn't feel like moving. My head was throbbing, and my bum right knee was swollen. I sat there by myself for a long time, untying my cleats without looking and silently cursing bad odors, yellow teeth and head-on collisions.

***

Rick Black had planted the seeds for my foul taste for football. Rick was the older brother of Ray Black, a neighbor and classmate and basic good 'ol boy. I probably wasn't quite Texan enough for him, seeing as I didn't have a pyramid of chewing tobacco tins in my bedroom, but he'd welcomed me into the neighborhood crew without much trouble way back when.

Anyway, his brother Rick was a basket case, a longhaired guy with a galaxy of white pimples, especially around his mouth. A senior and Picadilly reserve during our seventh-grade year, he introduced us to the world of tackle football while Ray was having a sleepover for the gang, about eight of us in all. We were all camping under his trampoline and trading baseball cards, content as could be, when Rick came out of the back door and decided to ruin my day. If you ask me, being under (and not on) a tramp was the only place to be. Ever since I'd gotten rocketed over the fence into the neighbor's yard when playing Break The Egg, I was pretty spooked by the things.

"Hey, hey, looks like we've got just enough for a good round of shotgun alley!" Rick howled.

Having seen the older kids play, I knew just enough about shotgun alley to cringe when I heard the words. It was basically like those joust things back in ancient times, only without horses or spears. In shotgun alley, the players were the horses, and their helmets were the spears. To me, it looked like 20 or so yards of sprinting toward agony.

Nobody looked especially interested in Rick, who appeared to be storing a cue ball of tobacco in his cheek. Nope, everyone was arguing about who had the best 'fro in the majors, Oscar Gamble or Lenny Randle. (It was Oscar, of course. The guy practically had to stoop over when playing in the Astrodome.)

Nope, nobody was interested, except for Ben Binford.

"Yeah, shotgun alley! Let's play, y'all!" Ben shrilled, shooting from the tramp's shadow. He thought Rick was the coolest thing since candy cigarettes.

He just had to go and do it.

Troy Thompson idolized Ben, so he jumped up. Skip Barnard worshipped Troy, so he did, too. Before you knew it, we were all in the Black's garage huddled around Rick. It was what the school counselors called peer pressure.

There were five Black boys - Ralph, Rick, Red, Ray and Reese - and they had like 100 football helmets in the garage. Most of them looked old and scarred with all kinds of colored nicks on them. That was the big thing on our block, to pound your head gear on the cement just to give it some character. That and doing a Pete Rose slide in the yard to make sure your pants were good and stained with grass. Moms hated that one.

"Let's see here now, this oughta fit ya, little guy." Rick handed me a Dallas Cowboy helmet. I'd been crouching in the back of the pack, waiting quietly with Shad Bryant, who was the runt of our class. Unless Rick had a Dixie Cup with a chin strap, Shad would be a tough fit.

My helmet, bright star on its side, looked shiny and new. It was really kind of nice. I twirled it around. On the back was a little sticker that said, "Not to be used for contact purposes." That wasn't so nice at all.

"A'right, hmm, let's match ya up," Rick said. We were standing in two bunches in the back yard, about 20 steps apart. The biggest guys were in the bunch that didn't include me.

"Okay, hmm, Paul and Ty, let's see what cha got. Now go getcha some, fellas!"

Paul and Ty peeled from the crowds and faced each other. Paul, by far the bigger of the two, got down in a three-point stance. Ty, who'd been the area's sixth-grade Science

Fair champion, did not. The only thing they really had in common was the fear in their eyes.

"And readeeee, setttttt, hutttttt!"

The sound was sickening, a dull thud followed by the thump of Ty's body hitting the ground. Paul peeled him off the turf and patted him on the butt, which we always did because the pros did, even if it didn't feel quite right. Ty started wobbling toward the wrong huddle, but Paul set him straight.

"Now that was a cotton pickin' hit!" Rick hooted.

"Gaddam, ya just gotta love football!"

Yeah, I thought, you just gotta love it. Five minutes earlier, I'd been all set to swap Ty my Ron Cey rookie card for his Mike Schmidt - plain robbery on my part - and now I was wearing a decoration and praying that the call for dinner would come before mine.

"A'right then, Ben, you go against, let's see now...." Rick searched our group.

I did the same and pretended to disappear. I eyed Shad, who looked like he was wearing a spaghetti pot on his head. He looked terrified, and I hoped for his sake that he wouldn't be called.

"How 'bout you, little Dallas Cowboys dude?" "Thank you dear heavenly God," Shad whispered.

So much for being a nice guy. Though I'd seen him 100 times, Rick still didn't know my name, but he didn't have any trouble matching me up against the toughest kid in the neighborhood.

Ben, who'd taken to drinking raw eggs after seeing *Rocky*, was the one guy who was actually enjoying it all. The kid plain loved football. He'd played ever since fifth grade, starring at defensive end on a sixth-grade team. He wasn't that big, but he played real big, and right then, standing straight across from him, he looked like a grizzly bear behind a T-bar face mask. Not a brute or anything, but definitely the meanest kid on his cul-de-sac. I was hoping he remembered that I helped him out in English hour all the time.

I couldn't chicken out, though. There was too much at stake. If a guy lost face in the gang, he ended up watching a lot of *$25,000 Pyramid* in the summer. Dad once said that if we got wiped out by a nuclear bomb, there'd be only two things left...cockroaches and that Dick Clark guy.

"Go get 'em, Jasp," Shad said. I buckled my chin strap and peeked out over the face mask. It had just one bar, like a kicker's. My left eye, always the left, started to twitch.

"And readeeeee, setttttt, hutttttt!"

The year before, I slammed into a closed sliding glass door in our porch room. It hurt tons and gave me two black eyes. But that was nothing compared to this. I was a small target, but Ben found the bull's-eye. For a second, I thought my head had left my body. Instead, it was only the helmet, which was laying a full five yards away from my outstretched right arm.

Half of it was, anyway.

Yep, my shiny Dallas Cowboys helmet, the one that by the suggestions of safety and laws of the state wasn't supposed to be used as a helmet at all, had split in half, right down the middle.

I turned my spinning skull toward the sky.

"Sheeeeettttt!" Rick shrilled. He was hanging over me on one knee.

Really, all three of him were, all with a bunch of whiteheads primed for the popping. Zits, I wasn't looking forward to them. "Are ya a'right, little man?"

"Yeah, are ya okay?" It was Ben. His helmet was pulled down over one eye, but his other eye looked pretty concerned. I think he knew he'd botched his only chance of passing our upcoming vocabulary test.

At that moment, I couldn't think of too much to say. Really, I didn't especially feel like talking at all. I let my head fall to the other side. Shad, his helmet spinning on the porch, was pedaling away on his bike. Smart guy.

Reese, the youngest Black brother, was standing just outside the back door. He was eight or nine and a maybe a little different. All I knew about him was that he really, really loved mayo sandwiches. No meat, just the white stuff.

"Hey!" Reid screeched, pointing straight at me. "You killed my brother's helmet!"

A little part of me, a miniscule spot deep down that hoped I might be the next great Picadilly Puma running back, died that day, too.

***

The Bingham locker room was completely empty, and Mario the janitor was sweeping up. He didn't know a word of English, but he was always smiling. I went to use the phone outside of Coach Max's office. It was almost 7:30. My folks would be wondering what the deal was, seeing as I usually called by 7:00. Dad hated to miss his shows.

Outside, the sky was completely black. Most of the locker room was, too, except for a little light bulb above the middle row of lockers. But as I reached the phone, I noticed a sliver of light peeking from the coaches office. Me and coach, we were both putting in a late night.

I had maybe 15 minutes to kill before Dad came. I went to the bathroom and combed my hair, slicing my part right down the middle and folding the wings up perfectly. I washed my hands. I watched Mario scrub the toilet, wondering how a guy who cleaned up after a bunch of crazy kids could ever smile. Probably seen us play.

The light still burned from the office. I didn't really want to talk to him. He was a nice man and all, but he was a grown man, and an old one at that. And at my age, you didn't often fire up conversations with grown men, even when they were named 'Dad.' But something, I don't know what, made me knock lightly and push open that door.

"Um, hey coach."

Coach Max was sitting at his desk, head in hands and in no hurry to change that. He slid his head above his right hand and looked at me with sleepy, half-closed eyes. The guy looked more than ready to call it quits.

"Oh, hi son, hello," he said, then slowly checked his watch. "I didn't know anyone was still here."

"Um, yessir, I'm just waitin' for my ride."

"I see, I see," he said. He turned toward me in his swivel chair and adjusted his specs. He looked at least 75 in the shadows, maybe older. "So, what can I do for ya?" It was probably more what I could do for me.

"Well, I just wanted to say that, well, that I wish I woulda said somethin' today. I mean, I wish I coulda said somethin'....but, well, the truth is that I didn't much know what to say."

Coach Max wrapped his hands behind his head and leaned back in the chair. He started to fall backward but caught his balance, and I swallowed back a laugh. "About what it takes to be a champion, you mean?"

"Yessir, about that."

He looked right at me, but I could tell he didn't really see me at all.

Finally, his eyes fell to the floor, and a deserted look stretched across his face.

"Son, I wouldn't have much known what to say, either."

Outside, a car honk. I turned to leave. I think we were done, anyway.

"Um, see ya tomorrow, coach."

"Yep, we'll see ya, Jody."

***

Friday practices were my favorite. Shorts, shoulder pads, stretching, plays run against a ghost defense and, best of all, no real hitting. Coach Max probably figured that we'd get hit plenty at our game the next day. The San Jacinto Bulldogs were the opponent, a team that had won two games and lost seven. Two wins, that was like the lottery around Bingham.

Still, our final practice was pretty crisp, probably because it was just that. That was motivation enough. It wasn't like we'd suddenly found our groove just to prove Coach Brooks wrong. Nobody had even mentioned the ape. It was almost over, that's all. After practice, we were supposed to watch some film of San Jacinto, but Coach Max said his wife had taped over their game footage with *The Love Boat.*

He called us over after wind sprints. We huddled around him and gasped for air as a group.

"No, no, don't bend over," he barked. "Straight up, hands over your head."

Coaches were always screaming that, to not bend over. But I'm sorry, when you felt like falling down, the last thing you wanted to do was stand up.

We rose and panted in unison, and for a moment he slowly looked us over, like he was trying to make eye contact with each player. I thought maybe a pep talk was coming.

"I wanna say somethin,'" he started and then paused for a long while. "And I want ya all to listen up good and to remember this." Another stop. "Boys, well, your jocks and socks have to be turned in immediately after the game. No excuses."

Again, I was wrong.

Except for in the old, grainy movies that I sometimes stumbled across on the tube, I'd never really heard a pep talk. Sure, I'd had coaches make bribes before games, like promising a trip to Mr. Fantastic's Pizzeria if we won, but nothing too inspiring. It was sort of hard to get all psyched up about pepperoni, plus we knew we'd probably end up getting it anyhow.

"And come by the locker room Monday to check in your uniforms," Coach Max called out as we wandered off. No problem there. Most of us would have gladly done it right then and there. "Oh, and maybe get some rest tonight, huh? Big day tomorrow."

He meant well, but the guy was all wrong. It was going to be a big night. Kurt was having a sleepover, and so was Katie Nichols, who lived just three streets over. As soon as all the parents nodded off, it would be Liplock Central. See, sleepovers weren't that cool anymore, but making out was becoming way cool.

Unfortunately, Katie's dad was either an insomniac or one sharp cookie. Kurt talked to Katie last at about 11 'o clock, and the guy was still up watching the tube. Said his head kept bobbing up and down, but he wouldn't crumble. I was fast learning that moms were pretty easy, but dads of girls could be real roadblocks. So we settled on talking about stuff, about sports and girls and the cars we hoped to one day drive, before sleepiness finally set in. By midnight, only Kurt and I were left, and I was fading fast, doing the falling-off-the-cliff thing.

"Ya know what I'd like to do tomorrow?" Kurt asked out of nowhere. It brought me back a little.

"What?"

"Win a stinkin' football game," he whispered. I heard him wrestle around in his sleeping bag. "Just one. I haven't done that since sixth grade, not once."

"Me either." David's words were soft but clear from across the den. I pried open my eyes and thought about it. They were both third-year Bingham students, and, more than that, both part of a class that had come up empty for two straight seasons. A loss to San Jacinto would polish off three long years of long Saturdays for much of our team.

I let the idea hang in the stillness. It was no different than a lousy haircut; there was no need to rub it in. I drifted off to sleep thinking about Andrea Woodall and the Bulldog defense, exactly in that order.

***

My game-day breakfast at home the next morning was no different than my regular school-day spread. Ten biscuits, all dripping with honey, and a glass of milk. Like always, Dad had them waiting when I got out of the shower. As I wolfed it all down, I considered that of my 100 or so pounds, probably at least half of that was biscuits and bologna.

The other half was pure skin and bones, a fact I realized once again as I pulled on my uniform in the locker room around noon. Game time was set for two o'clock, and Jay Lundy Gordon, the local singing weatherman who wore a toupee that made him look like a Sears mannequin, had called for another scorcher. Ninety-five degrees in the shade, the kind of day that could make a guy's meat fall right off the bone. At least I didn't have much to lose.

Judging from the general attitude in the locker room, neither did my teammates. The mood was carefree as the Buzzards geared up, and bad jokes and tall tales of the night before filled the air. A few guys treated the hours before kickoff as serious business, walked around wearing these stiff game faces, but basically it was like a bad sitcom.

Coach Max walked in 10 minutes later. His shorts were again too short, his socks too high and his shirt too white. He put a hand on his hip and leaned against a locker. A beam of sunlight reflected off his head. Basically, he resembled Mr. Clean with a whistle.

He hushed us down, no small chore, and ordered us over. From close range, he looked a little different, not quite so out there, maybe more intense. This time, I thought a pep talk was coming for sure.

"Okay boys, here's the deal," he said, rubbing his hands together. "One of the buses won't start, so we're all going to have to squeeze into the other one."

Ah, I'd just learned that one. It was what Mr. Stewie, my English Lit teacher, called poetic justice.

The ride over was brutal. There were about 50 of us, plus a portion of the band, the cheerleading team and a few trainers and managers. Geez, did our managers have it tough. Washing the jocks of winners was one thing, but scrubbing our grubby sack pouches must have been the pits. Coach Max, as usual, handled the bus like a hand grenade, racing along at a good 30 miles an hour. I shared the third-to-last seat with a trumpet player with huge sleep rocks in his eyes. Finally, after a good hour, Rackney Stadium came into focus.

It was a perk of our final game. Along, of course, with it being our final game. This would be our one and only appearance at Rackney Stadium, the home of the Picadilly Pumas and the Midtex Mustangs. It was almost brand new, having replaced ancient Barnett Stadium just a few years back, and was blanketed with that prickly fake turf. Like I said before, every other Friday, Picadilly always played before a jammed house, Midtex High about half that. On this Saturday, Bingham and San Jacinto would show their stuff before a slightly smaller crowd. There'd no doubt be a cast of dozens, all sharing our last names. Oh, and a couple of girlfriends peppered here and there, at least until halftime.

Still, that didn't matter. Rackney was the big time. The locker rooms were spacious and airy, and the pissers didn't even reek yet. We'd gotten the home locker room, meaning that we were suiting up where the future Picadilly stars would one day dress. Strapping on my shoulder pads, I knew I would never be one of them.

I'd decided that it would be my last football game. It wasn't a clear-cut decision, like picking out of shirt to wear. It had just kind of formed in my mind through the years, starting the day Ben Binford knocked me silly and continuing on until that very moment, when I realized my jersey was on backwards.

The pre-game drills were much like Friday practice, only in full pads. First we pretended to stretch, pulling hard when

Coach Max was nearby and dogging it the rest of the time. C'mon, no ordinary boy could really touch his head to his knee. We then scooted from station to station, running plays and doing drills and pretending to be totally focused. Slaps on the butt, rhythmic claps, the basic sis-boom-bah bit.

"Cmmmnnn, ltttsss ggggooo," a player in passing would mumble behind his mouthpiece. Some guys wore the things from the second they put on their helmets, muzzling themselves for the next two hours. I wished a few of them would wear them at all times.

Anyway, it was the same bit we'd followed for nine weeks. And for nine weeks, the result was always the same.

Sleepwalking through the routine on the Rackney carpet, nothing hinted that anything unusual was about to happen.

I sat in the locker room just minutes before kickoff, having already lathered up a decent sweat. Gordon was on the money; it was a scorcher. Some players wandered around, but most were propped on the backs of benches and chairs. I wiped my face on my jersey. I was number 46. I usually blamed my lack of production on it, the jersey, the number. I mean, a guy couldn't be expected to be fast or flashy wearing number 46.

The Bingham fight song filtered through the open door. I wasn't sure what the tune was, but it sounded too much like the theme from the *The Jeffersons*. It was a little off-key, and I couldn't help but think that maybe the bus ride over had taken a little out of our gang.

In the corner, David and Kurt were smearing black war paint under each other's eyes. It was the stuff that was supposed to act as a sun visor, the gunk you saw the pros wearing. I didn't see why Kurt really needed it on defense, but it would probably come in handy for David. As quarterback, he spent much of each game staring up at the sun from his back.

With three quick claps, Coach Max got our attention. He stood in the center of the room, holding a clipboard. I figured it was our game plan, though he never got around to telling us what the game plan was. Three plays and a punt, or maybe one and a turnover, that seemed to be the weekly attack.

"Well, boys, I guess this is it," Coach Max started. It was the last game of a last-place team, and there would be no pool party. Yep, this was about it. "I just want y'all to know how much I've enjoyed spending this season together. It's been an honor and a privilege to, well, to watch y'all grow and mature as young men and as a team."

I hoped nobody would laugh. We'd grown about as much as Coach's hair over the last three months. Zip.

"So let's get out there and, well, let's give it all we've got."

It wasn't legendary stuff - heck, most of it wasn't even true, and the last part was pure canned material - but at least the guy had tried. Of course, I wasn't expecting Knute Rockne. Anyhow, his final career pre-game speech spurred the Buzzards into a medium-fast shuffle out of the locker room.

***

We didn't pick up the pace much in the first half, either. The Bulldogs took the opening kick and scored four plays later. Somebody had mentioned something about their top running back being a speedster, but nobody had paid much attention. Wouldn't have made us any faster, anyway. The kid took a pitch and sprinted 60 yards around right end.

Two minutes in, we were behind, seven-zip.

We answered with a promising debut, driving a full 30 yards before sputtering when Payton tried to catch a third-down pass with his facemask. Then Jim Barry Ingram, one of the team's more reliable performers, sailed the punt snap so far over Joey's head that the ball rolled clear out of the end zone and may still be rolling today. A 50-yard snap, no joke. Nine-zip, them.

Our defense then tightened. From a knee on the sidelines, I realized that the unit was made up almost entirely of Bingham lifers, the owners of the lifetime 0-29 record. The group included Kurt, who gave us possession back with a fumble recovery in San Jack territory.

"Ltttssss dddddddoo itttttttt!" Kurt slobbered as he ran off the field. Those mouthguards, they did nothing for effective and concise communication.

The Buzzard offense, though, was an equal opportunity bunch. It only took us three snaps to give the ball back, courtesy of yours truly. I took a pitch at their 25-yard line and found the near sideline, for a second even seeing paydirt. But it was what I didn't see - number 51 - that made things head south. In flag football, fumbles resulted in a blown whistle. *Hey, that's okay little fella, you still keep the ball*, the officials would say with a soft pat on the head. But on this day, my bumble was grounds for a turnover at the five and a nasty rug burn.

And so it went, our spirited battle before a sitting-room-only crowd. We showed a few flashes, like when David broke free for a 35-yard scoot into enemy territory. But on the very next play, he went scrambling around and got cute, weaving and juking all over the place before stubbing his foot into the turf and falling. I actually think he tripped over the midfield stripe. Loss of 30. Drive over.

Our defense, which had allowed something like 8,500 yards against Northside, continued to hang tough. The Bulldog scatback called Alfie was stuffed for squat after the early score. And their air attack was every bit as lethal as ours. They tried two passes, one that ended up in Brock "Billy Goat" Battle's arms for an interception and another that whacked a mascot on the snout.

On the sidelines, things were the same as ever. Some guys had their head in the game, most didn't. For example, I went back to get a cup of water after my fumble, hiding as much as anything else. Danny Colantino, shoulders pads already off, was camping with a pretty twirler in the stands. He was a third-string tight end, sure but he was an Italian third-string tight end. Case closed.

Just seconds before half, we again slid into scoring position, advancing all the way to the Bulldog eight. A sharp little drive got us there, one sparked by some clutch plays and, more amazingly, no major goofs. It was pretty exciting, watching ourselves tick off plays like they were drawn up, like it wasn't even us.

Of course, success was pretty much a fluke for the Bingham Buzzards.

The last play of the half summed up our season to that point. David was supposed to throw a short pass into the left corner. He did that. But he wasn't supposed to chunk it right to a kid in a purple Bulldogs jersey. He did that, too. I almost caught him at midfield then again at the 20, but the little waterbug was toying with me. One last dive gave me another faceful of carpet. As he circled back toward the San Jack sidelines, he passed me and laughed.

***

We headed to the break, a tired and sweaty and defeated bunch. We were used to that, to being way behind, but this was a different feeling. This was anger. We'd beaten them all over the field, really we had, and had nothing but a 16-0 deficit to show for it.

Just ahead of me, Kurt and David were walking together. Kurt would no doubt play at Picadilly, where he'd finally taste victories and maybe even play a role in some of them. Like I said, he could fit in anywhere, even a starting lineup as an undersized linebacker. As for David, well, he'd forget about all of it in time. Poor guy had more concussions than completions on the season.

As we neared the locker room, I felt a stare. It was Coach Brooks. He was standing just to the left, up on the front row behind the railing, and crunching on a snow cone. As I passed him, he looked right at me, shook his head and laughed. His lips were stained orange, and, like I said earlier, I'd seen better teeth on a rake.

"Really showin' me somethin,' you piss ants!" His words echoed through the tunnel.

In the locker room, I wanted to say something, I really did. Something that would light a fire, ignite some burning desire in us to succeed. But first, I tended to my bloodied forearm, which stung like a scorpion. All the while, while

Doc Bunting sprayed red paint over the gash, I knew I'd say nothing.

But somebody, the least likely guy around, did.

"Huddle up, huddle up!" he screamed from the room's center. It wasn't so much the voice but the tone that made us obey. In seconds, we were clustered around him.

"Before we go back out there, I wanna say something," he began. For maybe the first time all season, our collective attention was focused on one target. "Here's the deal." A pause. "Well, first off, I don't think it really matters if we win or lose this football game. I really, truly don't. And I don't think it matters that Coach Brooks thinks we stink. I mean, we do stink. "But he said somethin' the other day, somethin' about us not havin' what it takes to be a champion. Well, I've thought a lot about it, and I don't buy it. I mean, who really knows what it takes? Does he have some kinda fancy math equation worked out? Is it, I dunno, weight times height divided by whatever else? What? Like Brooks knows?

The man teaches driver's ed. C'mon." Some muffled laughter, but just a little. "I mean, it's all about wantin' something, isn't it? Isn't it? I think we should just try an' figure out what makes us wanna be champions. And I'm not talkin' about a lousy football game, either. It's just a game, for cryin' out loud. So forget about Bingham Junior High. Forget about winnin' or losin.' Forget about screwin' up. Forget about the guy next to ya and forget about the other team. I just think that maybe we should all just wanna be good, want it really, really bad.

"So for the next hour of our lives, let's try and figure out what makes us wanna be a champion. Not for Brooks..." A pause.

"For you."

Silence followed. He stood there, split right in the middle of us, foot on a stool. You could almost hear people mulling it all over. We'd spent so much time figuring out how to be bad, we'd forgotten to consider the alternative.

He started to clap. Slowly, methodically. Kurt joined in first, followed by, of all people, Heath Meals. And then it started, a tribal roar. Soon it echoed through the room, 40 pairs of hands, 40 voices, 40 reasons for wanting to be somebody. The rafters began to shake above us. It gave me big, fat goosebumps.

"C'mon, let's goooooo!"

At that moment, I woulda probably killed for Coach Max. Not the coach - the goofy guy, the lifelong loser. And from the way we stormed onto the field, fresh off the best pep talk ever, the rest of the Bingham Buzzards would have, too.

***

The emotion didn't pay off at first. We went backwards on our opening drive when I fumbled a pitch, then booted the ball out of bounds trying to scoop it up. But our defense was out of its mind. Chad broke through and blocked the following punt, then hunted the loose ball down and raced to the Bulldog seventeen. It was a great play and all, but he'd talk about it for a good eleven months.

It took us seven plays, including a fourth-down run by fullback Ricky "Redneck" Ryan, a rodeo nut who kept straw in his socks to gnaw on during the game, but we finally stuck it in. David tumbled across from the one, riding the Mountain Man's back over the goal.

Five minutes into play, the Buzzards had their second offensive score of the season and first in several weeks. David really hammed it up after the touchdown. We kind of all did. Some famous coach once said that you were supposed to act like you'd been in the end zone before when you got there. Well, the Buzzards weren't there very often, so we lived it up, especially after Redneck stumbled across for the two-point conversion to make it 16-8.

"Yeah! Yes! Yes! Way to go, boys! Way to go!" Coach Max hooted as we trotted off the field. "Now ya got 'em on their heels! Now they're runnin' scared!"

As the game wore on, only two things kept us from creeping closer. One, the Bulldogs' ability to avoid any more major blunders and to run the football, if only in small spurts, before punting. And two, and this was pretty big, the fact that our offense was flat-out pathetic. There was no changing that, especially in the last half of our last game. Eighty yards might as well have been 80 miles. Anyway, the first thing was frustrating; the second was a simple fact.

With four minutes left and an eight-point deficit, we needed a miracle. Well, or Joe Loco.

If you want to be accurate and all, Joe was probably clinically insane. Along with the bird execution in shop class, he'd brought a homemade bomb to school in a *Herbie The Love Bug* lunch pail, put an art teacher in a headlock and gotten caught humping a girl on the roof of the school.

You could say he was a little unstable.

He was also the most athletically gifted junior high school player in town. Joe wasn't big or fast or strong. He was all three. And when he felt like playing, he was unstoppable. He wasn't a classic running back, no fancy jukes or anything; he was just too much for a hundred-and-nothing-pound safety to deal with. You just kind of shoved him the ball and watched him go.

But the thing was, he never really felt like playing. Sure, he showed up at practice, at least some of the time, but always did something before game day rolled around to cause a suspension or benching. The adults at the school didn't have the slightest idea about what to do with Joe, and neither did Coach Max, who was terrified of him. We all kind of were. The guy was a time bomb.

And while our defense was trying to get the ball back, I thought Joe was going to explode. I was trying to catch my wind on the bench when Joe, hair pick dangling from his gerry curls, strolled past and tapped Coach Max's shoulder. Joe hadn't played in weeks, which was a big plus for me because I would have been an instant bench warmer.

Their conversation lasted just three seconds or so, but Joe must have made a good point. He threw his helmet on, right over the pick, and was in the game by the next play.

I had to see. I hustled up next to Coach Max, who looked different than I'd ever seen him. His shirt was soaked with sweat, and his eyes were wild with intensity.

He actually looked like a coach instead of a mailman.

"Um, what did Joe want, coach?" I asked.

He turned to me for only an instant. "To play, son. To play."

And that he did. Though he hadn't played a snap on defense all season, Joe burst through the line and stopped Alfie for no gain. Then, on third and inches, he hurdled two blockers and collared their quarterback for a 10-yard loss.

When he wasn't so bad, Joe Loco was very, very good.

"Attaway Joe! Attaway defense!" Coach Max yelled as the defense left the field. Joe tried not to smile, but it slipped. Just a little.

During the punt, Joe snapped the water bottle from me. He sprayed his face with water, cracked his neck and turned to me.

"Next series, I'm in for you," he said blankly.

I couldn't really argue. It took a scrawny arm to bring me down. With Joe, it took an entire school. Someday, probably a SWAT team, too.

Our five-play, 75-yard drive that followed was a highlight reel of what could have been. Like a human wrecking ball, Joe slammed right for 18 yards, rammed left for 20 and hammered up the middle for 24 more. Finally, he took a pitch and, after flattening a pair of Bulldogs with nasty stiff-arms, he high-stepped into the end zone.

The Bingham sidelines went wild. Well, kind of.

Because of the heat, our fan base had thinned to about 30 people. My folks, figuring they were putting in their last mandatory football hour, were still around. On the far end, by himself, sat Coach Brooks. His hat was pulled way down, and his mirrored shades were almost as big as his head. Looked just like the guy from *Chips*.

Not Ponch, the other one.

It was 16-14, with a little more than two minutes left. We would no doubt try a two-point conversation and attempt to knot the score. All it would take would be a quick hand-off to Joe and an easy three-yard plow to paydirt.

I could live with that, a 16-16 final. I heard that a tie was like kissing your sister. Well, that was better than making out with your grandma with her teeth out, which is what getting drilled week after week felt like.

There was just one problem, but it was a big problem.

There was no Joe.

"What the...? Where the heck is he?" Coach Max asked, whirling around as the officials waited impatiently.

"What's it going to be, coach?" one ref barked. "Gonna go for two or kick or what?"

Coach Max froze up like Bambi under a floodlight. Of course we'd go for two. A kick wouldn't do us any good. Plus, there wasn't much choice, seeing as we didn't really have a placekicker. Todd Kipping did our kickoffs, but that was usually only once a game with the whole field to work with. He kicked straight-ahead style, like that plastic Super Toe guy, and often hit our offensive linemen on their backs with his practice tries.

"Where the hell is Joe Robinson!" Coach was frantic. And he even got the name right, so he meant business.

"Hey, there he is!" Kurt yelled, pointing in the other direction. "Hey Jooooe!"

About 50 yards away, walking along the track and away from the playing field, was Joe. Only in a span of seconds, he'd managed to multiply. On his right, he was flanked by a young girl, all of 16 years old and one I'd never seen before. Maybe the roof girl. On his left wobbled a young boy, probably two or so and wearing a blue doo rag around his head. He was holding Joe's hand. Huh, I thought, a junior Loco.

"Joe, hey Joe!" Coach Max's hands hung in the air like he was waiting to catch a pass.

Wasn't going to happen. Joe only raised his right arm and flicked it outward. Didn't even turn around. The three of them wound slowly around the track, then disappeared through the far gate. We stalled for a minute, but he was long gone. I didn't exactly get it, but there probably wasn't much to get. I figured Joe had proven himself to himself and, well, to his own team.

I turned to Coach Max, who looked like he'd just been left at the altar. "Well, whattaya waitin' for, get in there!" he screamed finally, tugging at my shoulder pads.

Sure, now he needed me.

Our two-point try was pathetic. The plan called for David to pitch the ball to me, then I would hand off to Redneck, who would hand off to Payton sneaking around from his wide receiver slot. In other words, the double reverse, the 'ol dipsy-doo from the glory years. But this wasn't the YMCA, and we weren't the Hedgehogs. Payton slipped on some of Redneck's loose straw, and the play lost 14 yards.

We still had one last hope - an onside kick.

A successful onside kick took touch, skill, finesse. Todd, trotting out with the tee in one hand and his asthma inhaler in the other, owned none of the three. I mean, he was a kicker on a team that didn't really need one, so that put him pretty low on the food chain. But our choices were few.

"Down!" Todd yelled, his left hand outstretched. Eight of us were on one side of the field, with a pair of Buzzards waiting on the other side just for show. "Set!"

With that, he trotted toward the ball. We did the same, tiptoeing at the line until hearing the soft thump of shoe to pigskin. We sprinted for the slow roller like rabid dogs. It was a race toward respectability.

The pile-up that followed was a mess, a cluttered heap of mangled bodies. I couldn't see a thing, though from the smell I knew Joel Schlichter was around somewhere. I couldn't shake the guy.

If the ball was down there, I sure didn't see it. Did get a nice slug in the nads for my efforts, though. Finally, as I was prying a mouthpiece out of my nose, someone found the buried treasure.

"I got it! I got it! I got it!!!" I kind of recognized the voice but wasn't sure who it belonged to.

We unfolded from the heap. Sure enough, Joel was standing right next to me when we reached our feet. The referee pushed me out of the way and knifed through the crowd. He reached a player and twirled him around, exposing both a Bingham jersey and the football.

It was Heath, the forgotten one. His smile stretched from earhole to earhole as Mountain Man gave him a bear hug and hauled him to the sidelines. Good for him, I thought as we gathered at the San Jacinto 42-yard line with 31 ticks left. Good for him.

Payton hustled in the play to David, who then turned to the huddle and repeated it to us. But as usual, David was doing the church mouse bit.

"Hummiddity, hummidditty, on two," David whispered.

"What?" we screamed together.

"X two-th...blah blah blah. On two," he repeated. For some reason, he always emphasized the snap count, so at least we would know exactly when to begin the play that we didn't know. Anyway, it was like going to Mass in that huddle.

"X236 cross on one!" Payton finally shouted.

David dropped into the pocket. The deep was designed to go deep to Payton or toward the near sidelines to Redneck. Those were his primary options. Really, though, running for his life was his only choice. He escaped out of bounds for a measly gain of two.

Second down, a screen pass to me. We'd run it once all year and should have left it at that. David drifted back, and back, and back. Way too far back. Finally, after pretending to block, I peeled away from the pack and nabbed his endover-end pass. One kink - I was about 15 yards behind the line of scrimmage. It took some fancy footing and a lifetime to peel my way back to the 35. I got mugged before reaching the sidelines.

Coach Max called our final timeout with 16 seconds to play.

Our unit gathered around him. He was out of breath, flustered and nervous. I think we all were. We were operating in strange territory.

"Okay boys," he huffed, sweat dripping on his clipboard. "We probably have time for a couple more plays. Let's go with, um, right 218 fade and, and, um, left 27 sweep." We started to hit the field.

"And men?"

We turned.

For the first time, at least to him, we were men.

"Let's make it count."

The first play, 218 fade, was all about Payton. It isolated him alone on the right side of the field and took advantage of his size and speed. We lined up hoping that, just this once, Payton's hands wouldn't go and get in the way.

"And readeee....hut!"

David pedaled straight back and stopped. He didn't pretend to have any other choices and didn't disguise his target. It was the bomb you drew up in the sandlots, the Hail Mary, the Last Chance Cafe.

He released the ball just before getting bashed.

Like I said, Payton had a lot to live up to. As if it wasn't bad enough that his dad was a local legend, that same dad had gone and named his only son after one of the best players in the NFL. Payton never said so because Payton hardly said much of anything, choosing instead to sing, but I think he hated that name.

But on that play, and maybe for the first time in his life, he lived up to it. Tightly guarded on both sides, Payton jumped as the pass neared. The two Bulldogs did, too, but not nearly as high. Or as gracefully. Or, in the end, as successfully. He must have been five yards above the turf upon catching the ball. It was almost perfect. Almost. See, he was also three yards short of the end zone.

We raced to the line like school girls. Everything was a blur around me, and I couldn't hear a sound. My chest was burning, and my knee was throbbing. I helped big Jesse Sewell drag along, giving the game clock a quick look. Six, five, four.

The smart move would have been to down the ball, to slam it to the ground and stop the clock. Then again, we weren't winless for nothing.

"Hut!"

David peeled to his right. The play, 27 run, was a designed sweep that was supposed to give the quarterback about four lead blockers. Picadilly ran it with amazing success and execution. We didn't. In seconds, he was surrounded. He reversed his ground. David must have been a huge Fran Tarkenton fan, because he was always zigging and zagging all over the place, even when he didn't need to zig or zag at all.

In this case, though, dodging was pretty much a must -- four Bulldogs were hot on his tail.

From my viewpoint in the back of the end zone, things looked bad. David was no speedster, and the pack was gaining on him. But out of nowhere, Mountain Man erased three of them. I think he might have clinically killed two of them.

We were still in business.

The interior line was still a big pile of bodies, a bunch of leaning lugs. But as David tore around the left side, about 10 yards from the end zone, one Bulldog was still on his heels. I figured that I should maybe do something.

As I snuck around the opposite side, it all came rushing back. David's shadow was Rick Black. He was Ben Binford. He was the Northside Gators. He was every linebacker who'd ever pancaked me. And, best of all, he had no idea I was coming into the picture.

Blindside hits weren't really fair. Then again, neither were a lot of things in life. I thought about all that as the Bulldog neared David and I closed in. Believe it or not, I did. Everything was moving in slow motion, like the halftime highlights on Monday Night Football. I could have swore I heard Howard Cosell's voice.

As we all reached the same point, right around the five-yard line, the Bulldog made his move. Maybe David would have broken the tackle, maybe not. Just as his shoulder turned downward from the pull of the tackle try, I made sure that we'd never know.

The collision was a little nauseating. It was kind of like a whipping from your dad. Probably hurt me more than it did him. Still, it did the trick. From an upside-down view, I saw David escape into the clear and leap across the goal stripe.

Ball game.

I slowly rose to my feet, my legs unsure, my head cloudy. I looked to my left, to where the fallen opponent was sitting back on his elbows. His eyes were a little crazy, but I recognized him. It was the little waterbug, the one who'd laughed in my face at the end of the half. Pain had never felt so good.

In the end zone, the guys were mugging David. Kurt was draped across his back, and the whole gang was bouncing together. In the corner, Payton was break dancing, head spins and all.

It was obvious that my dirty work was going unnoticed. That was fine. I was just enjoying the show. I stood there, still a little out of it, and felt a wave of emotions.

Happiness, especially for David and Kurt and Coach Max. Relief, in knowing that our tag as losers could be lifted, if only a bit. And hey, even a little pride in myself. I didn't have much to offer, but I'd left it all right there on that field.

***

The team lifted Coach Max and carried him off the field. I joined the crew and did one of those things where you clenched both fists together and swung them in the air on both sides of your head. No big reason. I just didn't think people did enough of that.

Riding along a wave of shoulder pads, Coach turned his index finger toward the sky. We weren't number one, or even number five in our conference, but that didn't matter. Maybe he was just showing the crowd how many wins we'd racked up on the year.

"Bing-ham! Bing-ham! Bing-ham!" we chanted. It sure felt good, the joy of victory thing. For once, we weren't that skier tumbling down the mountain, that agony of defeat sucker.

As we shuffled toward the locker room, Coach Max motioned for Mountain Man and Jesse to put him down. We stopped in a rush, like a freeway pile-up. Through a slit of light, I saw why. Standing in the doorway was Coach Brooks.

He was leaning to one side with folded arms and a wide smile. We moved silently and slowly forward. Oh God, I thought, the guy was somehow going to take credit for everything. We'd all had something to prove out there, and crazily enough had done just that, but I was pretty sure that none of it because of a guy named Hurricane.

Coach Max spared us the lecture. He found his footing and, with a quick wave, again stopped the team in its tracks. A few seconds later, he was face to face with the man who'd questioned the need for our very existence two days earlier.

I can't report what Coach Max said, but it wasn't for a lack of trying. The team as a whole stretched forward, leaning toward the two men in the shadow of the doorway. It wasn't a heated argument, but it was a one-sided conversation in Coach Max's favor. Anyway, we didn't really need to hear. Know how they say a picture is worth a thousand words? Well, this was like that *The Odessey* book that Dad had been trying to finish for most of my life.

At first, Coach Brooks did nothing but smirk. But after a while, his face changed. His lips tightened, and his eyebrows got all crinkled up. He adjusted his cap, then readjusted it. He started fidgeting and fumbling. The whole time, though, he said zip.

Finally, after a good two minutes, Coach Brooks put a hand on the railing above him, threw a leg over and pulled himself up. Slowly, he eased through our waiting, sun-drenched parents and ducked down the exit ramp. Somewhere, I hoped that Gipper guy was laughing his tail off.

"Whattaya think he said?" Kurt asked quietly. We were sort of hovering in a big blue-and-gray ball, waiting to see what happened next. "I think he chewed his ass out." "I hope he told him off good," David whispered.

"Say, did y'all see that blocked punt of mine?" Chad asked. It was already starting.

"I betcha he threatened to plant his fist in the sucker's face," Payton said.

Maybe, but probably not. Coach Max was probably more likely to plant daffodils in his garden. As for me, I just thought that the guy standing before us, looking again more like a mailman than a coach, had finally figured out what to say.

As we filed into the entrance, I found myself face to face with Coach Max. He put a hand on my elbow, stopping my momentum, and winked.

"We did it, Jody. We did it."

I nodded and grinned behind my facemask. My name didn't matter, anyhow. I was just a kid with a headache who wasn't sure what he was doing, and he was a washed-up ceramics teacher who wouldn't know what to do next.

But in our final game, we both got one last good lick in, and it had felt pretty darn good.

Bet Your Ass

I was 14 years old when I won my first girl in a poker game.

It was the summer between ninth and 10th grade, the three-month cushion between junior high and high school. It was all pretty cruel, really. Just when a kid started feeling like a somebody, boom, he got zapped back to the bottom lockers and older desks and stricter teachers, back to knowing nothing good at all. We were finally moving up to Picadilly, but it was really just a step down to Loserville.

Annie Sedgefield's life wouldn't change a whole lot. Annie wasn't popular at Bingham, and she probably wouldn't be at Picadilly, either. With her bright red hair and pale skin and mouthful of metal, she wasn't much to look at. If she had any less of a tan, the girl would have been clear. Heck, throw in her whiny voice and sour pits, and she wasn't much to listen to or smell, either. Sometimes she was kind of funny, in a weird sort of way, but mostly she kept quiet and looked sad and, well, someplace else. To think she would turn into a beautiful swan someday was a fairy tale. Nope, Annie Sedgefield was and always would be a duck.

But Annie had three things going for her in June of 1984: (1) Parents vacationing in Idaho or Iowa or someplace; (2) a big house; and (3) a swimming pool. And smack dab in the middle of a hot Midtex summer, that was plenty.

Word of Annie's party spread by the usual means - somebody told Amber Taylor. Amber was Bingham Jr. High's beautiful swan, only she skipped the whole ugly duckling part. She had blonde hair and bright blue eyes and a knockout of a smile, and her bod was way ahead of schedule. Oh, she was just 14 or 15, but she'd graduated from the Bingham boys years ago, and it was just wasted wishing to get goofy about her.

Even the sophomore or juniors were really no match for Amber. If you weren't a senior football player with some college scouts on your tail, then you were flat out of luck. She couldn't shake the whole Valley Girl bit and said 'like' like, every other, like, word, but that didn't take away from the pure, like, viewing pleasure.

Anyhow, nothing made Amber happier than to spread the good word. I was lounging in bed and lobbing a tennis ball to myself when my buddy Danny Allen called with news of the party. He'd heard from Deanna Carson, who'd heard from Stacey Hamm, who'd found out from Amber, who'd probably known about it all before Annie Sedgefield herself.

"So anyway, it's going to be cool, lots of chicks there and stuff," Danny promised.

"Well, when is it?"

"Later tonight, like around eight or so. So whattaya think?"

I caught the ball just in front of my face, making it 153 in a row.

"So?" he repeated.

I was still over 200 catches from my personal record, and even farther than that from having a life. "Yeah, sure,

I'm game."

Midtex summers were murder. There was always baseball in the evenings, but the days were long and slow and hot, with only our annual family vacation to bust up the boredom. Every August, we loaded up and headed to Missouri to see my mom's relatives at the farm or to Colorado to see my dad's family, where I'd hang out with my cousins and swing on trees or chunk crab apples at passing cars or sit around and swap lies or play some ball. I liked it best when we went to Colorado, because Missouri was a little too *Green Acres* for me.

I mean, the farming life was fine and all, if you weren't allergic to hay and didn't mind the general smell of crap, which I was and which I did, but wearing Cousin Randy's grimy overalls and milking a cow or chugging along on an old tractor with my Uncle Hilbert wasn't exactly Six Flags.

But even Denver was starting to lose its shine. It wasn't that there was nothing to do, because there was, or that I didn't like my cousins, because I did. Mostly, we were just getting too old to get away with the good stuff.

If it wasn't for Danny, I would have gone crazy.

Danny was like a brother to me, only one without a beard, and lived just around the corner, though we were never that far apart. We'd been linked at the hip since the summer before, after both being recruited by a Little League team called the Superior Trailers Titans. Know how some squads always had a brute that had to whip out his birth certificate, just to prove he was young enough for the league? Well, we Titans had about four of those guys.

Every team in West Texas was scared silly of us. If they hadn't been in my dugout, wearing the same sharp and shiny blue-and-red uniforms, I would have been, too. Our ace pitcher, a hulk named Bobby Brewster who looked way more like a Bob, was so mean that he once brushed back his grandma at a Downing school picnic during sixth grade. The teachers threw a fit, but I understood. It was only softball, but that didn't give granny a right to crowd the plate.

Anyway, the Titans were good enough to win 38 straight games, 33 by shutout even, and breeze to the state tournament in Brownwood. But see, Texas was an awfully huge place and just full of small towns and big kids. First we got shut down by a beanpole of a pitcher who struck out like 20 of us and, just to make sure, even snapped our best player's wrist with an inside fastball.

We won a couple of games after that, but then some orange team with a curly-haired slinger named Brandy whipped us good. Kid might have had a girl's name, but his fastball was nothing to joke about. I whiffed twice against him, then came up in the last inning with us down 5-3 and a runner on second. I did the sign of the cross before stepping in the box and whiffed at three straight pitches. Game over, season over.

I figured God had more important things on his plate than my batting average.

Anyway, I spent that summer hanging out in centerfield, which was a pretty lonely place to be considering our mutant pitchers. Mostly I just fought off mosquitoes, practiced my batting stroke, and waited. And waited. And waited. Unless the ball was poked over to right field, that is. More than once I had to tear over and snag a fly ball headed that way. Shakes Todd was our right fielder, and even though he owned the city's top seven all-time scores in Dig Dub, which was pretty cool really, the guy was terrified of the ball. That kind of worked against him in things like, say, ball.

As the Titans' catcher, Danny was much busier behind the plate, which seemed like a pretty scary place to be considering our pitchers. He would toss his floppy blonde hair back, pull on his mask and disappear into a tiny ball. A handful of sharp thuds later, he would slowly unfold, chunk off his gear and meet me for a seed-spitting contest or to chatter on the far end of the bench, all matted and crusty and red, even though we'd be up like 26-0.

It made me glad to be a lefty. See, there were two things I'd learned we southpaws could never do. One was math, because the math part of our brains were all screwy. And two, play catcher. I wasn't sure why, and I wasn't about to ask. Between the spiral notebooks and smudged-up hands and backward scissors, we lefties had enough to worry about.

Danny's folks ran a restaurant called Todd's Steak House, a place where you could get a hamburger as big as your skull. But they were hardly ever home, so Danny kind of became a regular around our place. We had to put our heads together to find stuff to do, but we always stewed up something. Whiffle ball in the backyard, with ghost runners. Knee football in the den, with skinned-up knees. Nerf baseball in the living room, with broken lamps. Crank calls, dirty movies on HBO, junk like that.

Oh, and knocking each other out. That was where you would crouch down and take a bunch of deep breaths, then stand up while the other guy clamped his hands tightly around your throat. In a snap, you were out cold for ten, 10, 15 seconds or so. I mean a real mini-coma. It probably wasn't all that safe, taking ourselves to the edge of death like that, but it was pretty good fun.

So if Danny was like a fourth brother to me, then we were sort of like his second family. He was a grade behind, so we didn't hang out as much during the school year, but in the summers we were practically like a Denny's and a La Quinta. The summer of 1983 was filled with winning and sleepovers and Slurpee races and brain freezes, and I couldn't see ever forgetting a minute of it. (Except for when we were in our pretend comas, of course.)

***

The summer of 1984 was different. For one, I had moved up to Pony League ball and on, by curse of the draw, to the Midtex Bumper Stallions. And the Stallions were no Titans, let me tell you. We had lame purple uniforms and a suspect roster full of little Timmies and Jimmies and Tommies who showed no signs of becoming Tims or Jims or Toms anytime soon. Nobody ever, ever checked our birth certificates. Our coach, a grumpy guy named Chuck, was like the dry cleaning king of Midtex, and his uniform was always so starched and stiff that I was afraid he would shatter into pieces when whacking grounders.

One more thing: Coach Chuck wore spikes. I mean real, careful-or-you'll-bust-your-butt-on-the-slick-convenience-store-floor steel spikes. I didn't get that one. We only won five games all season, so the guy should have had more on his mind than traction.

Having Danny as a Stallions teammate was the only saving grace. He'd moved out to shortstop, because his knees already sounded like farm equipment, and I'd moved in to first base, because that's what lefties did. We couldn't play catcher, but we were also banned from the really cool positions. Special scissors, special positions, all that.

But the changes were more than that. Being 14 with time to kill was like walking a tightrope between cool and goofy. You couldn't really go riding around the block on your bike anymore, because sure enough you'd meet up with a pack of eight-year-olds on their fancy Mongooses and feel like a putz. Dirt-clod fights and BB gun battles and hornytoad hunts were out, too.

Oh, hornytoads, that was one thing Texas definitely had on Ohio. They were these tiny dinosaurs that looked like frogs, except with horns and a lousy attitude. They supposedly spit blood out of their eyes when they got mad, which was like a superhero power if you really thought about it, but I didn't sweat them much. In fact, a few years back, my transition to the gang was smoothed over by my ability to corral the little critters. If a kid could hunt down a few hornytoads and ride a good wheelie, he was in.

But that was then. Now we had to find cooler things to do, like going to the mall, where kids my age packed around the entrance and pretended to smoke and to have things to say. But since we couldn't drive yet, we'd have to get dropped off, and moms and crowds were always risky. Just when you thought you'd made a clean break, they'd go and holler for you to tuck in your shirt or tie your shoes.

Anyway, just as I was thinking there should be a handbook for it all, a set of rules for growing up, the tennis ball slipped between my hands and bounced off my nose. Three hundred twenty-seven, not too shabby at all. My fourth-best run ever. I knew it was pretty silly, having a catch with myself, but a kid couldn't quit when he was shooting for a personal record any more than he could stop popping those bubble things around packages.

I sneezed and hit the showers.

I grunted to my mom that I was headed to Danny's and made the six-house, one-turn, 141-step walk over to his house while our next-door neighbor's weenie dog, Satan, growled and head-butted the fence. The little fella was probably harmless, but you didn't take chances with things named Satan.

Anyhow, if it had been Dad, I would have maybe mentioned Annie's party, because to him parties still meant yard darts and birthday cakes and pony rides. But he was off at one of his rubber conventions, and Mom knew better. After years of dealing with my brothers, she knew there came a time when guys didn't give a flip about yard darts, and not because they could take an eye out, either.

Steve, Danny's brother, was at the refrigerator when I let myself in the side door. He wasn't fishing for anything, just kind of standing there in the light and the coolness. I did it all the time. It was a guy deal.

He turned, leaned against the door and greeted me with the usual.

"What's up, dufus?"

"Oh, hey Steve," I grunted.

"So what are you two faggots up to?" If a couple of kids hung out a lot together, they were automatically faggots, at least to Steve.

"Um, nothing," I said, trying to sneak through the kitchen and back to Danny's room, where I could hear Bruce Springsteen howling away about something.

But it was no use. Steve was a couple of years older than Danny, but he was about half a foot shorter than his kid bro, though he was built like a fire hydrant, right down to the red hair. So it was pretty key that he leaned on someone every once in a while, just to keep his turf, like a dog squirting on the couch. He wasn't all the way awful and came in handy when we needed a third for hot box or an easy win in H-O-R- S-E or P-I-G, but he still never missed a chance to give me a noogie or just plain grief.

As if I was in the market for another big brother.

If there wasn't a holiday involved, Simon was the only real brother I saw much anymore. He had moved down to Midtex a year earlier and gotten a job at the rubber plant, leaving a girl back in Ashland, a pretty Irish one named Jan who'd been putting up with him forever. I hoped he would bring Jan down and marry her someday. She was nice and didn't act all girlish, plus she took me to the movies and to the carnival and bought me stuff like cotton candy. Blue cotton candy, obviously; a guy couldn't go prancing around with the pink stuff.

But I only saw Simon in spurts, for little whiles. He lived in a little pad on the other side of town and usually only popped up when Mom was cooking something good. He was big and strong and reminded me of the guy from the paper towels, so I guess he was what you would call handsome, if you had to call a guy handsome. Mostly, he would just show up and shoot some hoops with me or sit with Dad and talk about making rubber, then plow down some dinner and disappear until it was a steak or meatloaf night again. So I guess you could say my relationship with Simon revolved around his appetite.

Steve slammed the fridge shut and stepped in my path. I could feel a headlock coming on.

"So what's goin' down tonight?" he asked, smiling. If you put some blue jean overalls on him and stuck a smoke in his mouth, Steve was the spitting image of Mr. Allen, right down to the wide gap between his front teeth.

"Um, this girl is havin' a party," I mumbled while trying to swerve past.

"Oh yeah? Who?" he asked, blocking my path.

"Um, Annie Sedgefield." There was no way he would know Annie Sedgefield. People only knew Annie by accident.

"Red-headed, pasty-faced girl over on Derringer Lane?" He knew Annie Sedgefield.

"Yeah."

"Cool, we'll be there," he said, plimping my head with his school ring and rushing toward the back.

That's exactly what I was afraid of. See, it wasn't really Steve, because I had this feeling that behind the body slams and slugs that he really kind of liked me. Once, after flipping me off the bed and into the corner of the nightstand, he was even nice to me for a week or so. But his friends, especially when they were all glassy eyed and rowdy and, most of all, together, could be murder. And a lot of them were built like tanks, especially a loud, big, wide one named Jake Jacobson.

Danny was taking a nap and snoring away like Darth Vader. I woke him up and told him to get moving, and he stretched and groaned and rolled off the bed, saying he'd be back in 10 minutes. I didn't mind. I was a big fan of naps myself. I thought if everyone could toss down a mat and get in a good 15 minutes every afternoon, then the world would be a much better place. I really did.

In the other room, Steve had ditched the Boss and flipped on something twangy and Texan. Big brothers, even smaller big brothers, always controlled the tunes. My brothers, Matt especially, used to give me these fat eight-track tapes for Christmas when I was like five years old. And I'm not talking Sesame Street or Electric Company, either. More like guys named Mick and Alice and Molly. (Lot of guys with girl names in rock-n-roll.) I would smile and gush and pretend to be excited about the thing, then sling it into a pile in my room. Two days later, it would disappear, and Matt would be cruising around with some guy named Jethro screaming out of his red Plymouth.

Never failed.

While Danny showered, I flipped on the tube and watched part of *Urban Cowboy* for like the 33rd time. Man, I loved that movie. I mean, the Travolta guy would never pass for a cowboy in real life, at least not around Midtex, but he played a pretty good movie cowboy. And that Wes Hightower, the villain, well, he would fit in just perfect. I sometimes even found myself rooting for him, with his mesh and scars and felonies, even though I knew Bud would always end up with Sissy.

Through the swinging doors, the kind that sweaty cowboys busted through when they really needed a drink, I could see Danny in the mirror. He was shaving, though he didn't need to shave at all, and his face was good and lathered up. He caught my stare and gave me a shrug and a grin. I shrugged back. Having shaved just before coming over, I understood, even though, while having some soft, black fuzz above my top lip, I was also waiting around for my first authentic whisker.

A few minutes later, he pushed through the doors, his waist covered with a towel and shaving cream still smudged on his face. He grabbed some underwear and slipped them on before letting the towel drop. That was an unwritten rule with guys. Unless you were in a crowded locker room or streaking around the block on a dare at a slumber party, then hanging free and easy was a solo kind of thing. No one-on-one nudity allowed, especially with a big-mouthed brother in the other room.

"So who all's goin' tonight?" I asked Danny. He was the kind of guy who would know, another of those sorts who could drift between different packs and ages. He was pretty good with the girls, too, which was always a bonus in a friend, and I'd scored more than one movie date because of it. It was often a PUF – a plump, ugly friend -- but they seemed to try harder, anyway.

"Well, anybody and everybody from what I hear," he said, pulling on a New York Yankees jersey. Danny always said that Bucky Dent, the Yanks' shortstop, was a cousin of his, but I was still mulling that one over. Bucky was short and dark and looked like some mobster's kid, while Danny could have passed for Opie Taylor.

Still a good story.

He went on: "Stacy said that Heather said that Amber said that Annie told Amber to just tell people our age, but ya know how that goes. Supposedly a bunch of high school people are going to crash it later."

He slipped on some shorts and high tops, kept them untied like all of us did, grabbed a cap and squirted something on his neck that smelled like Scotch tape.

"Ready?"

I fixed a clump of hair in his Moosehead Beer mirror, which was hanging next to the Budweiser mirror, which was hanging by the Coors mirror, which made it pretty cool to have folks who got free stuff for owning a restaurant. I had a mirror mirror. Anyway, my cowlick was standing at attention as usual, making it harder to tell who had bigger horns, me or the moose. Plus, I was coming off an extra-bad haircut that I'd just gotten down at Slick Snips from a lady with a mullet.

A good rule to live by is to never expect a good haircut from someone with a bad haircut.

But if there were going to be high schoolers at the party, then it was time to impress, or at least not give myself away as a crazy-haired maniac before high school even started. I applied an extra layer of spit to my fingers and tacked the stack down. It popped back up. I grabbed a cap off the rack and pulled it on extra tight. "Ready."

***

We were out the door and off to Annie's when Danny's folks pulled up in their van. I was always glad to see the two of them, which wasn't that often, unless we wanted some free grub or happened to be up at like, say, three in the morning, which was when they usually came home. Mr. Allen was a jolly kind of guy, always smiling and showing off that gap, and you could always count on him having a cigarette dancing from his mouth, with a long ash cheating gravity at the end, and holding a mug of coffee in one hand. The guy was like Linus and his blanket, only with a cup of Joe and smokes. By the way, I had no idea why coffee was nicknamed Joe instead of Sam or Frank or Ted.

Mrs. Allen was like clockwork, too. She was small and blonde with a voice so teeny and so delicate that I thought it should have been marked 'Fragile,' if voices could be packaged anyhow. She was younger and prettier than most moms, but she did some things that gave her away as a mom. For one, she always told you to be careful, even if you were reaching over to grab the salt. Like, while the other kids were shooting off bottle rockets and blowing up stuff on the Fourth of July, Danny and Steve were always stuck spelling their names in the sky with sparklers.

She was also a fixer-upper, which meant they were constantly getting their hair fixed or their smudged faces mopped off by a wet finger. Those were all in the mom handbook. The lipstick on the teeth thing, too. And though I'd never been shoe shopping with her, I could easily picture her hollering out "How do they feel, honey?" to Danny across the whole store.

"So where are you two boys off to?" Mrs. Allen asked over the clunk of the engine and in her loudest whisper. Their van was kind of old and a little shoddy, with those bubble windows and a left blinker that never stopped blinking. As far as anyone knew, the Allens were always headed off to the left. That van made me think that maybe the restaurant wasn't doing all that great. I mean, people piled in the place, but they served like a cattle per person for next to nothing, so Todd's Steak House might have been dishing out more than it was raking in.

"Oh, just headin' out to a party," Danny shrugged. I watched the blinker. Left. Left. Left. Left.

"A party, eh?!?" Mr. Allen yelled, his ash wobbling but hanging tough. "Well heck, what kinda party?"

"I dunno Dad, just a party," Danny moaned. He always seemed pretty put out by his folks, but I thought they were a riot. That's the way it usually worked, from toys to girls to parents.

"Well, ya mean one with strippers and kegs and whistles?" Mr. Allen hooted.

"Steven Malone Allen!" Mrs. Allen kind of yelled. That was another mom trick, using a full name when she was mad or embarrassed. It must have worked on husbands as well as kids, because he ducked his head into the mug of coffee.

I didn't know about the whistles, but even though I'd never really drank or even seen a non-TV girl naked, other than my cousin Sylia by complete accident, I was all for the strippers and kegs part.

Danny nudged me. "C'mon, let's go."

"Okay boys, y'all be careful," Mrs. Allen squeaked.

I tapped Danny. "What about what we talked about earlier?"

"Oh. Yeah, and Mom, can Jasp spend the night?"

She looked over at me. I smiled, real sweet-like. "Oh, oh, of course he can, honey."

Danny and I nodded at each other and started off. "Now y'all promise to be careful," she peeped. "And, also, be careful."

Of course she said yes. It was an old, can't-miss trick, and we all knew it. See, moms always had the last say when it came to sleepovers, because dads always shrugged and grunted and pointed you that direction anyway. But it was a no-brainer if you just asked her right in front of the other guy. Only when you were really, really, really deep in the doghouse would she shoot you down.

I'd slept over Danny's a million times by then, but the first time was kind of awkward. It was the first move that guys hated to make. Some guys were all goofy about it, thinking that it was a gay thing to do, even though it was really just about hanging out and seeing some new things and chowing down someone else's food. But it was a big step, as far as guys went. I didn't know much about the steps you were supposed to take with girls, having not taken many.

But I knew I wasn't gay and, even though I wasn't too sure what gays did or said or looked or acted like anyway, I was pretty sure that Danny wasn't either. Still, we always kept a row of pillows between us in the sack, just in case.

"Race ya," Danny blurted out, taking off without giving me a chance to back down. I took off, but it was no use. There were probably bigger longshots in life than racing Danny, the fastest kid our age in town, black or white or any color, but I couldn't think of any. See, Danny was good at everything, not much bigger than I but plenty more gifted. A real stinking natural, the kind of kid who you handed a ping-pong paddle to for the first time, explained to him that the goal was to tap the ball across the net without missing the table, and then watched helplessly as he skunked you five minutes later.

If I didn't like him so much, I would have hated him.

***

He beat me to Annie's by two houses. I caught up and draped my arm around his shoulder. It was only a little past 8:00, with plenty of sunlight still to spare, and there was only one car in the driveway. A light crept from inside the big window on the first floor, with only darkness coming from the top floor. The garage door was closed. It looked like the party of a girl, well, of a girl like Annie Sedgefield.

"Think we're too early?" Danny asked. "I du...du...no," I heaved.

"Wanna go once more around the block?" He didn't even have the decency to double over.

"Le...le...let's go in," I gasped. "We...we don't...we don't wanna be late."

I needed to find a slower running buddy.

The front door creaked open slowly, with only a bony, spotted hand in sight. It was like an old movie, where some butler named Jeeves or Burle popped around the door and showed the people to a creepy study. But the doorman wasn't a butler. It wasn't a man at all. Out popped the oldest human I'd ever seen, at least the oldest one still breathing.

"Hello dears," screeched the lady. She had on those big, square, black glasses that old-timers always drove around with, and her face was more wrinkled than my shirt. Behind her right ear was a hearing aid as big as a banana, and her mouth was tiny and puckered. She couldn't have been an inch taller than three feet.

We stood there, speechless.

"Are ya here for the party?" she asked, even kind of cheery. But then she lifted her shades, exposing a pair of squinty, suspicious eyes. "Or are ya sellin' somethin'?" She stood there with her mouth wide open and waited. The older people got, the more they seemed to wait around with their mouths wide open and their pants jacked up.

"Um, for the party, ma'am," Danny answered.

"Yes, yes, then you boys come right on in then," she said, swinging the door open. "I'm Grannie, Grannie Sedgefield."

She offered her trembling hand, and neither of us rushed to take it. Still, I didn't want to leave grannie hanging. I reached out and grasped it softly, not wanting it to crumble, only to be crushed by her grip. I tried not to cringe, but the damage was done. Danny shoved me from behind as we shuffled in.

The house was quiet and dark. It was a nice spread, had that real clean smell to it, and the banister up ahead looked inviting. I didn't miss much about Ohio anymore, but that banister slide was still somewhere in my blood.

Except for a cat that pranced across the carpet and acted like it owned the joint, like only a cat or maybe Christie Brinkley could pull off, there was no other sign of any life. Nope, it was just me, Danny, Grannie and a Fun Machine. Oh, you know the one: that half-organ, half-piano that guys with thin mustaches and cheap suits hocked in the mall and that played snappy tunes and beats behind the pounding of the keys? They wanted to be loved like pianos, wanted it so bad, but it was hard to take anything seriously when some salsa crap was rat-a-tat-tatting away in the background.

And darnit if grannie didn't feel like giving us a free concert. Without a word, she motioned us onto a fluffy, green couch, waddled to the bench, and starting banging away. Every once in a while, she would turn toward us, her hands never stopping, her shades still in place, her feet dangling from the bench, her head rocking to the beat, and break into a big, toothless grin. Her teeth were sitting on top of the Fun Machine. Falsies, by the way, didn't seem like such a bad way to go. A guy could eat whatever he wanted, then just dump his teeth in a jar of gunk and, bam, good as new in the morning.

She kept playing; we kept sitting. It wasn't even that terrible, as far as hanging out with grannies and listening to wannabe pianos and fighting fat cats out of your lap went.

At least until she started to sing.

"Someone's crying looooordddd, Kuuumbayaaaaaaa.

Someone's crying Looooorrrddddd, Kumbayaaaaaa."

It was kind of fitting that she broke out the church stuff, because I was just praying that she would stop. Still, we sat there, frozen and hoping that someone, anyone, Annie, the milkman, God, would rescue us. I peeked over to Danny, who was trying not to laugh. I really hoped he wouldn't, because then I would explode, too. The domino giggle had destroyed us in church many times.

"Ohhhohhh Loooorrrrddd, Kuummbayaaaaa."

She took her hands off the keyboard and turned toward us. I didn't know whether to clap or tip her or what.

Anyway, it was over.

She faced the keyboard.

"Goooooo, teeell it on the mounnnntaaaaaaaain." It was just beginning.

We sunk back for fifteen more minutes that seemed like hundreds. Grannie got in a groove, rocking back and forth like Ray Charles with a fake hip as she went through her entire Biblical set. Even the cat hit the road during some tune about a guy and his trumpet, stretching and scratching and springing into the darkness. For the first time ever, I wanted to be a stinking cat.

She finished off "Jesus Loves Me" and cracked her knuckles. I made my move.

"Um, Grannie Sedgefield, Annie *is* havin' a party tonight, right?" I said it clear and loud, too, even though that hearing aid of hers could probably tune in conversations in Pittsburgh.

"Eh?"

That was old people talk for, "Huh?"

"Annie. Annie's party?"

"Ohhhhh, Annie, yes, yes," she said, adjusting her specs. "Yes dear, Annie is having a party indeed. A birthday party!"

"Well, are we early or somethin'?" Danny asked.

She looked at the clock above her. "Let's see, what is it, eight and 40 minutes?" She swung around and straddled the bench. "Oh Lord, heavens no. I'd say you're running quite late, dears."

Danny and I looked at each other and turned our heads like confused dogs.

"Oh dears, the party is out back, out in the guest house."

If you had fired us out of a cannon, we couldn't have disappeared any faster. We left the front door hanging open, a trap for the next sucker to fall into, like Bingo Holliday, a choir canary who was wandering up the front sidewalk. Bingo would like grannie. Heck, I liked her. Nice lady.

I just didn't care to grow old with her.

***

We pushed inside the guest house, and it was the usual bit. Everyone stopped and stared, a couple guys motioned and nodded, and everyone went back to their business. We hadn't missed much, because there wasn't much to miss. The ten or so people there were already clustered into the boy-girl groups, peeking over at each other and acting like the other was missing out.

At the three real parties I'd been to, the older kids did the same thing, but eventually the guys would start to circle around like lions in a nature special, and the girls would perk up like antelopes. But us, being sophomores-to-be and all, well, we mostly just stood around like dopes for the next 20 minutes and picked at the junk food from our separate buzzards. Amber tried to pull us all together, to make us play some goofy game, but it was no use.

It was kind of obvious. Thrown together, we had no idea how to party.

Annie changed everything. She appeared from nowhere, this blur of red hair and pig tails and bird legs, turned off the radio and pulled a chair in the middle of the room, which was draped in ribbons and bows and other girl stuff. She climbed onto the wobbly chair, put two fingers to her mouth and whistled. Not a half-bad one, either. Maybe there was hope for Annie yet.

"Ahem....I'd just like to say hello and to thank everyone for comin' to my 15th birthday party tonight," she started, to the weak applause of a few girls and the pop of Danny's gum. "There's punch and cake on the table, and there's chips and dips over on the counter.

"We have some real neato board games in the closet, and feel free to put anything you want on the record player and just have a good 'ol time."

With the last sentence, she added one of those oh-boy arm pumps, bringing about a group grumble. And yes, after double-checking with Danny, she had really said 'neato.' Record players, chips and Parcheesi. I looked back to the main house, to grannie.

Annie started to climb down but stopped. "And oh yeah, there's a full keg of beer by the pool in the back."

Drew Harris started the applause, and Angie Witherspoon followed. Soon the room was filled with hoots and hollers and thirsty kids five or six years short of the drinking age. Annie folded her hands behind her back and did one of those curtsy things, right there on the chair. Her green dress rose up, giving us a peep show that no one cared to peep at. Her legs were almost invisible, evident only by a mess of freckles, and her panties were white, with teensy, red polka dots.

Nope, there was no hope for Annie Sedgefield, none at all. But her party, well, her party was back in business.

Amber Taylor, like always, made the first move. Like always, we followed. We all drifted together to the back door, never leaving our groups, then re-assembled in our own packs near the pool. The pool was pathetic, by the way, all murky and muddy and green, and it had obviously been a scam to lure us all there. Not that I minded much, not being a very strong swimmer anyhow. In Midtex, bathtubs were about the biggest bodies of water around, and it was hard to work on your stroke in the tub. Still, it seemed kind of weird, to call a pool party and then to keep the thing looking like a swamp. I mean, if I was having, say, an ice-cream party, I'd probably at least buy some decent ice cream.

But we weren't thinking about Marco Polo anymore. The keg was the thing. It was plunked deep inside a green trash can, with fresh ice sparkling around it. I didn't know much about drinking and even less about kegs, having only seen them on commercials about softball players and at my brother's weddings, but I was pretty sure that there was good fun inside that fat tub. If Larry Mazzetti, my brother Matt's fuzzy best man, could duck out of the wedding reception with a couple of decent-looking girls, then there had to be something to it all.

Except for a few sneaks of my dad's brews, I'd never drank before. But I knew the drill, knew it well. Dad liked to pour a couple of martinis when he got home from work, heavy on the clear stuff and easy on the green bottle. I would watch him sip and think, think and sip, staring at Dan Rather and all the time sliding lower in his recliner. Mom always joined him with a glass of wine, always with one ice cube, always from a box. More than once, I'd seen her yank the guts out of that box and strangle it right down to the last drop.

I knew it was wrong, to be hitting the sauce and all. But there wasn't a grown-up in sight, and everyone else had flocked to the keg after Amber had snagged a red cup, filled it to the top and started pounding like an old pro. So it all felt like one of those tree-and-forest things--if someone old enough to smack us didn't see it, then was it really happening at all?

"Aren't ya going to have any?" Danny asked. His cup was almost empty, and he was sporting a foamy mustache.

"Um, well, bet your ass," I snapped, swiping the cup from him and filling it right over the rim with the keg pistol. Bet your ass. It just flew out, and it felt good to say, real smooth. I thumped away the top layer of fuzz, took a quick sip and nodded to him. Bet your ass.

I found out a few things about beer over the next hour or so. For one, it tasted pretty good, real cold and airy and, well, golden, if golden could have a taste. It went down with a sting and left a little kick, but it was a good pain, and a guy couldn't help but let out an 'ahhh' and a burp after a long swallow. And the more swallows I took, the funnier everything got. Like on his very best day, Terry Deering never got more than a couple of courtesy laughs for his impression of Bill Cosby. Well, at a tiny party at a nutty girl's house, with a full keg of beer, it got knee slaps and high fives and even a hug from Marlene Fitsch. That wasn't exactly a good thing, seeing as Marlene had gotten sent home from school twice with head lice, but you get the idea.

Yep, beer seemed like the perfect party favor. Without even the insistence of Amber, our packs slowly meshed together, right by the shallow end, until before long we looked like a real party. The dozen or so of us stood and talked and laughed and drank, sometimes in pairs, sometimes as one, as the sun fell and a full moon began to climb in the sky.

I even talked up a few girls, filled their cups for them, laughed at their stories, drank like I knew how. Usually, each word out of most any girl's mouth seemed more confusing than the last, but tonight, there was something magical and whimsical about Angie's 10-minute story about her bunion.

After my third cup, I was pretty much on top of the world. It was like that WD-40, the beer. I could talk easily, listen closely, stay cool under pressure. Once, I caught Amber looking at me, or at least looking in my general direction. Didn't even flinch. Nope, I just smiled, held it for a sec and looked away, real slick, real calm, real easy, like Isaac the Bartender from "The Love Boat." I thought about maybe heading over to her, proposing a toast or something classy like that, but, man, did I have to pee.

I was waiting for Darla Simpleton to get out of the can, my head propped back against the wall, and the room started to twist. Not a bad kind of spin, just a slow, steady glide, like I was moving my head without having to move it. I smiled and closed my eyes. Beer. Maybe it was the answer to making that move from junior high to high school. A guy didn't need to figure out what to do next or how to do it right.

He just needed some suds.

"Hey, poker game in the garage!" It was Trapper Kincaid, leading a parade of people into the back. I gave up on the can and started that way, not sure what the deal was with girls and bathrooms. If anyone was going to need 15 minutes to powder their nose, it would be me.

Trapper had always been a starter. He started rumors. He started fires. And he started fights, lots of fights. The last one gave Clay McGill a broken face and Trapper a six-week ticket to the Midtex Juvenile Center. And he never even tried to hide anything, so he always got busted, usually by opening his gigantic trap.

Except for Trapper, nobody liked Trapper.

"So who's in? Huh? Who's in?" By the time I wandered in and propped against the wall next to Danny, Trapper had already cleared the frills off a table and pulled up four chairs. "Trapper wants to play some cards. Who's brave enough to play with Trapper, huh?"

Oh, that was another thing with Trapper. He was a first-person guy. To those of us who knew him, he was Trapper. To those who didn't, but found out the hard way, like Clay McGill, he was Theodore. And to Trapper, he was Trapper.

"I said Trapper's ready to play some cards, babeee! Who dares to tangle with Trapper?"

Danny shrugged at me. I shrugged at him.

"So what happened to the group outside?" I asked. I'd gone and starting thinking we'd gotten the hang of it all.

"I dunno, got boring I guess. We started havin' a gleek contest, and the girls got all weird about it."

"Oh. So who won?"

Danny smiled, exposing the front-tooth gap that ran in his family. He came from a long line of gleekers.

The girls passed us and giggled, formed one of their little huddles by the music and giggled some more. I still didn't know what the heck girls did in their little groups, or why they always surrounded the stereo like it was a campfire, or what was so darn funny. The only thing that could cause a bunch of guys to scrunch up so close and laugh was a good fart contest.

Trapper continued to shuffle like a madman. His fingers were thick and short, just like the rest of his slug body, but his hands were surprisingly fast and sure. It was really pretty impressive. Guy looked like he could change the string off a weed eater without even shutting off the thing. Phil Davidson had already pulled up a chair, as had Andy "Smiles" Telford. In the middle of the table sat two full pitchers of brew, with a punch bowl of Cheese Cruncheroos on the far left, reminding me that I was starving. I'd only had a jam sandwich for dinner – you know, two pieces of bread jammed together.

"Wanna?" I asked Danny.

He whirled around the room. Drew and Anthony Walden were already playing foosball, spinning their men and trying to rack each other with the prods, making the whole game a pretty tough sell if you asked me. The girls had fallen back into full antelope mode. Only Annie sat outside of their gang, a blank stare plastered on her face while she sipped from a Hello Kitty cup. For a birthday girl, she sure didn't seem too festive. Anyway, our choices were pretty squeezed.

"Sure, let's go for it," Danny said.

***

I really only knew two things about cards, and I'd learned them both from my brother Simon. One, don't get drunk. And two, no matter what, don't cheat. With those tips and about three lifetime hands of poker under my belt, we settled into our chairs.

"Ok, empty out your wallets, boys. Trapper's going to clean you out!" I didn't carry a wallet and hadn't since I'd lost my one with the snazzy Velcro fastener back in eighth grade. It was always empty, anyway. Danny and I had mentioned something about maybe getting summer jobs, but jobs seemed like a lot of work. I mean, I knew my dad had hauled a wheelbarrow full of bricks up a hill (both ways) all summer for about a dime a day when he was only nine, because he'd reminded me like 4,200 times, but those were footsteps I didn't care to follow. Besides, just how much character did a 14-year-old kid need?

As it was, I leaned back and dug three dollars and 81 cents out of my pocket. If you asked Dad for a few bucks, that was pretty much what you got.

Danny pulled out maybe half that, all in silver. The summer before, he bussed tables at the restaurant a little and would nab a buck or three from the tips, then we'd go live it up. But he got nabbed by his mom when she found 59 George Washingtons in his pocket, and now he never had green. Those were the days, back before purple uniforms and crisp, spike-sporting coaches named Chuck.

Smiles threw down a pretty fair-sized wad and, of course, smiled. The guy never quit. He had plenty to be happy about, seeing as his dad operated on feet or noses or some other expensive body part and that he was the richest kid around, but it didn't really matter either way. You could tell Smiles that the world was ending in like four minutes, and you'd get nothing but pearly whites from the kid.

Phil struggled out six bucks. Phil had what you would call an arcade build, meaning that the most exercise he ever got was shoving another dollar in the change machine. Probably couldn't curl a Rubik's Cube, though he could fix one perfectly in just under two minutes. He was skinny and weak, with greasy black hair and glasses too big for his narrow head. Real clumsy too, and not super bright.

Know how people say they are having one of those days? Well, I think the guy was having one of those lives.

But Phil liked me, for one reason. Back in sixth grade at Downing, he managed to make the basketball team as our 12th man, the guy at the far end of the bench. He never, ever played, but Coach Doolittle put him in during the last quarter of our last game, along the time that most of the dads were grabbing their wives and swearing that they could do a better job of coaching. Anyhow, there was a turnover near midcourt, and Phil, sweatband and knee pads and all, ended up with the ball in the clear. So he took off, kind of half-stumbling and half-dribbling, and made a basket, even as we were begging him not to. See, it was the wrong basket.

Well, while everyone was laughing and hollering and pointing, I took the inbounds pass, dribbled down the side and flung the ball to Phil, who was trying to duck out of door near our bucket. He turned around just in time, wiped his face and banked in a deuce as the horn sounded, becoming maybe the only guy to ever score twice and to never really score at all.

There was nothing too normal about Phil. He was either moping around by himself or bugging people with these magic tricks that never quite worked. He was a lot like his dad, who was salesman and sold those get well remedy drinks that nobody ever really got well from. Everyone always ragged on his old man, called him nuts. Now, Smiles' dad was a little off too, seeing as the guy walked around our block every morning and had long conversations with either himself or his stick, nobody could be real sure, but the adults never called him nuts. They just whispered that he was "eccentric."

But Phil never hurt anyone, probably couldn't hurt anyone. He just wandered through the days and disappeared after school to the arcade, where he worked evenings and destroyed all of our high scores and hung out with Zeezo, the even creepier guy who owned Zeezo's Magic World next to Chess King.

"Alrighty now, let's see how much dough Trapper's going to win," Trapper hooted. He poured his hands through the small pile of bills and coins. "Whatta we got here, hmm?"

"Let's just play, huh?" Danny barked.

"Oooo, somebody's in a fat hurry to lose his money, huh?" Trapper snapped back. "Okay, let's let it roll then.

How 'bout some five-card stud, sevens wild?"

We all shrugged, and he dished out cards faster than the human eye could follow. I gathered my cards and bent them up. I didn't actually know how to play five-card stud or seven-card stud or any kind of stud, having mostly only played War and Go Fish, but I was pretty sure that two aces and two sevens off the deal was pretty rich. I bet it all. Only Smiles hung with me through the whole hand. He smiled and plopped down a pair of threes. I raked in six bucks.

"Not bad, not too damn bad, Schitt," Trapper said, pushing the stack of cards to Danny. "Now sit on back and watch what 'ol Trapper can do."

Thing was, as the hands played out, Trapper couldn't do much of anything. Neither could Phil or Smiles or Danny. See, 'ol Jasper was on a roll. We played three more rounds of stud, and I won them all. Every time I flipped up my cards, my hand looked like a photo album. There was no strategy involved, only good luck and sweet cards. Trapper turned red and made us switch to Black Jack, but my luck didn't change. If someone else had 19, I had 20. If I had 11, they all had 24.

The whole time, I hid behind a beer and tried not to laugh while my stash bulged to over 20 bucks. Along the way, I bankrupted Danny, who was drinking more than betting and starting to look a little cock-eyed, and milked Phil down to a few quarters and a wad of pocket lint.

Smiles had about five dollars left, but it didn't really matter. The guy probably had three hundreds tucked in his left sock, and even if he didn't, everything was still peachy by him.

Trapper wasn't as psyched about it all. He was pretty mad and really loud. He'd thrown down some good hands, but not good enough, and had some close calls, but not close enough. By the time he'd spit out some cuss words that I'd never even heard, and spun them into cuss phrases that didn't exist, he was down to three crumpled dollars and a thick, purple vein on his forehead.

"Here, go get us more beer." Trapper shoved the pitcher at Phil, who nudged up his glasses and grunted something but did it just the same.

Trapper had picked on Phil for years. No real reason, just because, the way a stupid fly will pick you out of a crowd and buzz around your brain for hours. Didn't jam him into a locker or anything, just constant needling. And there really wasn't one thing Phil could do about it.

"So what's next?" I asked, eyeing my loot. Sure beat wheelbarrows and rocks and hills and dimes.

"I'll tell ya what's next," Trapper snarled. "Yer going to run out of luck soon enough, and Trapper's going to be sittin' right here when ya do." He snatched the full pitcher from Phil, spilling a good part of it, and plopped it down, spilling another good part of it.

"Well, I'm out," Danny announced, sliding his chair away from the table. He pretty much didn't have a choice, but you still had to jump on saying stuff like that in cards.

"Tough luck, Danny," I said, tipping a beer in salute toward him. I would have spotted him some dough, but he had folded on 18 earlier, so I figured it would be like tossing money down the gutter.

"Yeah, think I'll just watch, too," Smiles giggled. I was kind of sad about that. I'd figured out that even though his face always said royal flush, the guy never had squat.

"What about you, dorko?" Trapper asked Phil.

Phil bit his bottom lip, the way I sometimes did when I danced to the music of Kenny Loggins or Richard Marx, and looked at his crumb of coins.

"I'll play."

"And you?" Trapper asked, nodding at me. "Now don't go and tell me yer going to take the money and run."

I thought about it. Trapper was right - luck did have a way of changing, and fast. Just the week before, out at Sunshade Golf Course, I'd bounced my five-iron shot off two trees and a sprinkler head to within four feet of the cup, then watched as a prairie dog made off with the ball. Wasn't about to chase after it. Those things were guinea pigs with fangs. (Besides, I gave myself the putt anyway.)

Still, like an idiot, I poured another beer, took a quick slug and squinted just like Dirty Harry.

"Count me in."

Like I said, half the fun was saying stuff like that. And I even got a high-pitched 'oooo' from a couple of the girls who had wandered in a little closer to the game. That was usually how the antelopes ended up biting the dust. I just looked their way, nodded and stabbed a handful of Cheetos. Of course I was in.

Bet your ass.

***

The cards continued to fall my way. It took five seconds to get rid of Phil. He asked for a hit on 12, and I gave him a queen of hearts. Pretty much summed up his existence. He punched the air and pouted a little, but Annie broke out a Video Pinball game for him, so that glazed things over. Then I won two more hands from Trapper and squeezed him down to four bucks before Mother Nature called.

"Lemme drop a load, and then we'll get to playin' some serious cards," Trapper said. I shrugged, and he stumbled away, throwing his shoulders back and bowing up. I wondered what it was like, having to act tough and terrible all the time. Or if deep down, away at detention, he was really as scared as the next guy. I believed that if the world was completely honest, then everyone, even guys, would just stop and sometimes throw their hands up and just scream and scream. Not wanting to look stupid was the only thing that really kept us all in line, if you asked me.

While I waited, everyone bailed on me. Danny went and started dancing with Pam Honeyshade, a gawky blonde who'd been his puppet for two summers. Whatever he wanted her to do, whenever he wanted her to do it, she was game. Susan, her PUF (plump ugly friend), was waiting nearby, wearing pants so tight that they made her face turn a soft shade of blue. I thought that tight clothes should be a privilege, not a flat-out right.

As for the rest of the party, Butch Berry and Zelda Stearns were swapping spit next to Susan, and Drew and Anthony were still spinning away at the foosball table.

Marlene and Angie and Darla were hanging around Terry, who was twirling on his back. Terry got hooked on the break dance thing back in eighth grade, quit sports and everything and started wearing gloves all the time, but he wasn't all that good. After a few seconds, they turned toward each other and started taking baby sips from their cups.

Smiles somehow ended up on the dance floor with Annie. They were swaying slowly next to Danny and Pam but didn't fit together as well. She was too tall for him, and he was too everything else for her. They clumsily rocked away, until Annie pivoted toward me and made me realize just how much she looked like Peppermint Patty. After a revolution, Smiles was facing me. For the first time ever, I saw him frown. Not one tooth. It wasn't supposed to turn out that way for rich kids.

Amber was alone, over in the far corner, looking out a little window, sipping and probably searching for someone to show up with a driver's license. It was a little past 11:00, but there was still no sign of them, the high school guys. That was fine by me. They'd be wrecking our lives soon enough. Least they could do was give us a few hours of peace and quiet, a few more hours before swiping our pride and our girls, who, by the way, were looking better and better by the brew.

I can report the exact day that I started looking at girls instead of just seeing them. It was a Thursday morning near the end of seventh grade, in Miss Calhoun's third-hour Life Science class, and Sandra Sage pranced in and plopped down in front of me, just as usual. Now, until then, Sandra, who looked decent but never said anything good, had been handy to cheat off of, and that was about it. Well, we were taking a test on bugs or bacteria or something, and I got stumped early. So I leaned over to take a little peek at Sandra's paper, just to get me in the right frame of mind and all, and instead got an eyeful. See, it was 1,000 degrees outside, and she had on a baggy tank top with no bra and lots of room to breathe. So I spent the whole hour studying her anatomy, none of it caring about that of a cockroach's and made a 68 on the test.

But you have to know that wasn't the point.

I still wouldn't pick a girl over any sport other than soccer or choose one over a good plate of spaghetti, but they were starting to grow on me a little. Like if the movie stunk, they were right there to fall asleep against. And if you ran out of things to say, they were right there to slobber on. Plus, if you didn't have any place to stash your stuff, they always seemed to have pockets and pouches all over the place.

So even though girls yakked too much and, more than that, often wanted me to yak back, I could see where they could come in handy. Here was pretty much the deal: I felt the same about them as I did with ice hockey. I liked them okay, even if I didn't really understand the rules.

"A'right, Trapper's 10 pounds lighter and ready to roll!" my opponent screamed upon his return from the can, louder and prouder than any guy with four bucks left should have been. He flopped down and flipped out two cigars, the skinny jobs with the white mouthpieces. After jamming one into his mouth, he offered up the other one to me.

"Here ya are, have a cigar, bro!"

It felt like a good poker thing to do. I mean, I'd seen *The Sting* and all.

"Um, okay," I said, taking my first official cigar. I lit it, took a little puff, coughed, hacked and chased it down with, by then, about my seventh official beer. Funny, but I'd always seen myself having my first brews with my dad or maybe my brothers, not with this guy.

"Now, let's play some cards," he said.

For whatever reason, Trapper Kincaid came out of that bathroom a changed man. Over the next hour, I watched my stack shrink into a pile, my pile wilt into what my folks would call a get-together, and my get-together dwindle into next to nothing. It didn't matter what I did or what I didn't do. Fold or hold, raise or call, drink or smoke or whatever, it was hopeless. Like I said before, Trapper usually did something to land himself in hot water, but it never happened. We played 10 hands; he won all 10. All 10. No doubt about it, Trapper was on fire.

"Sweet holy shit, Trapper is on fire!"

See.

I was woozy. I'd shattered Simon's poker rule, the don't go-and-get-plastered one, and I knew it. Want to know how?

As I slouched there with my two inches of beer backwash and stinky cigar and stinking 97 cents, I watched as two Trappers and his four hands arranged about 14 piles of stash in a row. And you've got to believe me when I say that one of him was plenty. The whole time he had two big grins on his face, and I realized I'd fallen right into his trap. Have a cigar, bro! Here, lemme pour ya another beer!

Yep, the 'ol South Side Shuffle.

Oh, and by the way, here's a tip: when you smoke your first cigar and start sucking on your first keg, pace yourself. I was a sweaty mess, and the cool glide in my head had turned into a Tilt-A-Whirl spin. I pushed away my cup, realizing that, unless you were asking what made your head feel like a turnip, beer wasn't the answer, not at all. Heck, I couldn't even remember the question anymore.

"So, whattaya say? Ready to get cleaned out?" both Trappers drawled.

I shut an eye and looked around. Except for the light above our table, it was now pretty dark, but I could make out a clump of couples on the couch by the music, including Danny and Pam. I could tell it was Danny because he had his cap turned backwards, which I think was a rule for catchers, even ex-catchers. No more foosball. No more break dancing. No more baby sips. Smiles had slipped away from Annie and started in on Susan, leaving our hostess solo in her chair again. No more giggles, only lips and smacks and The Police. That was maybe the best thing about making out - no talking needed.

I couldn't believe it, but Amber was still around. Still over by the window, still alone, still waiting. She looked over to me and smiled, but it was a lame one, a hafta one. It was almost midnight, almost the witching hour for most of us.

"So what the hell? You in or what?"

Anyway, the party, at least the G-rated crowd, had pretty much cleaned out. Why should I be any different?

"Sure," I sighed. "Let's do it." With less than a buck, I wasn't sure how much I could do anyway.

"Want some help?" It was Phil, the game in one hand, a hunk of money in the other and a smirk on his face.

"Whattaya mean?" I asked.

"Well, looks like you're pretty short there."

"Well, yeah." Short? Yep, I was Gary Coleman short.

"So?"

"So, I'll loan ya some money."

"Where did ya get it?" It musta been 50 bucks, easy.

"I work."

"Oh." So that was the secret to having more than three dollars at one time. "But...why would you give it to me?" He looked straight at Trapper. "Just cuz."

I looked to Trapper. Though I'd taken a crash course on the smoking and drinking and losing and winning, I wasn't sure if getting late-night loaners was a poker kind of thing to do.

"Man, Trapper don't care," Trapper laughed. "Shit yeah, I'll take the sucker's money."

Phil sat down and slid over his riches. I didn't know what to say, so I didn't say anything. I just perked up in my chair and turned my hat backwards, not like a catcher but like a kid meaning business.

I was back.

Trapper grabbed the deck and started shuffling. He tried to get fancy and it ended up in a 52-card pickup. He laughed it off. Another bridge, another mess. He was now going with the one-eye thing, too, and he looked like crap, all puffy and pink. Trapper might have been a better drinker, but he was no better of a drunk. He pushed the cards to Phil. The shuffle king was dead.

Phil dished out the cards slowly, like he was really concentrating, and we started back in on Black Jack. Trapper hit a hot streak and milked me down to 20 bucks, but I hung in there, mostly by taking a fat pot with a ballsy hit on 15. I started to focus on every hand, on every card, as if I was facing a pitcher that I had no business hitting. Real slow, real careful, measure him out then, wham, a clean rip to center. I could take this guy.

Of course, I tended to strike out sometimes, too. Trapper went on another run, this time about wiping me dry. I was trying to think, trying too hard probably, but thinking and betting and blinking and breathing all at the same time had become way too tricky. When a guy had to think about thinking, he was in trouble. By the time Amber slid into the open chair and put her head in her hands, Trapper pretty much had my allowance and poor Phil's paycheck stretched out before him.

Maybe I couldn't take this guy.

I took a deep breath and cracked my neck, first to the right. Phil looked mad. Seeing as there probably wasn't much money in the family elixir business, I couldn't much blame him. And then to the left. Amber looked bored and beautiful. I tried to focus straight ahead. There they were, both Trappers, thumbing through their money. I hated them both.

"Hustle it up, huh dweeb?" Trapper sneered. Phil did as he was told, the poor kid, and started shuffling.

"Wait," I said. "Let's just....let's just quit."

"What? Quit!?! When we're havin' so much damn fun?"

I'll tell you, I really wanted to make a comeback. I wanted to go back to getting the girls' squeals, back to the attention, back to feeling 14 years old and back to having 37 bucks. Back to feeling like a lion.

But I had no weapons left, nothing up my sleeve. And I didn't expect Amber to pull a Phil and to float me a loan.

C'mon, girls didn't go around pulling out cash unless they absolutely had to.

"Yeah, I'm out."

We sat there in silence for a minute. Trapper gloated. Amber sulked. Phil pouted. From the darkness of the corner, I heard a zipper. Then, from out of nowhere, Trapper decided to start something again.

"Well, shoot, Trapper's got a helluva idea."

The last great idea I remembered Trapper having proved to Skip Donahue that enough helium balloons really could pick a kid up and carry him away, just like in cartoons. Hadn't seen Skip in years. But since the zipper I'd just heard probably came from the pants of either Danny or Pam, maybe both, I had time to listen. Plus, Amber, bored or not, sulking or not, smelled just like peaches, and I was a big fan of peaches.

"What is it?" I finally asked.

"Well, how 'bout we play one hand of Black Jack, double or nothin,' for the whole thing?" Trapper proposed.

"How's that sound?"

It sounded pretty darn good, especially since I had nothing to lose, and he had nothing more than, let's see, 94 cents to gain.

"Trapper, this is all I have," I admitted, spreading out my coins. I was more suited to play three games of Gallaga than high-stakes cards.

"Well, how 'bout we make a deal?"

"A deal?"

"Yeah, a deal."

"Whattaya mean?" In the corner of my eye, I saw Amber lift her head from the table.

"Well, see, this is what Trapper's got in mind," Trapper said, propping his hand on the table. "See, I have this stupid community service thing to do next weekend, just some cleanin' up and stuff out on Route 142, but the thing is, Trapper's got better things goin' on."

"What'd ya go and do?"

"Oh, just a little candy bar thing." Trapper had been stealing stuff since he was old enough to grab, usually just for the heck of it. He was a topper and a taker.

"Yeah, so, what's in it for me?" I asked.

"The cash, moron. Like I said, we'll play one hand. You win, you get the cash. Every cent of it." He leafed through the money. It was a lot of lunches.

But with first-person guys, there was always a catch.

"And if you win?"

"You do the work."

Phil put down his video game. And for Phil to put down a game, it was serious.

"So, whattaya think?"

I dug deep into the bowl of Cheetos and picked out a handful. There weren't many left, and the stragglers were all broken and ignored. It wasn't like burned potato chips, which got passed over by most but gobbled up by me. I loved the burned ones. "C'mon, how 'bout it?"

Here was the deal. I wanted the money back, if only to pay back to Phil. And I wanted to bury the guy. But I wasn't nuts about the work thing. A day with Miss Anderson was one thing, but covering for a criminal was another. For all I knew, I'd get busted and get stuck with an orange jumpsuit and a trash stabber for life.

"Like, what are ya going to do?" It was Amber, spitting out her first sentence in hours. I hadn't really minded.

Good-looking girls didn't need to talk to be appreciated.

"Well, I dunno," I said. And I didn't.

"Well, I think it sounds, like, super cool," she said, her voice coming to life. "I mean, that's, like, just like in the movies."

She was right. It was a straight out of a Western, a winner-take-all kind of thing with booze and cigars and everything. But something was missing. I looked at Amber.

She looked back to me, her blue eyes as big as pies, and I felt a rush. Not where you're thinking, either. Somewhere above my belt, right where I got a lump when a pitcher lobbed a moonball right down the pipe.

Something was missing.

Of course, the girl.

So I thought I'd take a swing at sweetening the pot.

"Well, I'll do it if I get the money...and a kiss from you."

Swear to God I said it. Then, get this. I shrugged, like it was no big deal. Like a, well, like a lion full up on antelopes.

"Oooooo!" It was Trapper, squealing like a Theodore.

Phil hid behind his hands. From the corner, I heard a zipper zip back up. As for Amber, well, I waited for a smack.

I got a smile.

"Well, like, okay. Okay Mister Jasper, like, you can kiss me if ya win, fer sure I guess." Swear to God, she said it. Just like that, too, give or take a 'like.'

"So what if Trapper wins, baby?" Trapper asked. "Does Trapper getta little tongue if he wins?"

"Gross, gag me."

He flipped her off and punched Phil in the arm. Hard. "Deal." I figured he meant it both ways.

We were back on.

***

Phil shoveled a card to me, then to Trapper. I turned mine up, looked it over and looked at him. He turned his up, looked it over and looked at me. I hoped I didn't look as bad as him. More than that, I hoped he had a deuce, because I had a measly three.

Phil flipped over my next card, face up. A stinking five. Phil gave Trapper a jack. Trapper gave me a grin. He didn't have a deuce.

"How's it lookin' over there, pardner?" Trapper squawked. "Got any plans next Saturday?"

I looked at Amber. She didn't look happy or sad, disappointed or excited, just kind of present. Tell you the truth, I could be wrong, because I didn't notice anything but her juicy, glossy lips. I looked at Phil and realized the money meant nothing to me anymore.

I wiggled my finger at Phil. "Hit me."

He flicked it over. Another five. Thirteen total. Wasn't much.

Trapper waved Phil off. "Nuh-uh, Trapper here's good to go."

I wasn't. I wiggled. Phil flipped. A three. Sixteen. I pulled off my hat and ran my fingers through my matted hair.

Trapper leaned forward. "Well, well, whatta we have here? Sixteen showin' with one card left to play, huh?

Whattaya going to do now, slick?"

Good question. I could freeze on the 16 and hope Trapper was bluffing, but Trapper was probably too cocky to bluff. Or I could play it out and hope for, well, hope for another baby card. Sixteen was like green beans. Not too bad, not too good. I was stumped.

"How 'bout it? Feelin' lucky, slick?"

I looked over to Amber again. She smiled, and not even because she had to. "Go for it," she whispered.

You've got to know that was enough for one last wiggle.

Phil angled toward me and let my fate fly from his right hand. The card spiraled through the air, landed just left of my stack and skidded to a stop.

I looked down.

I smiled.

"Shhhiiiiiiiiiittttttt!!!!!!"

I never knew what Trapper had. Never would, either, because the pitcher and the bowl and the beer and the snacks and the money and the cards all went up together in a heap when he turned over the table. The only card that mattered fluttered down last and settled on a dollar bill, face up with no face at all.

The five of diamonds.

Now, diamonds might have been a girl's best friend or however that saying went, but I was feeling pretty high on the things about then, too.

Trapper hopped up from his chair, threw his hands on his hips and stared at the pile. His chest was heaving hard, and three new forehead veins appeared.

"Like, omigod, that's, like, 21!" Amber screamed.

"I know it's 21!" Trapper yelled. "Don't ya think I can count?!?"

It was an easy set-up, but I wasn't about to say anything.

The guy could still pound me.

"Well, looks like ya got some cleanin' to do," Phil said, pointing at the mess. It kind of shocked me, the way he said it, real snappy. "A lotta cleanin' to do."

"Aw, shut the hell up, dork," Trapper snorted. He kicked the pile, soccer style, and stormed out.

Phil looked at me, smiled and winked. It took me by surprise, because Phil wasn't a wink kind of guy, not one bit. Winks were for smart alecks or guys trying to get away with something.

Or ones who'd just gotten away with something.

Turned out I didn't break Simon's main poker rule.

I didn't cheat.

Hadn't even thought to, even though Dad always said that a guy had to make his own luck. Well, not when he had a slick-dealing, card-tricking geek in his corner. And especially not when that geek was dishing out a lifetime of revenge and returning an old favor, all in the simple turn of a card.

"So, like, I guess I owe ya a kiss or somethin,'" Amber said with a shrug.

I didn't cheat, not one bit. Phil did. And man, was I glad.

I can't be like all those people on the radio call-in shows who win concert tickets and get all misty and gurgle that they'd never, ever won anything before. I had. Back in sixth grade, I nabbed the runner-up gift in a church raffle, a bowling ball made for someone with sausages for fingers. Father Tom walked away with the grand prize, a trip to Disney World or Disney Land. (I never knew which was which.) Father acted surprised as heck when the lady called out his number, but I still say something stunk about it.

Anyway, by law, Father Tom was out of the running for Amber. So I walked over to her and bellied right up. My head was light, and I still had a little of that bulletproof feel to me, but my heart was hammering away so hard that it felt like my lungs were using the thing as a trampoline. Still, she held her ground, didn't budge an inch, like someone had ordered her to stay. But she was no dog, let me tell you.

"So how, like, do ya wanna, like, do this?" she asked.

She was smacking her gum. Peppermint or spearmint, or some member of the mint family. It felt good to be close enough to guess.

I only knew one way to do it. I'd learned at a party back in seventh grade, when the bottle spun to a stop in front of Lacy Chase and she laughed and leaned over and stuck her tongue clear down my throat.

Seemed pretty sick and sloppy at first, but it grew on me. Could have done without the audience, though.

Well, Amber and I didn't have an audience, not really.

Soggy bill by soggy bill, Phil was gathering his money, and Annie had hopped from her chair and joined him. They reached for the same bill, and their hands touched, just like in a sappy coffee commercial or something.

"Sorry," they said at the same time, pulling away.

"It's okay," they said, again together, this time laughing.

Jinks could be great fun.

Annie scratched her head and shrugged. "Um, I have Ms. Pac Man up in my bedroom, if ya, I dunno, if ya wanna play."

Phil lit up. And off they went, Phil with the only two ladies he could score with, Annie with the only guest who'd thought to bring a present to a birthday party.

***

In the corner, make-out central was still in session.

Danny and Pam. Smiles and Susan. Butch and Zelda. And Sting. I would have thought that Trapper's tantrum might have broken it all up, but priorities were priorities.

It felt sort of goofy, like a huge *have to* on her part, but I went for it. I slid my hands between her arms and reached around. I rubbed her back, starting at the shoulders of her tight, white tank top and working my way down. She didn't seem to mind too much, so real slow and sneaky, I headed toward a butt that even the crusty teachers at school couldn't help but steal a stare at. She reached behind her and stopped me just south of her bra strap.

Eh, worth a shot.

Still, even wading in a sticky puddle of brew, it was all nice and warm and maybe even a little romantic. And I have to report, she didn't even seem to be hating it. I put the clamps on her and pulled her super close. I puckered up, and she reached into her mouth and snatched her gum. No distractions, no rules, no gum. It was time.

But you know, a guy can only get lucky so many times in one night.

"What the hell is goin' on here? You call this a party?" I knew the voice. It was Tripp Donley, one of Steve Allen's buds. He was the son of the head golf pro at the Midtex Country Club, one of those toothy guys who turned up his collar, but Tripp was better with the sauce than the sticks. The guy was always blitzed. Still, he wasn't that awful, though it was hard to really trust a guy named after a verb.

"So, what, nobody speaks 'round here?" he yelled. He stepped inside and looked back over his shoulder. "Jake, you mean ya dragged us to some party with a whacked-out old lady and a bunch of retards?!?"

And there he was, Jake Jacobson.

He didn't so much appear in the doorway as he did become the doorway. Jake played most of the offensive line for Picadilly High and had already locked up a full ride to Arkansas or Texas or another of those schools with a stadium bigger than my hometown. He was wide and tall and strong, a human muscle contraction and also captain of the school rasslin' (AKA wrestling) team, a guy who terrorized people for the pure joy of it. I knew him only through Steve but knew enough to stay away from the guy, especially when he was tanked. See, when he drank, Jake got red. And the more he drank, the redder he got.

And standing in the doorway hugging a 12-pack box, Jake looked like a German sausage.

It didn't so much bother me that Amber broke away from my grip at the sound of Tripp's voice and sprinted over at the sight of Jake and buried her head in his barrel chest. Or that Jake looked massive and moody and all the things that would cause some local sportswriter to nickname him "The Picadilly Pulverizer." Or that his attention was aimed right at me. Naw, it was kind of all three.

Anyhow, the bet was off, and I figured my head would soon follow. "So, like, where've ya been Jake?" Amber whined.

"Aw, some crazy hag and some girlie dude trapped us in the main house," he snorted. "Been singin' freakin' churchy songs at us for a half-hour."

See, I knew Bingo and Grannie would hit it off.

The whole time, he kept staring at me. His eyes were dark, which was fine, and glossy, which wasn't. I mean, Cujo, that killer dog from the movies, had dark eyes and was cute as could be. But when they got all crazy and glazed over, he started eating people. I fidgeted but stayed put, hoping that maybe Jake would remember that we'd played a little hoops together just a few weeks before in Danny's driveway and I'd let him run all over the place without calling traveling on him even once. Not many things funnier than a meathead on a basketball court.

I was, as you might figure, so wrong.

"So who's this guy?" Jake sneered, motioning toward me.

"Oh, that's just Jasper," Amber chuckled. "We were just, like, playing cards and stuff."

The way she said my name wasn't any different than if she'd said she was going to go take a dump. I didn't mind, not one bit. Really, I was super with it. With no Amber, there was no us, and with no us, there would be no bloodshed. But we hadn't had time to cover our tracks.

"So then what's all over your back?" Tripp slurred.

"Like, huh?"

Jake spun Amber around, and there it was. It was as if someone had been finger painting all over her white tee, and the artist was big on orange. I slowly looked down at my hands, then made two tight fists, wincing at the thought that Cheetos were going to get me crunched.

"Yeah, just what the hell is goin' on?" Jake grunted. "Are you messin' around with this little guy or what?" Amber was, like, speechless. He looked back to me. It was pretty dark, but I'm pretty sure I saw him lick his lips.

A guy named Schitt didn't go through life without getting in a fight or three along the way. I was probably about 4-2 lifetime, with a whole bunch of draws and stretched-out clothes and a scar above my right eye from Troy Simpson's sneaky fast right hook. Here was usually what a fight at school got you: a shirt suited for a clown, either a sore hand or a sore face and a sure trip to the office.

I started some, finished others and tried to never back down. A guy had to protect his name, even when it was a goofy name. Especially then. I figured fighting wasn't so different than yanking out a nose hair. Sometimes you had to do it, even though it hurt like hell.

"You stay right here," Jake said to Amber, directing her against the wall. She folded her arms and said nothing. The social butterfly had gone and clammed up. Tripp stationed himself against the wall, too, but kept his distance from Amber. I would have done the same from the very start, had I known she was Jake's girl. I was a little dumb, but not plain stupid.

As Jake closed in, red as a rose, his eyes filled with rage, I knew there was a first time for everything. For beers. For cigars. For running. See, I didn't much care about my shirt. I had plenty. Or my hand. I had two. But my face was, well, it wasn't the best, but it was the best I had. And there wasn't a teacher or parent or grannie or cop in sight to keep it from getting rearranged by the fists of a blue-chip baboon.

My left eye, always the left, started to twitch.

There was still one person who could help, though, help by just being his same 'ol miserable self.

"Say, what's all this? Trapper's not ready to call it a night yet!"

He stumbled in just as he'd stumbled out. Wobbly, rowdy, drunk. And, here was the beautiful thing, hungry. The guy had a Cheetos mustache fatter than Magnum P.I's.

"Now who the hell is *this*?" Jake yelled like a guy getting impatient to pound someone, anyone.

"No, who the hell are you?!?" Trapper snorted back.

Jake turned toward him with an open-mouthed look. It was a good sign, at least good for me. I'd lost the spotlight. Remember when King Kong set down the pretty lady for a sec when the planes starting wailing on him? Well, same thing.

It was a small break, but it bought me some time. Time to run, maybe, or time to throw a cheap shot. I wasn't completely above that. But more than anything, it gave me time to wash my hands of the whole mess.

It hit me from the side, so softly that I barely even noticed. Not from the darkness of Lip City, where it was business as usual. Someone had put on Air Supply, so it was light's out over there. Instead, it came from the opposite corner, from an open window above the foosball table a few feet away. It was a wadded-up shirt, barely more than a scrap of cotton, but it was enough. I scooped it up, turned my back to Jake and rubbed so hard and so fast that I probably wiped the fingerprints clean off my hands. I could feel the threads tearing in my fingers as I wiped away the evidence and flung it back out the window. Just like that. Didn't know who it came from. Also didn't care.

"So what is it, you boys tryin' to come and steal Trapper's woman?" Trapper snapped, nodding and winking at Amber. She swallowed back a smile and looked expectantly at Jake. I figured she didn't much care who got pummeled, as long as it happened over her.

Jake only shook his head and returned to the reason why he was 18 inches from me. He reached out an enormous paw, took my left hand and examined it. Then my right. They were clean. Sparkling. Spotless. Well, maybe not spotless. I was 14, and a guy at that.

I smiled and shrugged at him. He did neither in return.

"Lucky sonuvabitch," he growled, dropping my hand. Then he headed toward Trapper, leaving me alone and dizzy and broke, but alive. Trapper lost his cocky smile and swallowed hard. See, Trapper was a starter, but Jake was a finisher.

Not wanting to cheat death and all that, I made a break for it, stepping real lazily past Tripp and Amber and then breaking into a sprint so fast that Danny would have choked on my dust. I think, in poker talk, it was called cutting your losses.

"Heyyy, ouch, Trapper don't like that!!!"

***

Later, back at Danny's, I didn't feel all that lucky. I wasn't about to go home, not with my mom's superhuman sense of smell, not with the Allens still safely serving up three shots of bourbon for the price of one at the steakhouse. But sleep wasn't in the cards for me, either. I was looking out the window and laying on my stomach, trying to hold my guts in and reminding myself that the Tilt-A-Whirl was a favorite of mine when I saw a figure moving slowly up the sidewalk. I took it for Danny, but as the shadow got closer, I realized it wasn't. It was Steve, a shirtless shadow carrying a wad of cloth, a brother that I didn't want but was sure glad I had, if only for one fuzzy night.

Danny came home a little later but he didn't come to bed. Nope, he made a beeline for the bathroom and started spewing. His heaves and hacks and gurgles were contagious as yawns, because my mouth started watering, my jaw starting shaking, and I hustled in to join him. I broke through the swinging doors, the kind that sweaty cowboys busted through when they really needed a drink, and gave every one of mine back to the sink, plus some lunch to boot.

Some lion I was.

"How ya feelin' in there now, ya friggin' wimps!" Steve hooted from his bedroom. He might have been a brother, for real to Danny and for rent to me, but he was still a big brother.

I tossed a washcloth to Danny. "So what happened between Jake and Trapper?" I had to know, ya know?

He wiped his mouth. "It was ugly."

"Really?"

"Yeah, real ugly."

I nodded and spit, happy there was always someone bigger and meaner, feeling a little better. A little.

Danny carefully rose from the floor and leaned next to me against the basin. He splashed some water on his face, then lifted it slowly.

"Say, would you wanna ride our bikes or somethin' like that tomorrow?"

It was maybe the best idea I'd ever heard.

"Bet your ass."

Out Of Tune

Everyone wanted to hang out with Billy Hamilton.

Except, of course, until they'd hung out with him.

Billy wasn't like the rest of us. He didn't try to be cool, mostly because he didn't have to. It just kind of followed him around, like a shadow in shades. And the girls followed right behind, at least with their eyes. He was like The Fonz, only with better hair. I mean, that Henry Winkler guy was getting up there. The thumb, the jacket, the motorcycle, none of it was really fooling us anymore.

Billy had things that every guy wanted, even the big-time jocks or the face guys, though they'd probably never admit it. First off, he drove a red Trans Am that he parked backwards. It had an engine that purred like a lion and a stereo that made the teachers cringe. And he fit it, too. He stood about six-foot-two and had light blonde hair that floated down to a set of broad shoulders. But he didn't use a comb. He just did this hair flip thing about every four steps in the hall. I tried to do it once and got one of those shocks shooting through my neck. Figured you had to know the technique.

It was hard to explain, but everything was a little different about the guy. He dressed different, impressing without trying to impress. He walked different, bending back at the waist and letting his head bounce a little. And when he saw people he knew, he did another little head nod. Not the downward nod that old people did or his trademark hair flip thing, but similar and every bit as smooth.

Nobody exactly knew what to make of him. He'd moved to Midtex during the Christmas break of this, our junior year, and just sort of gotten tagged as someone to watch. Supposedly he was from somewhere up north, but nobody was really sure. See, here was the big thing about Billy Hamilton. He was a complete mystery. Maybe that was why the girls, even the seniors, turned and watched him strut past. The guy was a side attraction, the 10-inch horse at the fair.

I know it sounds kind of creepy, me going on and on about the guy. But I like girls, I swear I do. I'd known that since the end of sixth grade, when Deanna Renshaw let me peck her on the cheek at the roller rink. I asked her to go with me right then and there, and she said yes. Then she broke up with me after one stinking lap. Two songs later, she was out doing the backwards skate with Andy Rifkin. Then came the T-shirt incident with Sandra and the kiss-that-wasn't with Amber, with a few hits and more misses along the way. Anyway, I was hooked.

Just wanted to get that good and straight.

New students, especially ones who threatened to swoop in on the action, usually got the cold shoulder at Picadilly. But it was hard not to like Billy. He smiled all the time, a wide, inviting smile, and said hello to most everyone. Teachers, janitors, brains, blockheads, wide girls, skinny girls, language clubbers, science goobers, everyone. He was just known for being known, like that Nipsy Russell guy.

Even the jocks took to him. He didn't play sports, though he was bigger than most of the varsity linebackers and probably could have snatched up my starting spot on the junior varsity baseball squad. But I don't think he had the time, because he was always roaring out of the parking lot right after the sixth-period bell. He would salute people and cruise past as Night Ranger or Triumph or sometimes even Kenny Rogers blared from the cab. Then he would slowly roll down Howell Drive, honk at the smokers at Duncan's Drugs and screech off to the north, his hair blowing in the wind.

You never knew which Billy was going to show up. Sometimes he dressed like a cowboy, all decked out in Wranglers and a western shirt and maybe a Davy Crockett jacket. Other times you'd see him in a fancy shirt and nice pants, or a white tee and flip-flops, or a ballcap and sweats. And he was never with the same person twice. You'd see him walking with some no-name freshman dude, then the next hour he'd be high-fiving the star running back. Same thing with girls. A tall redhead one day, a short brunette the next, but never more than once. Most people had their own circle and hardly ever crossed the line. A jock was a jock, a redneck a redneck, a thug a thug. But with Billy, the line was all over the place.

At school, he took weird, out of-the-way classes. Drafting, steel shop, car repairs, junk like that. It was like he had worked out an all-elective schedule. The lady who fixed our junior classes, Mrs. Daly, must have fallen for him, too. Anyway, there was a side wing just for those courses, and

Billy always ended up strolling that way after the tardy warning bell. I couldn't wait to get out of high school, if only to stop hearing bells and whistles and fire alarms all the time.

I think maybe that's why people liked him. He wasn't from the sticks, and he knew about the other stuff. At least we liked to think that he did. A bunch of guys, especially seniors, tried to pretend to have all the answers, especially in front of girls, but we all knew that it was an act. Some were just better actors than others. And the girls, well, who knew what they were thinking.

You could say that inside of six months, Billy Hamilton had been branded as a ladies man, though nobody ever saw him out on a date. And as a good friend to have, though he always cruised the drag by himself. And as a good student, though nobody who was anybody had a class with him. He just appeared and became this larger-than-life person. I'd lived in Midtex for almost six years, had had a bunch of different short-lived girlfriends, never cruised the drag without at least two other buds and was an honor student. And as far as I knew, I had no reputation at all.

It was like he'd figured out how to have fun, no matter where he was or what he was doing. Nobody made being alone look like such a gas. And laughs were hard to come by in Midtex, trust me.

He had a secret, and we wanted to know it.

Well, one night, the least likely person ended up spending an entire Friday night with the guy.

Me.

***

I'd never said a word to Billy, and except for on my way to chemistry sometimes, never really crossed paths with him. He was more of a rumor than a real person to me. We'd nodded, but, like I said, the guy would nod and smile at a fire hydrant.

The only person I knew who'd talked to him was Coby Cane, a weak-hitting right fielder on the JV who took steel shop because his dad was a mechanic. I hoped that my dad didn't expect me to go into the rubber game after graduation. I had bigger plans. What they were, I had absolutely no idea.

"So what's that Billy Hamilton guy like?" I asked Coby once in the locker room before practice.

"I dunno, it's hard to say," Coby replied, pulling black batting gloves on both hands. I didn't know why he even bothered. The guy couldn't hit a lick. "He mostly just heads to the corner and kicks his feet up and smiles and laughs. Nods a whole lot, too. Can't say I really know him though."

I found out soon enough.

It was a Friday afternoon, and everybody was hustling to get out of the fieldhouse parking lot. Coach White had cut off practice early, which was a miracle. He was one of those coaches who liked to go over the fundamentals a trillion times, then start over and do it all again. I understood to a point, because that's what separated the chumps from the champs. But he was a maniac about it. I mean, it was only JV ball, and it was real clear that Cecil Mudge, a back-up outfielder, was never going to hit the cut-off man with any consistency. I wasn't sure if Cecil, who wore those goofy sports goggles, could even see the cut-off man.

But Coach White was young and still full of spirit and claps and pumped fists. He actually cared, even about winning a JV game against the Weller High Whips, short for Whippersnappers. Someday, he'd get old and beaten down and start slouching like the other coaches who didn't coach football, but not just yet.

High school, by the way, wasn't so bad, and wasn't so good. It was just plain school, and I figured even if you lived in like Hawaii and had coconuts staring at you from outside the window, it was always going to be just plain school. Living in Midtex probably made it easier, because there was nothing much to stare at or to think about anyway. High school was like junior high, only with more hormones and less homework. Oh, and still bigger boobs.

Anyhow, I was tearing toward the exit that afternoon. There was really no need to rush, because a bunch of cars were already stacked and waiting to leave. They were in all shapes and sizes and colors, but mostly used. There wasn't a ton of money floating around Midtex in those days, not since the oil bust. Dad said there wasn't enough oil left around anymore to part your hair.

But the student body of Picadilly didn't care much about that, not with the weekend in our sights. Girls and guys hung out of their rides and waved and honked at each other. Some guys flipped each other off, which was the same as screaming 'hey,' but only without having to wave. I saw Bridgette Berry, probably the hottest chick in the entire school, pull up right next to Jimmy LeClair's Monte Carlo SS, lean out and plant a sloppy kiss on him. Tongues and all, flapping around right there.

Man, I thought, I should have stuck with football.

Actually, I had given it one more shot. Kurt talked me into playing my sophomore year, but it was a short and sorry comeback. During preseason workouts, I took a pitch from Jeremy Bruce and, about two steps later, took my usual beating. Wobbling back to the huddle, I noticed that I was dragging my left leg like a pirate. I wanted it to come along, but it wouldn't obey. Doc Richardson, a kooky-eyed trainer who looked off in six different directions when he talked to you, lugged me away to the trainer's room in a black golf cart.

"So when does it hurt, kid?" asked Doc while pressing on the purple, swollen thing.

"Well, when I walk or run mostly. Kind of when I breathe, too."

"Oh, I see, I see." He scratched his head. "And it's just the left knee?"

"Well, yessir."

"Hmmm." He reached into a jar and handed me four white pills. "So it really only hurts half the time, right?"

Dr. Dunn, our family doctor, had a different opinion.

And his theory was backed up by X-rays and a fat bill.

Seemed the cartilage in my knee was shredded like lettuce.

Three days later, I went under the knife.

They said I could be back in six weeks if I worked real hard, but I knew it was a career-ending injury. I acted like it was a big bummer, but it felt more like a black-and-blue blessing. Wasn't exactly the Purple Heart, but it was a war wound of sorts, and at least I hadn't just up and quit. Besides, I got to crutch around school for a month and get out of class early and answer questions from seemingly concerned students.

Nobody asked questions to a second-string halfback and back-up deep snapper.

"So does it hurt super bad?" Jan Kretzmeyer asked me one day on the way to history class. She was dragging my backpack along, another plus.

I shrugged. "Naw, just a little. Like when I try and run sprints on it." At the time, I could still barely walk.

"Oh no, don't do that!" she gasped. "Promise me ya won't try and overdo it!"

"Oh, well, okay," I sighed.

"No, Jasper, ya gotta promise," she pleaded, clutching my shoulder.

"Okay Jan, I promise," I said. And I promise that she carried my books every day for the next three weeks. I asked her out when it became good and clear that I was just walking along with my crutches. It took her two seconds to turn me down.

Said she was dating Brady Cobb, who played football.

I decided to stick with baseball and hoops, my two best sports. At least in those, a girl could actually see your face. Oh, I still rooted for the football team, went to all the games, talked smack to the enemy. It was kind of fun to be a tiny part of probably the best football school in all of Texas, which was probably no less a deal than having the best beer in Germany.

But I didn't miss it. Never, not once. Maybe the baseball players, especially the JV guys, didn't have their names plastered all over the walls - Go, Go, Go, Big Harvey! Declaw the Cougars! - but we did get to the parties in one piece or look worried all the time.

Seemed like a fair enough trade.

We weren't going anywhere fast in the parking lot, so I thought about taking a detour. There was a little side lot by the tennis courts, over where the band practiced. Don't tell anyone, but I always kind of respected the people in the marching band. They practiced like mad, then got nothing out of it but five or 10 minutes at halftime and a sure reputation as a nerd. I didn't dare hang out with any of them, but you had to respect their determination. All I could play was the car horn.

After school, the druggies always took over the band lot. They were never in a hurry, happy to just puff away and have stereo wars. About four cars up, Jimmy and Bridgette were practically naked. And they were seniors with patches plastered all over their letter jackets. I was still patchless, so it wasn't like I could honk at them. So I gave the side route a go.

Billy had the same idea. Two cars ahead, I saw him tear out of line and fly toward the courts. I followed, though not as quickly or impressively. My car was red and had four tires and a steering wheel and all, but the similarities stopped about there. I drove a 1983 Pontiac J2000, a Christmas gift from my folks during sophomore year. I'd found the keys at the bottom of a big, bowtied package, then raced outside in my whitey tighties to find part of it peeking out from behind my mom's Camaro. The front of it was sparkling and sporty and pointy, but, after seeing it in full, it became practical and sensible in a hurry. The J2000 was a wannabe sports car with a go-cart engine and speakers no bigger than walkie talkies. Don't get me wrong, I appreciated it and all--one guy on our baseball team drove a hunk of steel that steered like a tanker and was older than he was-- but it was no Trans Am. Not even close.

We rolled through the thugs, passing through the haze and the heavy metal and the hickeys. I wondered how much Rush a guy could listen to in one lifetime. A few of them I didn't recognize were lying on the hood of a Pinto and appeared to be barely alive. Up ahead, I saw Billy's hand fly out of his window and make the peace sign.

"What's up duuuuuuude!" one of them hollered. The guy knew everyone.

***

Allison Rickles helped introduce me to Billy. Allison was supposedly the great-niece of Don Rickles, that bald comedian who always used to get so ripped at those television roasts they had for Dean Martin. Anyway, she was a looker, really leggy and giggly, and we were pretty decent friends. Study buddies, like that. I'd wanted to upgrade the whole thing for a good two years. I had needs, and, most of all, no real prospects for the prom yet. It was three weeks away, and I knew I had to get cracking. Girls got snatched up quick, usually by guys who had no business taking girls like Allison. The slackers, like me, ended up going stag and swearing it was by choice.

I'd almost asked her a few hours before. I was hurrying to fifth hour when I spotted her over by the vending machines. But T.J. Ranzotti, a senior who looked exactly like The Karate Kid, was tilting the machine for her. The thing never worked, but it would spit out Funyons, Lemonheads, powdered donuts, anything if you knew the right way to rock it. Once I got eleven Whatchamacallits for two quarters. But T.J. was all in Allison's face, so I decided it could wait until later.

She was walking toward her car near the tennis courts. I wish you could have seen these legs. They were long as ropes and thin as Pixie Sticks, and she was bouncing along in all the right places. And the big bonus was that she was parked right by the exit that I was sputtering toward.

I wasn't a very good driver. It's okay, I can say it. I think the only reason I'd gotten my license was because the instructor, a little Chinese fella with a massive clipboard, exploded into a sneezing fit just as we left the DPS lot. He sneezed when I forgot to turn on my blinker. Four times. He sneezed when I ran a red light. It was yellowish red, by the way. He sneezed when I tailgated so close to a school bus that I could see up the nostrils of the little punk sneering out the back window. The guy just kept sneezing and checking away.

About the only time Mr. Clipboard stopped blowing was when I parallel parked. Or tried to, anyway. After my third try, the nose of the J2000 was facing the middle of Yucatan Drive and assuming the role of a roadblock.

"You jusss go 'head," he hissed. I saw him make a big 'X.' Then he sneezed again. I passed with flying colors, though if you want to get all picky, I probably cheated on my driver's test.

I gave the courtesy wave when people let me in and parked between the lines and everything; I just didn't pay much attention. People were always throwing up their arms and mouthing stuff at me. There were just too many distractions and rules. Marquee movie signs to study, songs to sing, sunflower seeds to chew. And c'mon, 35 miles an hour was barely even rolling. And that wasn't even counting the biggest distraction of all--a cute, boyfriendless, bouncing girl walking to her car. Alone.

It all happened in a blur, much like life in general. Allison was unlocking her car. I was rolling down my window. Billy was nodding at a traffic guard.

"Hey Allie!" I yelled, poking my head out of the window. We were good enough friends so that I could shorten her name.

She waved. I did the same, steering closer to her.

"Hey, wait up a minute!" I was thinking about asking her out to dinner to, you know, plant the seeds for the prom thing. I was also thinking that the wave she'd just given me looked way too much like a "but we're such good friends that I don't wanna ruin it" wave. Next she'd probably punch me in the arm and say "o-buddy-o-pal-o-chum."

But there was one thing I definitely wasn't thinking about as Allie leaned against her car, squinted into the sunlight and showed me the wonderful benefits of paper-thin, white outfits and a general distaste for bras.

Stopping.

It wasn't a huge crash, nothing like the ones we used to stage with model cars and firecrackers. In fact, I couldn't have been going any faster than seven or nine miles an hour. But it was enough to throw Billy's head forward, then back. And it wasn't one of his cool head flips, either. It looked more like those dummies from the driver's education movies, the bloody ones that were supposed to scare a guy into paying attention when he, for instance, drove.

I wrote notes during driver's ed. *Sorry so short. Write back soon. Why did you cheat on me.* You remember the ones.

The impact did nothing to me, except send a feeling of horror through my spine. Judging from the way he whirled around in his seat, Billy wasn't hurt, either. My only hope was that his car, which was probably worth more than my life, wasn't bent out of shape.

We met at the same time, the three of us, at the rear of his car. Allie looked freaked out like only a girl could look. Billy had on these dark shades that covered most of his face, but his eyebrows were hanging high above the frames, and his forehead was all wrinkled up. From head to toe, I felt like I'd just come from the dentist.

"Are you okay, Jasp?" Allie asked. She knew me well enough to shorten my name, too.

I nodded. I wasn't worried about me. Billy was crouching and checking the rear bumper of his car. I kind of checked mine, though I really couldn't care less. All I could find was a tiny nick. Billy was more careful, running his hands across the fishtail like it was all a prize on "The Price is Right." Though it probably only took a few seconds, it felt like I was in the stands at a Picadilly football game, and the refs were stretching the chains to see if the 'ol Pumas had made a first down.

Billy stood up. Unfolded, really. I'd never realized just how big and broad he really was. He was at least four inches taller than I, with shoulders wider than a Chevette and a long neck. And a big Adam's Apple, too. I noticed that because I was staring right into it. Anyway, the guy looked like he belonged on either a rescue show or a fake ID.

For a few seconds, he froze like a statue. It wasn't the hallway Billy, the one that we all loved but hardly knew. And then, with a nod and a king-sized smile, he was back. "Hey, we're cool." He flipped his hair back, the good hair flip.

I let out of rush of relief, for my insurance company, for my parents and for my own health. "Good. Geez, I'm so sorry about that. I was just lookin' over at Alli...."

Holding her hair up in a bun, Allie looked so pretty that it made me stop in mid-sentence. Her hair was probably my favorite part about her, because it was straight and actually fit in the photo boxes in our school annuals. Most Picadilly girls had this hunk of hair, this claw thing, hanging down in their eyes. Allie liked hers pulled back. Anyhow, maybe it was my brush with death, but I wanted to grab her and kiss her right then and there. Or at least ask her to go eat at Red Lobster.

"Sure you're all right?" she asked again.

"Yep, I'm fine." I turned back to Billy. "Are you alright?"

"Hey, still crazy after all these years," he smiled.

I nodded, recognizing those words from somewhere, though I couldn't remember exactly where.

That about wrapped it up. Nothing was hurt except for my ego, and the wreck had at least given me some quality time with Allie. A scratched bumper for a potential date, a guy couldn't ask for a much better deal. Anyhow, there wasn't much more to say.

Billy thought of something, though.

"Say, are you all goin' to the Def Leppard concert?" He hadn't made it to the 'ya'll' stage yet. Damn Yankee. Still, I thought I'd heard the word 'death' in there somewhere, so I needed a repeat.

"Huh?"

"The Def Leppard concert tonight at the coliseum. Are you all goin'?" He tilted against his car and propped his leg up on the bumper.

Ah, Def Leppard. They were a rock band that was pretty popular around Picadilly, especially in the stoner lot. Their music was pretty hard, but not the kind of hard that made people go all whack over the devil or anything. And their drummer only had one arm, so that was neat.

I'd only been to one concert before, the Beach Boys. It was right after our last day of seventh grade, an afterschool deal behind Midtex Coliseum. They trucked in all this sand and made a big, fake beach, right there in the parking lot. It was really more of a dirt pasture, but it was the big thing to do, so a bunch of us piled in Adam Sipple's mom's van and headed over there. But it was pretty weak. The guys were old, the songs were old and it was at least 184 degrees. All I really got out of it was a crappy shirt, a sunburn and a bunch of sand in my crotch.

But a lot of guys were concert fanatics and went to every single show. For some crazy reason, all the big acts passed through Midtex - Ratt, Ozzy, Cheap Trick, Bon Jovi, REO Speedwagon, Whitesnake. They all played in the coliseum, which also hosted the circus, the rodeo and any other major town event. I'd only been in the place once, to see the Ringling Brothers show. Two steps inside the front door, it became clear that the steers and lions and horses and elephants left more of a mark than Tom Petty. Man, was it rank.

The unofficial school uniform on the Monday after a concert weekend was the concert tee. They were usually pretty ugly and almost always black with those three-quarter sleeves, but some people loved to show them off. I wasn't one of them.

"Um, I haven't really thought about it," I replied to Billy. That was an understatement. I looked to Allie, who now had her little buddies shielded with folded arms. Sooner or later, girls always figured things like that out.

"Oooo, I'd love to see Def Leppard! They're awesome!" she gasped, her eyes wide as a trout's. Hmm, I thought, I had no idea she was a concert person, but, again, I didn't know her half as much as I wanted to.

"Yeah? Well, I've got some extra tickets to it," Billy said, alternating his attention between us. "And a buddy of mine's buddy is workin' security, so they're choice seats.

Whattaya think?"

Well, it wasn't exactly a romantic dinner for two - more like Taco Pancho and loud music with 3,000 people - but being crammed in next to Allie while getting to hang out with this Mystery Man didn't sound like such a bad night, not at all. By the way, most restaurants in Midtex started or ended with the word 'taco," and it was hard to get a meal that wasn't swimming in queso. Around our parts, milk was a part of the cheese group, not the other way around.

"Sure, sounds cool," I said to Billy.

Allison smiled. I was on my way. "Oh, I can't. I have a date."

"With who?!" I shot out too quickly and too loudly. "I mean, really? Um, with who?" It was probably too late. My cover was busted.

"Well, with T.J. Ranzotti."

I'd lost my prom date to some stinking Funyons.

"Aw, too bad," Billy said. Then he nodded at me. "Well, looks like me and you, amigo, if you're still in."

I shrugged. Sure I was in. I mean, free was free.

"Cool beans. Say, what's your name?"

"Jasper," I said, stopping there. I usually let them find out the punchline on their own.

"Jasper, cool name, reeeeeal cool. I'm Billy, Billy Hamilton."

"Yeah, hi," I said. And we shook hands. He gave me one of those multi-grip shakes where you ended up pointing at each other.

"Cool beans then. A concert with a kid named Jasper. Ain't nothin' cooler." He hopped in his car and peeled away. After some worthless small talk, Allie was gone, sliding away in a 280ZX that looked like a sports car from front to back.

And so it was a date, sort of. Not exactly the one I'd wanted, but something different to do at least. Before the wreck, I was planning on meeting some guys up at the mall arcade for a video football tourney. You might remember the game. Roller ball? Little X's and O's? Pinched palms? Anyway, a concert sounded better than blood blisters.

Al Fowler had pretty much tanked the weekend for everyone anyway. Zach Lee, a sophomore whose parents were always out of town, had had a huge party the Saturday before. Couple hundred of his closest buds. He made some trash-can punch, a green concoction containing about 10 liquors and a few pills, and Al ended up getting rushed to the hospital for a stomach pump. He was fine, but the parents and police of Midtex would be on full alert. Stomach pumps and hospitals always set the house party scene back for a good month.

***

Entering my neighborhood, I noticed for the umpteenth time in just what a desolate place I lived. Midtex was full of wasted space; at least that's what we called it in photography class. Empty fields, empty buildings, empty oil wells. There was so much room to grow, but Midtexans either lacked the dough or the imagination. Maybe both.

Nobody tried to pretend. Maybe that's what gave the place its appeal. Midtex was just plain Midtex. Nothing less, nothing more. And the people were friendly, always telling stories and jokes and punching you in the arm. Good people, except for the murderers, anyway. Midtex had been named the "Murder Capital of the U.S." for like six years straight. At least we were good at something other than football.

Anyhow, I figured living in an ugly place with friendly folks beat living in paradise with a bunch of shits. And somehow, it didn't seem quite so hot anymore. My skin was broken in like a good mitt, which was a plus.

Al Fowler or not, Ponderosa would still be packed. Ponderosa was really a fancy name for a deserted field just north of town, a patch where people met and hung around a little bonfire and drank beer. Anyway, for the time being it was called Ponderosa. Soon it would get busted, and everyone would move to another field, throw down some logs and call it Bonanza or Mesquite or some other cowboy-sounding name.

A few months back, some guys from Midtex High came over after a basketball game and starting swinging baseball bats at a few Picadilly football players, but mostly the place was all about peace and love and back seats and smelling like a barbecue pit. It had supposedly been going on for years, the cat-and-mouse game with the cops, but teenagers never ran out of pastures in West Texas.

My parents were pretty cool about things. I mean, they couldn't really think that I went to the movies every Friday and Saturday night of my life, though I really was a big movie buff. Still, as long as I was home around midnight and didn't smell like a brewery, I avoided Mom's lit cigarette glowing in the kitchen and the third degree that followed. If I did break curfew, she would usually just holler that she'd thought I was in some ditch somewhere and that now she'd have to call off the search party.

I remembered her pulling the same bit with my brothers, so I didn't sweat it too much. Wasn't sure why she thought we all hung out in ditches. But no matter what, here was a given: the later I stayed out or the weaker my alibi, the earlier Dad would be mowing under my bedroom window the next morning.

Here was the plain truth: I didn't have a set of super-hip, just-be-home-by-dawn parents. I had good parents. Most of the time, I'd take good over cool, because good didn't fade or gray. Besides, you could just rent the other parents from friends on weekends.

I might have to do that, I decided. Concerts didn't fall in the range of normal things to do around our house, though my mom had gone to see that Tom Jones guy a few months back. She was all gooey over him, so much that I'd noticed Dad wearing an extra layer of aftershave the night of the gig. But going to see Def Leppard on the spur of the moment with some kid they didn't know - and that I really didn't know - well, that was cause for some creativity.

"Hey Mom, think I'm going to spend the night over at Mike's," I announced at dinner. I was talking about Mike Handler, a longtime pal.

Mom picked at her food. "Oh, you are? What are you boys going to do?"

"Something like a something!" yelled Dad from the porch room. He was trying to solve a puzzle on *Wheel of Fortune.*

"Oh, we dunno yet," I answered, securing some spaghetti around my fork like a cocoon. "Probably catch a flick, play on the computer, shoot some hoops, somethin' like that." I figured if I threw out enough options, she'd bite at one of them.

"Oh, well, okay then. Just don't give the Handlers any trouble."

"Cooked like a goose!" Dad had nailed another one. I think he had a secret fantasy to be a contestant so he could win big and tell Pat Sajak he wanted to purchase the $925 ceramic Dalmatian. We were pretty good players in our family, but we sat all there like vegetables during *Jeopardy*, so it all evened out.

"May I please be excused?" I asked, already knowing the answer.

"Yes you may, but wash off your plate," Mom said, pecking at her own. With four boys, she was a pro at rationing.

I didn't like to lie. I didn't. But I didn't know many kids that didn't, at least sometimes. There was only one type of person who told their parents everything; we called them girls. My friends and I weren't out looting liquor stores or anything, just trying to find something to do in a place with nothing to do, like standing in burning fields.

But the worst part was that I couldn't even use my imagination, which was pretty lively. Since my brothers had already snagged the good stories, I was stuck with seeing *The Natural* for the 23rd time. I sometimes tried the tall-tale approach, but my fiction was pretty useless against their powers.

I was ready for the day when I didn't have to lie anymore. It was exhausting.

"Ninety-nine luftballoons go by!" I belted out under the rain of hot water. Singing in the shower was a favorite hobby of mine. I didn't really know the words, since there were only like five American ones in the whole song, but the girl on the video was a cookie, and the tune was catchy.

Sometimes I dreamed about singing in a band. I did. But I couldn't much sing or play anything or imagine being stared at, so that was all working against me. If I did ever have a band, I wanted to play the tambourine. No big reason, just because.

Standing in front of the mirror, I poked my head through the little circle I'd drawn through the steam and rehashed my earlier phone conversation with Mike.

"So if she does call, which she probably won't, just tell her that I ran up to the store," I said.

"To get what?"

"Doesn't matter."

"So why didn't I go with ya?"

"Well, because you had to stay and watch your brother."

"Why didn't my parents just watch him?"

"Because your parents aren't home."

"But what if one of my parents answer?"

"Mike, just answer the phone if it rings."

"But what if I wanna run up to the store for something?"

I was a little nervous, because Mike was a big worrier and sometimes cracked under pressure. He only had about five chest hairs, but they were already gray. Still, it seemed harmless enough.

I plucked a hair off the tip of my nose. My face was finally growing into the thing a little, and I didn't feel quite so out of kilter anymore. I'd let my hair grow out in the back, long enough to get bugged by coaches but not too long to get benched by them, and my face was finally clearing up. I thought I looked like a mix between the guy from *Valley Girl*, except probably not that good, and that Alf character, except hopefully not that bad.

The steam started to clear. Yep, still pretty much a dork.

I wasn't exactly sure what to wear. I usually favored the general jock outfit - a tee, jeans and tennies - but this was different. I thumbed through the closet and came up with a tee, jeans and tennies. But the shoes were old and torn, if that counted for anything. My feet had been size 11 since I was about five years old, and my brothers thought I was going to be the next Jerry West. But I seemed to be petering out at a little under six feet, and I could just barely scrape the basketball net, so I was probably more likely to be the next Jerry Lewis. Before I headed out, I cut a little hole in the tee. Seemed like a concerty thing to do.

"Byeeee, I'm leaving," I hollered on my way out.

"Bye, have fun honey," Mom called back, stretching out from the kitchen. "Aren't you going to tie your shoes?"

"Buy an 'u', buy a 'u'! You jacko!" I heard Dad scream.

***

Thought I'd pick up some beer on the way over. Seemed only right. I was just 17 and had no need for a fake ID, except maybe to get into the Crazy Colt Strip Club. Kurt and I had snuck into a couple of watering holes in town, but it seemed like they were always full of a bunch of men and a few ladies not especially looking for men.

Anyway, there was a drive-through place near Billy's house that sold to all the underage kids. An Indian guy was always working, and he'd poke his head through the open window and practically have the beer on ice for you. No questions, nothing, just a nod and a smile and a return to his dirty magazine.

It was our idea of a convenience store.

It was only about seven o'clock, but the drag was already filling up. The drag was about a four-mile strip that consisted of two turnaround points, one at Pizza Paradise and the other at Pizza Palace. In between, people just drove down 43rd Street and waved or yelled at each other. Then you passed them on the way back and repeated the scene. Every once in a while, you found out about a party or hooked up with a carload of girls and cruised around together, but that was rare. Girls didn't tend to want to pile into J2000s. Mostly, it was the same, goofy routine.

"Hey duuuuuuuuuude!" It was Sammy Erwin, flying past me in his low-rider van. He was alone, because girls tended to not want to pile into low-rider vans, either.

"What's uppppppppp!" I shot back. If I stayed out and cruised, I'd see him again in a half hour or so. It was all as strange as being a teenager.

But on this night, I had bigger plans. More mature plans I turned left onto Buckner Boulevard, away from the Pizza Palace and from the thumping bass in the parking lot, and headed north. Billy lived in a tiny subdivision called Pecan Grove, a good ten miles from Picadilly. There was a crumbling baseball complex where we played our summer league games, but I didn't know anybody who actually lived out there that wasn't a pecan farmer.

I tried to read the address that was scribbled on my hand. 192..some- thing...2...Ch...something...ee. I'd showered, you know.

Anyway, it wasn't too hard to find. There were only two other streets and a dozen or so homes in the whole area.

Didn't see a single pecan, either.

19212 Cherokee, that was it. I parked in front of the house, a good distance from Billy's car, which sat alone in the driveway. Cars like ours didn't much belong side by side. I picked some pepper out of my teeth, grabbed the six-pack of Busch and headed toward the front door.

"Over here, Jasper baby!" It was Billy, just to the side of the house, his head poking through an open screen door in the ground. His hair was wet, and he was sporting jeans with no shirt. The guy had more chest hair than the entire JV baseball team combined.

"Oh, hey." I detoured to the right.

"Glad ya could make it, dude." he said. I reached him, and we exchanged another of those complicated handshakes. I reminded myself to work on those. "I gotta finish gettin' ready, cool?"

"Cool."

He noticed the brown sack. "No way! Brewskies?"

I nodded.

"Hey, ain't nothin' cooler," he said, swiping it from me. "C'mon in." I took the three-step drop to the basement level. Some people called the things storm or tornado or bomb shelters, though Midtex never much faced any of the three. I think it was more of a make-out shelter.

"I'm almost there," he said. He rubbed a towel through his hair and headed for the closet. "Go ahead and take a load off, make yourself right at home."

It really kind of was its own home. The room wasn't that big, but it was divided into three sections by hanging sheets. The middle section was the bedroom, and the waterbed still swayed with motion. The room to my right was lined with a beer bottle pyramid and velvet paintings, the kind that people peddled from the back of vans at the corner of College Drive and Ninth Street, and the room on the left was sectioned off by a black sheet with a 'Trespassers Beware!' sign stapled to its front.

All in all, it was very hip, very smooth, very Billy Hamilton.

At our house, my room wasn't big enough for dividers, and Mom was already licking her chops to turn it into a sewing room someday.

I wandered into the velvet room, which also included a stereo, a couple of chairs and a wheel wagon table. And records, tons of records. I was already way into cassette tapes, but Billy obviously wasn't ready to make the switch. The only person who I knew with more records was a kid named Trey

Duncan. His dad owned Duncan's Wild, Wide World of Music. Trey said they were starting to get in these more compact metal records, but that they would never last.

Only big would fly in Texas.

I fell back into one of the chairs and cracked open a beer. "Buschhhhhh," I said, smiling a little.

His voice filtered through the sheet. "Hey, why don't ya spin some vinyl."

I fingered through the albums. He had a little bit of everything. Hard rock, soft rock, in between rock. New, old, real old. Country. Blues. Even some comedy albums. I thought about putting on Steve Martin -- he had this old gag about shoes that was a riot - but decided on Def Leppard's most recent release. You know, to set the mood and all.

"Yessss, excellent choice!" His approval made me feel good, and I took a long drink of beer. I sat there for a few minutes, listening to the music and wondering what it would be like to have some kid sitting around in a torn tee waiting to go see me in concert.

For a few reasons, I was pretty excited. Some of it was hanging out around someone new. I liked my circle of friends, but it had been the same circle for years. After awhile, I guess it was sort of like a marriage. We ran out of things to say. But most of all, it was the feeling of the unknown. It had been a long time since I hadn't known pretty much exactly the way things were going to turn out.

"Yo, Jasp, c'mon back!" His voice was muffled and strange. I squeezed out of my seat and walked to the bedroom. It was empty.

"Nuh-uh, back here, buddy," he said in the same distant tone. I leafed through the curtain and poked in my head. The room was small, dark and, most of all, smoky. It held only two chairs, a lava lamp and Billy, who was wearing a Joan Jett shirt, stiff jeans and Vans, which I thought were extinct. It was an odd ensemble, but it fit him. He was everybody, all rolled into one.

And oh yeah, he was wearing a gas mask.

Seemed he had a different way of getting in the mood.

At first I thought it was a Stormtrooper. But it was Billy all right, arms stretched out like he was about to conduct an orchestra. The smell was powerful and ripe and sour. I'd wandered into, well, into the pot-smoking room.

"Hey hey, welcome to my palace," he echoed through the thick, green plastic. "Come and get ya some!"

The rolling smoke jolted my memory, and I realized that I'd smelled marijuana three times. In Ohio, I walked into our garage once and stood quietly behind a huddle of guys who were passing around a cigarette and laughing uncontrollably. I wondered then why they didn't just use their own. The things couldn't be that expensive, because mom choked down a couple dozen cancer sticks a day. Anyway, Matt spotted me and swooped me away, but the smell stuck somewhere in my head.

I caught it again at the Beach Boys concert, when I burrowed up close to the stage and got sizzled on the shoulder by a guy with another of those tiny smokes. Same smell, too, like a scalded potato chip.

And earlier, the odor floating from Billy's car was definitely the one I'd filed away.

I wasn't thick enough to think that it wasn't around. I mean, the stoners at school were called stoners for a reason. But the guys I ran around with stuck to cheap beer and chewing tobacco, so I never crossed paths with it in person.

Until then.

In the ways of pot, I quickly learned that gas masks worked opposite. Instead of keeping smoke out, they let smoke in, and in bunches. At least that's what I figured out after Billy pulled off the thing and instantly looked like Los Angeles.

"Here, your turn," he exhaled. Then he let loose with a thick, deep cough that reminded me of the waiting room at the doctor's office.

I wasn't the greatest at peer pressure. I was the type who needed somebody there to yell *no* at me or to slap me around a little. Otherwise, I usually just went with the flow. Stick something in my face, throw in a few eyeballs gawking my way, and I was pretty much history. But up until then, the worst thing dangled in front of me had been a bottle of Scotch. And even I was experienced enough to know that you had to be at least 60, maybe 70, to drink Scotch.

***

My head wasn't really made for a gas mask. Billy tightened the straps, but it was still loose and shaky. It was like my first football helmet, only made for a different kind of hit.

"So, um, what do I do?" I asked.

"Just open up and say 'ah,'" he said, firing up a match and dangling it in front of a patch of green. "Then when ya feel the heat, suck in hard and enjoy the ride."

"Oh, okay." My voice was distant, as if it wasn't even me talking. I couldn't believe that it was. Five minutes later, after two tugs on the thing, I felt like a human pin cushion.

"Ain't nothin' cooler than that, huh?"

So I was enjoying the ride to the show. A guy didn't get to roll around in a red Trans Am with a high-dollar stereo every day. The music tickled the back of my neck, and my head was heavy as I watched the headlights buzz by. Up ahead, the Midtex Coliseum came into focus, and the marquee sign flashed bright lights, one by one. It wasn't funny, but I couldn't help laugh. Just to the left, a Kentucky Fried Chicken sign promised a bucket for $6.99. Man, it sounded almost as good as Def Leppard.

The gas mask had fit well enough after all.

At the stoplight, I glanced over and caught a sweet blonde looking at me. She turned away quickly. I kept staring. And staring. She had to have known. Girls, they always knew. When the light changed, she tore away, never looking back. That was another difference between us; guys had much longer attention spans.

For whatever reason, I thought of Vickie Sorenson, my first car date. It was our sophomore year, and I wasted about three hours and 30 bucks on the softball toss trying to win her a prize at the carnival. I ended up with a sore arm, Vickie got a John Stamos mirror and a Wham! keychain, and the con man with the patch eye got a bigger hug from her than I did.

Later, her dog busted open the bathroom door while I was taking a crap at her house. That was bad enough, but her folks were in the next room playing Sorry! with a bunch of friends, so pretty much the whole block got a peek and a whiff. Then there wasn't any toilet paper, so I had to waddle out of there.

It was our first and last date, and I wasn't too Sorry! about that.

"Doin' alright there, capt'n?" Billy asked as we edged into the parking lot.

I nodded and smiled.

I didn't feel ashamed, and I didn't feel proud.

I just felt really hungry.

"Out of sight," he said, backing into a spot like only sports cars were allowed to do. "Good tunes, good buzz, ain't nothin' cooler."

He flipped off the car and hoisted a beer. "To tonight." Sounded good to me. I raised mine and clanked it to his. "To tonight." The beer tasted like tin on my thick tongue.

The coliseum was packed. As we pushed past the ticket booth and through the turnstile, I struggled to get my body to come along. My head rung with the buzz of conversations that bounced off the walls, and my eyes were fixed on the stampede of bouncing heads. I couldn't ever remember feeling more awake and less aware. But I hung close to Billy, who seemed a seasoned pro at mastering crowds. He grabbed my arm and together we shuffled, sideways walked and ducked through the mob. In minutes, we were just right of center, about fifteen rows back.

"Here ya go." It was Billy, joint in hand, chest drawn in deeply.

"Um, no, think I'll wait." I thought it was a good idea, since I could no longer feel my legs.

"Hey, your call," he said, shrugging. He took a big drag, and the tip turned beet red. Didn't even look around first. I did. The guy on the other side of me, the one with the spiked wristbands, was smoking the stuff out of a corn-cob pipe. He looked mean, and his tattoos even meaner. Never that crazy about spikes or tattoos, I scooted closer to Billy.

It wasn't the Beach Boys crowd. These people seemed bigger and hairier, even the women. I felt small, not in size as much as in experience and intention. These were concert people in search of a big show and a bigger buzz. I was a radio listener and a foot tapper with a bigger buzz than I cared to have. I probably had some friends scattered throughout the stands, but not down there, not with the leather-and-chains crew.

For the first time, I wondered how the video tournament at the mall was going.

"Sure ya don't want a hit?" Billy again offered up the joint, which was by then no bigger than an eraser tip.

Sounded like he'd been slugged in the stomach.

I shook my head. I loved the feeling and all, but I didn't like it too much. Plus, I was starving to death. Good thing that Ghandi guy didn't smoke, I thought. And that made me giggle a little. Heck, everything made me giggle a little. I wasn't alone, though. Everyone in the section had smiles cemented on, like a bunch of Ronald McDonalds.

Soon the lights fell and the opening act started. The group was called Loud or Crazy or some adjective. Never heard of them, but the name sure fit. Weren't very good, just a screaming gang of long-haired dudes, but they sure were loud. It was all a four-song blur anyway.

During the break, Billy went to the can. I decided to stay put for a basic lack of confidence in moving and tried to take it all in. The crowd clapped, stomped its feet, chanted. The guy next to me reloaded his pipe. He caught me staring and gave me a quick nod and a smile, just like Billy always did in the halls. It was all beginning to all make a little sense.

The lights again faded, and the crowd went wild as Def Leppard hit the stage. The blonde guy with the mike told us that his very favorite place to come was Midtex, and everyone started screaming. Then they started playing. No Billy. They sang a song I recognized from the only rock station in town, then a real wild one I'd never heard. That drummer made more racket with one arm than I could have made with three. Still no Billy.

Finally, halfway through the fourth song, he slid in next to me, his eyes wide and crazy.

"So where've ya been?" I asked. I'd started having bad thoughts.

"Sorry, had to wait for the shitter to clear so I could getta buzz on," he said, sniffing. "Had to change gears a little, ya know?" He wiped his nose. "Mmm, ain't nothin' cooler than the first one." Another sniff.

"Oh, ok." I turned back to the stage and tried not to smile so much.

I had to admit it: Def Leppard put on a pretty good show. They were a little faster than I was used to, but not fast enough to keep a guy from tapping his toes. After every song, the lead singer, a happy guy called Joe, kept telling everyone how much he loved Midtex. We all knew that we were just another tour stop, that tomorrow night he'd be drooling all over Lubbock or Amarillo, but he still managed to make us feel kind of good about ourselves.

Or it could have been the weed.

I wasn't a very good concert person. All around me, people pumped their fists or played air guitars or rocked their heads with the beat. The guy next to me, though a bigtime safety hazard, had taken me in and made me give him at least 25 high fives and three to five head butts.

Up just ahead, a herd of girls rode high on people's shoulders. One was topless, which was nice. I was all for that.

In the stands, a lot of people just sat back in their chairs and clapped or swayed, but claps and sways didn't fly on the 15th row. I tried to strum my air guitar once, but it didn't feel right. Some people were all-out dancing, but I was born without beat. Mostly I just stood there and tried to work up some spit in my mouth. On the bright side, by about the sixth song I didn't feel like Mr. Potato Head so much anymore.

Finally, I snuck away to grab a bite. The foyers were almost empty, leaving an open shot to the snacks, to the chili dog I'd been fantasizing about since the lousy lead-in group. But in turning the corner, I found the most sickening, disgusting sight of my life. The concession stand guy was closing up shop.

"Wait!"

He paid no attention and continued to close the flap.

"Kid, we're out of shirts."

I reached him and tugged on his arm. "Sir, I don't want a shirt. I want a chili dog."

He leaned against the wall. He was thick, short and greasy, like a sausage.

"Please, sir, please. I'm beggin' you. I need a chili dog. I need it." The guy must have worked concerts before. He understood, like a mom understood when you needed a hug. He just knew.

"I need it."

***

I'd eaten three and split a fourth with Spike's wife before Billy showed up again. He was having a blast, but Def Leppard could take little credit. It had taken him a song-and-a-half to find a make-out partner, a short-haired girl with buck teeth and a rose tattoo on her right shoulder. She was pretty nasty but seemed to be an expert kisser. When you closed your eyes, it didn't really matter that much. That was my theory, anyhow.

For most of the concert, they went at it like two hummingbirds. Every third song or so, he would turn to me, say something that I couldn't hear or understand, then return to her. They kissed, smoked, kissed, disappeared for twenty minutes, sniffed, kissed, smoked. In between, random people came up to him, slipped him a handshake and disappeared. Turned out, Billy wasn't much of a concert person, either. Not one pumped fist or nothing.

I was starting to feel pretty normal again. By the time the band left, came back, left, came back and left again, my head and my senses had hooked back up.

I felt an arm fly around my shoulder. It was Billy, or at least a distant relative of the kid from the school hallways. Gone was the boy next door, replaced by a human sweatshop with three blue hickeys and the beadiest, reddest, slittiest eyes I'd ever seen.

"Man, what a show!" he screeched. "Ain't nothin' cooler than a kick ass concert, huh?"

I shook my head. Of course there wasn't. I guess.

He led me through the people, who were still begging for one more, and again threaded through the crowd like Houdini. I still felt a little heavy and slow, but we finally reached the front door. The thick, West Texas air had never felt better.

He unlocked the car, then squinted at me through his slits. "Say, ya wanna go to a kick ass party?"

I looked at the flashing clock on the marquee. 10:14. Still early, plus I didn't have any place to be. To my right, the Pizza Palace lot was stacked with two lines of cars, one heading out, another heading in. Soon, most of them would make a pass and take the two-beer trip back.

"So? The party?"

It was still early, I promised myself. "A party? Uh, sure."

I wanted to listen to some tunes, to feel the music ripping through me like before, but Billy felt like talking. And so he did. He talked about living in L.A. and getting a job laughing for those tapes that they played in the background on sitcoms. I'd always known that that Kirk Cameron guy wasn't really that funny. He talked about living in New York and partying with Adam Ant, the punk singer. He talked about playing the drums in a metal band called The Weeping Sores in Chicago, about picking up older women and sleeping with friends' moms, about stealing a speedboat in Florida. He also said he'd left an "old lady" back in Chicago, a 26-year-old with the special suction powers of a vacuum cleaner. I nodded and hoped silently that if I ever called a girlfriend "my old lady" that she'd pound me.

Billy was either the world's greatest liar, the best-traveled student in Picadilly High history or 34 years old.

I didn't care much either way. I mean, I appreciated people with an imagination. But he talked in a rebellious tone, like he was almost daring me not to believe him. It wasn't that bad, just a little annoying, like a guy who made left turns without using his blinker. Plus, I noticed as we turned onto College Drive that Billy didn't use his blinker, either, so that was kind of a double whammy.

I sat there and nursed the last beer. It tasted warm and stale and didn't even make the 'buschhhhh' sound when I opened it. I studied his hickeys, which were welling up good and would soon be brands of passion. I never really understood them, hickeys. Given the choice of getting bit and bruised, well, I'd just as soon shake hands. But try telling Mary Tatum that. I once showed up to basketball practice with two Mary Specials that I'd caked over real nice with some girl's makeup. Coach Patton had two unbreakable rules -- no fighting and no hickeys. Anyway, the makeup melted away like wet paint once I broke a sweat, and I ended up running bleachers for an hour after practice.

Billy rambled on. All the while, I said nothing and tried to swallow a lot. The cottonmouth thing was murder. After hearing that he once went skinny dipping with Cher, I figured telling him about my life wouldn't hold up. See, like my Uncle Gary, Billy was a big-league topper; if I had a foot, he had 14 yards.

My first consecutive words of the entire ride stopped him cold.

"So whattaya your parents do, anyway?" It was a fair enough question, seeing as he'd taken ten minutes to lap my entire life.

"Aw, fuck my parents." That was all. He snatched the beer from me and turned it up, peeking with one eye to see the road while draining the can. He tossed it in the back.

"We need more brews."

We pulled into the Fast-N-Cheap, an all-night place next to Bingham Junior High. Billy reached into the ashtray and pulled out the fattest collection of bills I'd ever seen, except for on cop shows. It wasn't a briefcase full or anything, but it was at least a year's allowance. I realized the concert had been more of a business trip for him.

He opened his door, then leaned back in. "Say, ya wanna drive?"

Hey, sure I did. The car was sex on wheels. "Really?"

"Yeah, dude, really. Slide on over."

I did. The seat was tilted back too far, but I didn't mind. I figured it was some state law that you had to lean back and drive with one hand if you owned a hot rod. If I drove that thing, I was positive, I'd have a better social life. Or at least think I did.

"Be back in a flash."

And he was, twelve-pack in hand. One snag, though. The old guy from behind the counter was right on his heels, baseball bat in hand. With a pretty nice up-and-under move, Billy ditched him near the dumpster, dove into the passenger's seat and flung the beer in the back.

"Drive dude!"

So I did. Didn't know what else to do. I bounced the curb, leaned on the horn as we tore into traffic and screeched between a blur of honking cars. I felt like either Starsky or Hutch, though I couldn't recall which was which.

"What was that?!?" I cried out as the old guy became a waving, screaming speck in my side mirror.

Billy tossed both his arms up, as if he was reaching the highest peak on a rollercoaster. "Hey, that was a yahoooooooooo!"

Fresh off my first career robbery, I pointed the getaway car into College Gardens. I felt sick. We got lost, then got more lost trying to get back to square one. All the street names were golf related and circled into each other. Augusta hit St. Andrews, which wound around to Masters, which turned into Dogleg Drive. Anyway, we were looking for 1121 Ben Hogan Street, but we ended up behind a pickup truck on Tee Box Lane. There were three scraggly kids in the truck bed, all facing our way, their heads bouncing along. I felt pretty turned around, too, in more ways than one.

"So which way do ya think?" he asked.

"I dunno."

"Well, you're the one that lives 'round here."

I really had no idea. We were in the really, really rich part of town. I lived in the pretty rich part. "Well, let's see,"

I tried. "Guess I'll just go straight."

"Dude, never, ever go straight," he returned, then grabbed the wheel. We swerved wildly to the right, then bumped to a halt at the corner of Bermuda Boulevard and Sand Trap Circle, right under the street lamp. He laughed and dug into his pocket. A few seconds later, a crumpled, plastic baggy full of sugar was hanging between two fingers.

I wanted to believe it was sugar, anyhow.

"Aw, what the hell, let's just make our own party," he said.

Things weren't so funny anymore.

My left eye, always the left, started to twitch.

"Um, what is that?" I asked, afraid to hear the answer.

"Whattaya think it is?" he laughed. "It's snow, man.

Blow, candy, cocaine. Dude, where've ya been?"

He grabbed the keys from the ignition, dipped one into the bag, scooped out a little and covered his right nostril.

With a quick sniff, the powder was gone. Just like that. Didn't spill a flake.

"Wanna snort?"

If I had a nickel for every time I'd heard that one, I'd only have a nickel. But like I said, I wasn't very good with the peer pressure thing. I felt a pull when he offered up the keys. I did. It wasn't so much the desire to do it, but more of a curiosity thing, like putting your tongue on a square battery. Plus, I'd be the first guy on the block to do the stuff, far as I knew. Stinking peer pressure, I thought as I took the keys.

I didn't know too much about coke or candy or whatever. I'd never seen or smelled it, if it even did smell, but did know that it made people run around in circles. And that it was way illegal. And that it had wiped out like half of the Kansas City Royals a few years back. And that a small bundle cost a big bundle. And that it made people do stupid things.

"Hey, what cha doin,' dude?" Billy asked as the engine came to life.

"I'm startin' the car. I want you to take me back to your place."

Heck, I didn't need an expensive, illegal, team-trashing drug to do stupid things. I could do them on my very own, had proven it many times over. Besides, he didn't seem much like a peer anymore.

But it wasn't that easy.

***

"Okay, dude, c'mon," he pleaded. "I know of one more fiesta. If that's not totally rockin,' we'll blaze right back to my pad, no prob, no prob at all."

Well, it wasn't even 11:00 yet, and I still had all night to kill. On the other hand, the guy was shaping up as a convict.

"I dunno...."

"Aw, c'mon." He stretched a hand to my headrest. "Jasper baby, sometimes ya gotta let it all hang out, ya know, dance like nobody's watchin.'"

It was a sucker for stuff like that. "Well, um, okay."

"Cool beans," he said. And we were off. See, I didn't need cocaine at all to do stupid things.

The Hollidome was the setting of the party. It was the probably the most modern building in town, but it was really just a Holiday Inn with an indoor pool. There was also a bar called The Giddyup Saloon where the older crowd hung out. While their precious children snuck around and drank suds and wine coolers, many of the parents in town did the same at The Giddyup.

We got off the elevator and headed for the party. Down below, a few couples were scattered around sipping out of plastic cups by the pool, but besides that the place was still. Except for room 219, which was alive with laughter and music and smoke.

We pushed through the cracked door, and everybody stopped. A record didn't screech or anything, but somebody did trip over the cord to the jam box. The room was pretty packed, and the twin beds were propped against the back wall. I picked up three quick signs that it wasn't my scene. One, it smelled like the concert. Two, it looked like the concert. And three, except for Billy, I had way too many teeth.

"Um, I dunno anyone here," I whispered under my breath.

"Hey, I don't either," Billy said over his breath. Then he had to go and do it. "Hey everyone, I'm Billy Hamilton, and this is Jasper....

I thought about lying, but I was just too tired. "Schitt."

"Sch...," he said before hitting the brakes. It happened a lot. "Say what?"

"Schitt."

The room exploded, just like back in Mrs. Burnett's fifth-grade class, just like so many times in my life. Only this crowd looked more likely to sniff paste than to eat it.

"Dude, you're a riot," Billy said with a nudge.

"Ya'll c'mon in," said the guy with no shirt. "Beer's in the tub."

Someone plugged in the music, and Billy Squier started hollering again. The guys in the corner squished back together, the drinking game at the table started up again and the couple on the floor went back to dry humping. We were in, accepted. Sometimes my name was a real icebreaker.

"Hey, I'm going to grab a brew," Billy said. "You in?" "Sure."

I was all for parties, because parties meant girls. But there weren't any girls in room 219, only women, and not the kind of women who swapped plastic containers or had those fondue parties. These were party women, and from the look of things, they belonged to the party men in the smoking section, which Billy had joined. He was holding two beers, as promised, but was in no hurry to get back to me. Over there, he was in his element. As for me, standing in the corner next to a tableful of Pat Benatar impersonators, I was way out of my league.

My options were simple. I could leave, but thanks to the chili dogs, the beer stop and the lies, I had just under two dollars left with a night to burn.

Or I could stay.

"I've never given head to someone in an elevator," said the lady with the black eye.

Yeah, I stayed for that.

Everybody laughed, nodded and drank. Except for me. We were playing "I never...," a drinking game where a given person made some off-the-wall remark and the others took a swallow, but only if they'd ever done it. Anyway, the girls had been throwing down beer after beer; my first and only one was half full. But I was playing by the rules and all. It's just that I'd never given head to anyone anywhere at anytime. Like I'd ever drink on that one anyway.

"Okay, your turn, Schitthead," said the one with the purple hair. She wasn't trying to be mean, just funny. I didn't mind. I was honestly beginning to believe that Jasper Schitt was much better than Joe Smith. Really, I was.

"Okay, um, I've never woken up with a whole bunch of strangers," I said with a shrug.

Everyone laughed, nodded and drank. I did, too. I never had, but I thought my night was leaning that way, so what the hell. For a half hour or so, it had been kind of fun. But after three times that, I was learning way too much about my playing partners. I mean, I thought it was sort of cool that two of them had a birthmark down there, and even cooler that they'd shown them to me, but there was a limit. It was 1:21, and my lids were heavy. Plus, I didn't think I could hear Billy Squier belt out "Stroke Me" one more time.

"Yer so cute!" said the lady with the chew. She scooted a little closer. Yep, definitely time to go.

I made my way to the bathroom line. For the past hour, people had been ducking in there and coming out all white and distant, like zombies. Hadn't seen Billy the entire time, though I heard an echoed 'ahhhh' or 'yesss' every now and again. He made friends more easily than me.

I pushed to the front, past men twice my age. "Hey buddy, wait your turn," one growled.

But I was tired. Of waiting. Of Billy. Of the whole thing. The night reminded me of those paddle boats you could rent. They were fun at first, but after awhile they just sucked.

The bathroom was small and smelled like piss and beer. Except for Billy on the toilet and the curly-haired guy at his feet, there wasn't room for much of anything else. Oh, except for the needle, which was sticking out of Curly's left arm.

Aside from my lifelong fear of them, I didn't know anything about needles. Didn't care to know either, though I could guess that Billy wasn't giving out free booster shots.

"Jasp!" Billy caught me near the front door. "What's up, man?"

"That's just too much, Billy," I said.

Tell you the truth, a lot of the night had been too much.

"Aw, c'moooon, maaaan," he purred. "It's all about the heartbeat, man. Besides, hey, like I said, sometimes ya gotta dance like nobody's watchin.'"

But everybody was watching. Stillness had filled the room, and I could feel the weight of their stares as Billy hung over me. His eyes were barely open, with blue circles forming under each one, and he wore a crooked smile. Billy might have seemed like everybody and everything all jammed into one, but it occurred to me in the smoky stink of a hotel bash that he was really an elective-taking, Vans-wearing, drug-pushing nobody. A loser, a nothing.

"Billy...I can't dance."

And I couldn't, either.

His smile disappeared. And after sneaking under a hug attempt from the snuff lady, so did I.

From the shag carpet in the lobby, I saw that the party didn't make it much longer. A skinny guy in a blue jacket knocked on the door, talked to the purple-haired lady and walked away. A few minutes later, the same skinny guy and a security guard knocked on the door, talked to the purple-haired lady and leaned against the railing. Thirty seconds later, the room was empty, except for Billy Squier.

The guard was a fake cop, but he carried a real gun.

Billy came out last. He stumbled left before drifting back to his right. Using the railing as a crutch, he wandered down the hall, getting smaller and smaller. I wondered what would happen to him. I figured that pretty soon he'd run out of drugs or friends or heartbeats, maybe all in the same night. Maybe before the sun came up.

So I was waiting for a cab outside, wondering how I was going to pay the driver, when I got my first break of the night. Jimmy Kroger's dad came lunging out of The Giddyup, laughing with and leaning on a painted-up blonde. Jimmy Kroger had red hair. So did his mom.

"Um, Mr. Kroger?"

They stopped in a heap and turned to me as one. He moved a step nearer, shut one eye and stretched his neck out. "Jasper? Jasper? Is that you, Jasper?"

"Yessir, yessir it is."

He gave the blonde a stiff-arm, separating himself from her by three yards, and wandered up to me. His breath was sour and hot, and I noticed a tan line on his bare wedding finger as we exchanged, finally, a regular handshake. "Jasper my boy, what are, uh, what are you doin' here, son?"

The question could have worked both ways. "Well, it's kind of a long story, but I need to borrow some money."

He couldn't have been nicer. I probably could have gotten more out of him, but twenty bucks was fine.

Besides, we both had dirt, and I was no snitch.

Head over Hormones

Sometimes I figured a guy had to shoot for the moon.

Forget term papers or final exams or sheepskins. Mandy Drake was my senior project. Had been since the fifth week of senior year, when Mrs. Clifton, my World History teacher, broke up the pre-class buzz and announced her arrival.

"Class, I'd like to introduce you to Mandy Drake, a transfer student from Athens, Georgia."

It was tradition, of course. Ever since I'd almost been laughed out of grade school, new kids were always being herded in front of the class and thrown to the wolves. Usually an awkward silence would follow as the poor sap shuffled to the back row. Sometimes a 'hello' would come from a teacher's pet looking to score points. But this was the first time I ever heard applause, and it came from almost every boy in the room.

I was no exception. Hey, I'm not too proud to admit it. You really couldn't help it. It was either clap or fall out of your chair, and that would have been too obvious. Standing in front of the U.S. map, she bowed her head and blushed. I shifted my attention and saw Kip Hebner, a football player with one eyebrow but a sweet car, nudging another jock strap to his left. Kip would be trouble.

The girl was a knockout. Her blonde hair was lynched into a long ponytail, exactly how I liked it, and through her wide smile her teeth looked like perfect piano keys. She was about five-foot-six give or take, a perfect height to tilt up and look into the eyes of a six-footer like, well, like me for instance. I'd dated a hoops player named Nina Pritchard the summer before, and even though she had a deadly jump hook, it was no picnic making out with a girl who could hardly fit in the back seat of anything less than a four-door jalopy.

And the body, well, there was the body. She wasn't wearing anything special, a pair of Jordache jeans and a hot pink Izod shirt, but she made it special. It looked like her outfit had been welded on, and I gave a quick thanks to the heavens for tight clothes and tighter bodies. The "Sports Illustrated" models hanging all over my bedroom wall had nothing on this girl. Well, maybe a little, but Cheryl Tiegs wasn't standing in Mrs. Clifton's World History class in September of 1985.

Just looking at her made your heart do a Mary Lou Retton.

"Hi y'all."

Two words. I swear that's all it took. It wasn't a trailer park twang, like so many of my classmates had inherited and perfected. It was a real-life drawl, a smooth invitation to come on over and stay awhile. At least that's what it sounded like humming around Margaret Finkle's fried hair at the back of the room. Mandy was that Scarlett O'Hara lady with a wicked tan.

I saw us running through the field together like a couple from some dream sequence on a movie of the week. I saw our children with her flowing hair and golden skin and my, well, and her everything. Okay, I'll cut it out. But I did see her blur by Kip and slide into a desk right next to me.

"Hi," I whispered before she even had a chance to blink.

"Hello," she returned softly, with a warm smile to boot. "I'm Jasper." I offered my hand.

"Hey, Jasper, I'm Mandy."

She left me hanging for a sec before reaching out. Her hand was as soft and warm as a fresh bagel. I might have held on too long and too tight, because you would have thought she was starting a mower when she pulled away.

Still, it was a start.

Mrs. Clifton, who had a reputation for falling asleep during her own lectures, called the class to order. But she might as well have been Charlie Brown's teacher, because I understood nothing she said for the next 51 minutes. Pure vibrations. After all, fate was three feet away. Why else would Mandy have ignored the scattering of empty desks up front and made a beeline for the back? We had locked eyes briefly, when she stood at the front with more confidence than I'd ever seen from a person, and I'd given her my best stare. The attraction was undeniable.

At least it was to me.

***

Turned out, it wasn't to her. Mandy lasted only two days in our class, two hours that saw me make no progress beyond that stiff introduction, before she was transferred into Texas History. Happened that she'd heard the same World History routine back in Georgia. I didn't see why she couldn't take it again, make an easy 'A' and all and let me ease into things, but the suits of the school didn't give a flip about my hormones. Neither did she, judging from the fact that she never once looked my way or spoke to me again. As it was, the window had slammed right on my libido thingee.

Tell you the truth, there wasn't much of an opening anyway. Mandy was what we called a dude magnet, instantly becoming the object of every guy's obsession whether he had a shot or not. It looked like a tennis match when she walked back and forth between classes, and she soon acquired a daily pack of drooling escorts. There was Bobby Cauble between first and second, Todd Gillard between second and third, Kenny Williamson between third and fourth. I usually didn't see her during the second part of the day, but I figured there were plenty more Bobbys, Todds and Kennys waiting their turn. Anyway, the line was long, and having lost my only edge, I was clear at the back of it.

Still, a guy could fantasize, no matter where or who he was. I mean, nobody ever closed his eyes in class, played a game of pocket pool and thought about Janet on *Three's Company* or Thelma from *Scooby Doo.* Chrissy and Daphne, they were the ones.

So I had hope, if no real chance.

"Whattaya think she'd say if I asked her out?" I asked

Mike Handler one day between classes. She sped past with James Vicks, giggling at something he'd said and flashing every tooth in her perfect head. I'd known Jimmy since seventh grade and had never once heard him say anything funny. That was the thing about babes; they brought out the best in a guy.

"Asked who out?" Mike was finishing my Algebra homework, a regular deal for writing his English papers, and hadn't noticed or even smelled her stroll by. He hadn't missed a math problem in like four years, so numbers always came first.

"Mandy."

"Mandy?"

"Yeah Mike, Mandy."

"Mandy from Health and Nutrition?"

"No, the new Mandy right over there." I pointed to her as she turned the corner.

He only caught a glimpse, but her back was almost as good as her front. "Ah ha, not bad."

He tidied up the last worthless word problem, leaving only my signature left to seal the deal. Did anyone really care how long it would take eight pigs to finish off a 44-gallon trough of slop? Working our way through tests was trickier, but we'd devised a system including large numbers and small distances. He cradled the paper to his chest and smiled a little.

"So, whattaya think?" I asked impatiently. The bell was ringing, and Ruby D. Johnson, our wig-wearing teacher and a lady who probably pre-dated the abacus, wasn't hip on tardies.

"Quick, whattaya get when ya add a negative to a negative?"

I was no math whiz, but I knew that one. Grade-school stuff.

"Negative."

"Exactly," he said, tossing me the homework. "Same as with you and this Mandy. Negative."

With that, he escaped into the room. The paper floated to the floor, right along with my spirits.

I knew he was right, because, for starters, Mike was almost always right. The smartest kid in school, or at least the smartest kid with a name you could pronounce, Mike also found time to become a pretty good athlete and all-around good guy, a know-it-all who didn't act like he knew it all.

***

We had loads in common from the start. He moved to Midtex from Pennsylvania in sixth grade, just a year after me, and stood in the front of the class with a Shazam! T-shirt and red Toughskins while Mrs. Garner introduced him. He looked so lost, standing there like a big fruit rollup with wavy black hair that curled up at the ends, and I knew exactly how he felt.

We were a natural fit. We still rooted for our hometown teams - he the Phillies, Eagles and Sixers, me the Browns, Indians and Cavs - and talked often about our shared longing for snow, or at least a rush of cool air every once in a while. Some Texans had actually still never seen the stuff, snow. I mean, we'd played basketball the year before on Christmas day. And gotten sunburned.

Mike did go a bit overboard once over his admiration, maybe even passion, for Dr. J by ordering some Philadelphia 76ers cologne that smelled like bottled sweat. Who knows, maybe it was. Still, he was a good guy with an even better house.

See, the Handler home was the hub of entertainment on our block. Name something that a kid wanted, and the Handlers had it. A ping-pong table, a swimming pool, a hoops court complete with a free-throw line, the first computer on the block. And it wasn't one of those blocky, science fiction computers with the big wheels and flashing buttons, either. He had Asteroids, Space Invaders, Tron, the works. People said that one day we would do everything by computer, but Asteroids for now was just fine with me.

It was like the Boys Club or the YMCA, a clubhouse where bored boys with nothing to do could find anything to do. And you didn't even have to be a member. Mike wasn't filthy rich or anything - I think his dad was a numbers cruncher, and his mom was a teacher - but you couldn't tell a kid from the block that. It was a funhouse, a play palace, and guys flocked there. I told Mike he should have charged a membership fee, waiving mine of course. I'd been there from the beginning, through Mike's oily hair and bad complexion and headgear and into his gradual graduation into coolhood. Over the years, the Handler house became the place to be.

***

In May, after senior year floated by much like all the rest, it was good and primed to become the setting of my first time.

My first time.

Now, don't get me wrong. I'd made out with my share of girls, starting with Suzy Brown in the summer after seventh grade and continuing all the way to Angela Green the weekend before. Come to think of it, counting Shelly Black my freshman year, I'd covered almost every primary color.

And though most of the girls I dated reminded me of the Picadilly defense, giving up some yardage but not many touchdowns, I'd been real close once.

The summer before, I did the backseat tango with Kelsey Lanier, a lanky sophomore who dropped her pants almost on command. Anyway, I thought I was on my way until she told me about her monthly "little friend." Hadn't seemed like a friend to me.

So anyway, I was a virgin.

What of it?

In my general circle of friends, or even in a wider circle of non-friends, I think I was about the only one left. See, in a small town, there wasn't a heck of a lot else to do but make out. And judging from all the locker room talk, everyone was scoring. Billy Cross had even been with two girls in one night, having ditched the bonfire with Amy Bigsby and come back later to fetch Cara Clark. The guy got more action in two hours than I'd had in 17 years. Twice as much, even.

Even Casper Morgan claimed to have bagged Tina Chase, a thick girl who wore even thicker glasses. I guess her specs must have fogged up plenty, too, because Casper, while a solid defensive end, was the spitting image of Lerch from *The Addams Family*.

"So guess who 'ol Casper nailed in the Burger King parking lot last weekend?!?" he croaked.

Whoops and hollers.

"I always knew she was a prime piece of burger!" Whistles and towel popping. Stuff like that.

I always bagged it during such story hours. Nobody wanted to hear about second base, or even about getting tagged out at home. Slam-bam action, that was the ticket to attention in the showers. Sometimes I thought about flatout lying, maybe stretching a long single into a home run, but always decided against it.

See, here was another thing about small towns; you lied about getting some ass, and it came back to bite you right there. I showered next to plenty of the proof every day.

I did okay with the girls because I knew my place. I wasn't filthy rich or especially great looking or an all-state anything. But I also wasn't poor or a goon or a spaz. So I just dated the girls who liked sort of rich, not real ugly guys who could play a little ball, the girls you didn't have to worry about all the time and who didn't make guys go around trying to slug people and walls and windows.

I was probably like the abstract paintings we learned about in Art. Some people dug it; some didn't. Besides, being super popular meant wearing and saying and doing all the right things all of the time. Seemed like a lot of work.

I figured I'd ride out the slump. There was no shame in that. Maybe I didn't have any notches on my belt, but at least I had a belt. I was probably one of the lucky ones. There was no locker room talk for people in the Latin Club. Heck, they didn't even have a locker room.

***

Mandy's was one name I never heard being dished around after practices. She'd gotten snatched up early in the year by Andy Copeland, a two-sport star and basic Mr. Everything around our campus. Andy was rich, tall and, I'm not ashamed to say it, pretty darn handsome, and girls were always getting all flustered over him. Plus, he worked at Chess King, so he wore cool leather outfits with lots of zippers and pockets and stuff. It was darn near impossible to compete with someone in a Don Johnson jacket.

Guys like Andy always ended up with the Mandys of the world. Put together, they looked like a wedding-cake top working the halls, and there were even rumors that they might tie the knot after graduation.

I had Andy in two classes during spring semester, and we were pretty good friends. Not homework swapping buddies or anything, but casual friends. During Mrs. Sharp's English class one day in late-May, just a few daydreams before graduation, I thought I'd ask him about Mandy, pour some salt in my wounds and all that. "So Andy, I hear ya might be gettin' hitched."

Andy, who despite his many attributes wasn't the sharpest tack in the wall, crinkled his eyebrows.

"To what?"

I needed a simpler approach. "Gettin' married. To Mandy."

Andy didn't look up, instead concentrating on the construction of a paper football. Thumping a folded square between finger goalposts was big sport at Picadilly, and Andy, damn him, was probably the best I'd ever seen. A real paper football god.

"Dude, I broke up with her. That's way over."

It was all news to me. In fact, it must have been breaking news, because such priceless info would have already spread like one of those grease fires. The Romeos would be flocking.

I pressed on. "Really? Wow, I, um, didn't know that. Um, since when?"

The paper football was good and pressed. Andy gave it a ferocious plimp, and it whirled end over end toward Stacy Sanderson's skull.

"Second period," he snorted. "Ouch!"

"What's goin' on back there?" Mrs. Sharp hollered.

That's all I got out of him. The guy wasn't much one for conversation anyway, and he really didn't need it. You drove a sports car and lived on your own block and looked like Ricky Schroeder, you could pretty much grunt your way into the sack. That was practically law.

"Now don't forget, class, your research papers are due Friday," said Mrs. Sharp, waving her finger at us as we gathered our books. "If they're not on my desk by 4:00, not one second later, you can forget about graduating on time."

Mrs. Sharp was always making threats like that, like a guy's future balanced on passing a weekly spelling quiz. But since our senior research papers were worth 40 percent of our final grade, it was pretty important that I at least got started on the thing. She'd given us a list of lame topics to choose from, and I'd picked Daniel Defoe, some British writer who'd been dead forever. Never heard of him before, but I was pretty sure he hadn't written any of the sports books that lined my bookcase at home. And Pete Rose hadn't been an option.

By the way, despite her crabby ways, Mrs. Sharp was my favorite teacher. Somewhere within the punctuation rules and the painful sonnets, she had taught me a love of words. Not like the Shakespeare stuff, which seemed like a maze of fancy phrases that only teachers with cheat-sheet teacher books understood, but regular stuff like, well, like this. I actually enjoyed writing, liked wrestling around with sentences until they didn't suck anymore, and even thought of one day pursuing it as a career.

Sure it was a longshot, but, with no interest or skill in too much of anything else, I was looking for anything to latch on to. Besides, nobody ever dreamed of being a pipe fitter or a carny; people just kind of became one.

As we shuffled out of class, I thought about a code that Mrs. Sharp lived by. Whenever she gave us a grammar or spelling rule, she would always wander to the chalkboard and point at a little, neat paragraph etched in the upper-left corner that said, "This is the rule. But remember: there's an exception to every rule. There's even an exception to this rule."

I wasn't exactly sure what it meant, scribbled there in bright orange against the green backdrop, but Mrs. Sharp loved it, even threatening the life of anyone who erased it. It was her favorite threat. Sometimes, when she was out of the room, a kid would grab an eraser and act like he was going to rub it out. Everybody would laugh and egg him on, but the kid would inevitably set the eraser back and return to his seat to a round of *boos.* Deep down, though, we all understood. Behind her round glasses and bright-red blush, Mrs. Sharp was built like a furnace.

I personally kind of liked the saying, because to me it meant that anything could happen. An 'i' didn't have to come before an 'e.' A sentence could sometimes end with a preposition.

And a Mandy Drake didn't have to date the most popular guy in school. As I laced up my spikes before ball practice, I knew I'd fallen off the wagon. Mandy was my addiction all over again.

Really, I was obsessed for a couple of reasons. The first, the physical part, was a gimme. But it was also because of the Kevin Petrie Effect. For years, Kevin was this scrawny kid in my grade who nobody really noticed, a missing person who wasn't really missed. At least until the hiccups. Kevin started hiccuping early in seventh grade and kept it up for almost two straight years. Anyway, along the way somebody called the folks at *That's Incredible*, the show about people who could do kooky stuff like drive nails though their tongues, and that foxy Cathy Lee Crosby lady came down and did a big story on him. Saw him on national television, just hiccuping and burping his brains out.

After that, he was the most popular kid around for a good month or two. Got so close to the U.S. record that the Guinness people started sniffing around, but he finally kicked the habit when Sue Nagorski snuck up from behind and scared him. He tried to get it rolling again, but it was no use.

Couldn't much blame him; 'Ol Sue Nagorski was pretty spooky.

But Kevin had a good run, and people still talked about it. Well, dating Mandy wouldn't exactly land me on prime time, but it would make me a hit in the showers.

***

It wouldn't be easy, because the break-up wasn't classified info. On the way to practice, I saw Terry Bice walking with Mandy, his Picadilly cap pulled down to his eyeballs and his chest all bloated like a peacock on steroids. Bowing up was nothing new for Terry, but he looked especially puffy walking next to the school's top trophy.

Mandy, as always, looked like a door prize. Over the months, she had taken to letting her hair fall loosely down her back, her wings peeled on both sides of her ears, and her skin was still bronzed and smooth. Even with Andy at her side, there was always a parade of peeping Toms and Todds and Jims between classes. Moving on to these skimpy skirts as the Texas sun started getting serious, she always seemed to know how far she could stretch the school's dress code. Not that Mr. Dosh, our principal, would have done anything. The guy was a pushover, and Mandy was a killer.

She approached with Terry, weaving through the freshman hall. Her walk was more of a wiggle, and her breasts were ample and alert. The freshman boys slugged each other and laughed as she passed, probably not really knowing why yet but at least recognizing quality when they saw it.

"Oh, hey there, Jasper."

I didn't, maybe couldn't, make a sound in return, and she disappeared out the C-hall door. But that wasn't the point. She actually remembered me from that first week of school, back when she was a nobody and before the thought of her belonged to every stiff around. She remembered my warmth and kindness, the way I reached out to make her feel welcome.

Okay, so at least she remembered my name.

"So did ya hear that Copeland trashed Mandy Drake?" Ricky Fletcher's words shot across the diamond. I was a varsity first baseman/pitcher by then, while Ricky was our third baseman who was even better at dishing out scoop than taking outside pitches to the opposite field. His throw had barely reached my mitt before the chatter began to fly around the horn.

"No freakin' way!" yelled Lazarus Gonzago, our slick-fielding shortstop. Laz was no threat, having just used up three of the eight or so English words that he knew.

"Dude, she's mine!" returned Hut Kurch, a squatty second baseman. Hut was dating Rhonda Ronstein, a girl half a foot taller and at least fifty pounds heavier than he.

Not a prayer.

"She'll cry on my shoulder all night long, baby!" It was Ricky, who pretty much picked out girls like Babe Ruth called his home runs. Definitely a contender.

"Hey now, that's enough. Let's turn two."

Those final words came from Coach Davie, who always had the final say. Coach was a stern, religious man and former minor leaguer who had little patience for either small talk or missed signs. Wasn't what you would call a baseball genius, but he had skippered a pretty average team to an 18-9 record and second place entering the last week of the regular season.

Baseball had hardly become Picadilly's national pastime, not even close really, but I'd still spotted a couple of football players at our games. They were there for the pep girls, but still.

Around Midtex, there were some hard-to-miss differences between baseball, my favorite sport, and football, most everyone else's favorite sport. The football team had won like six state titles and earned at least as many trips to the title game, while the baseball program had made a couple of quick trips to the playoffs. They had a glass trophy case; we had a wobbly trophy shelf littered with a few wobbly trophies. They had pep rallies; we got popcorn balls in our lockers on game days. Their coach, a stout, stern guy named Jack Wilson, had a shiny company car and his own postgame television show; Coach Davie had a rusty Subaru Brat and a television in his office, which was no bigger than a wide receiver.

We both had Gojo, but it seemed to work better on the football field.

You get the picture.

They probably deserved the attention. I mean, those guys milked more out of their talent than that Martin Mull guy. A few months back, Picadilly made it to the state finals behind the heroics of a knobby-kneed kid named Justin Herron, a quarterback who couldn't really run or throw or do much of anything but win. Herron was harder to knock down than a Weeble, and you could imagine him saying "must....win.....game" like Superman fighting off kryptonite. Somehow, he and his gang of misfits - heck, even six Bingham Jr. High alums started - always found a way. They got waxed in the championships by an all-black, big-city team whose players had mustaches and kids (also with mustaches) in the stands, but it didn't matter by then.

People either loved or hated Picadilly, and I'd done my share of both, but I was sold on the Gojo thing. The stuff was mystical, magical, marvelous, at least when mixed with a bunch of rabid fans and kids who were terrified to fail.

***

After infield and during the monotony of batting practice, when players took their hacks and then trotted to the outfield to swap stories and hock loogies, the subject shifted from Mandy to Skip Day.

"So who'ths bailing th'morrow?" asked Lucius Thayer, our catcher and a kid unlucky enough to have been born with a lisp. It hurt to hear the poor guy try to say his own name.

Every year on the last Friday of school, just before exam week and only four days away, any senior worth his diploma would ditch class and head out to the Monahans Sand Hills. A desert within our desert, the dunes were about 40 minutes away, a bald stretch paved with nothing but sandy peaks and valleys for miles around, and the site of an all-day, once-a-year blowout. Kegs, volleyball, sand surfing and backseat brawls were the norm, with sobriety and sanity being the exceptions. At least that's what everyone said.

Although skipping was a Picadilly tradition, and I was a traditional kind of guy, I still hadn't decided to go or not yet. After all, I was scheduled to take the mound against Abilene Cooper on Friday, and the Cougars were in first place and ranked third in the state. I was pumped. I wasn't our best pitcher by any stretch, but Cooper seemed to struggle against lefties, and besides a pint-sized scab named Harlan Carpenter, I was our only southpaw. And Harlan didn't take much to pressure, having hyperventilated and fainted during his only at-bat of the season.

Plus, my research paper was due the afternoon of Skip Day, and that Defoe guy was still a complete mystery to me. I've got to admit, school didn't do that much for me. I always wondered why we didn't take classes about how to have a good marriage or how to raise a kid right and were instead force-fed those logarithmic equations and stories about stuff that had already happened.

Still, writing was kind of big to me, and, strange as it sounded in my own head, I didn't want to let Mrs. Sharp down.

Driving home, my thoughts shifted back to Mandy. Word was out. She was a free woman, fair game. Plus, after getting canned, she might even be on the rebound.

Sometimes the only way to get a girl was when she was good and down. The guys in her classes would have the inside track, but there would be plenty of competition. Only one thing went faster in Midtex than football tickets - a peach. I had less than a week to do the impossible.

***

For the next three days, I followed the same pathetic pattern. I stationed myself smack dab in her between-bell path at school, hoping for an opening. None came. Mandy was always closely guarded and sometimes even flanked on both sides, like her looks were worthy of the Secret Service.

Wednesday nights were hoops night at Mike's. Usually there was a good-sized game worked up, maybe a three-on-three war, but on a sticky night during exam week it was strictly one on one. Mike was a dead eye of a shot, but his lack of height and glaring slowness worked against him in the full-court game. Didn't make the varsity squad, and that bugged me as much as it did him, but he was a heck of a half-court warrior.

I dribbled in place and searched for an opening. "Say, Mandy Drake is available right now, and I'm thinkin' about askin' her out," I said, then snuck past him and banked in a bucket. My overall game didn't hold a candle to Mike's, but I could blur by him almost at will. Sheer speed had landed me a spot near the middle of the varsity bench, and a complete lack thereof had sent Mike to P.E. with the asthmatics.

It was a cruel, cold world that made little sense.

"Yeah, you and the rest of the school," Mike smirked, whispering in a jump shot. "Jasp, the girl probably already has a date until next November. Good luck, buddy boy."

It would take more than luck, and I knew that. What I needed was a plan.

"So whattaya think I should do?"

Mike muscled me inside. Even though he'd spend a bundle on these "How to Jump" space boots from the back of a magazine, you still couldn't slide a piece of paper under his vertical leap. But he had a family butt, and the force of it always sent me moonwalking. His strategy didn't work against the taller players, but he had my number in the paint.

He banked in a deuce. "Man, you should just stick to the plain ones," he said. "That way, ya don't have to always worry about her gettin' hit on when ya go take a piss at a party."

"C'mon, I'm serious," I said, stopping the action.

"So am I." He swiped the ball and drilled another jumper. Mike went out with Betsy Buckner, a sweet girl who was shaped like a mushroom and always had food and gunk stuck in her braces. Mike could take a bathroom trip to Pluto, and poor Betsy still wouldn't get hit on.

It was good logic and all, but I was in too deep. "C'mon, help me out here. I mean, it would be pretty cool to at least hang out with the girl."

"Well, let's see," Mike said, dribbling over to his favorite spot. "Why don't ya just take a shot..." Swish.

"...and who knows, maybe you'll score?"

I needed to hang out with someone who used fewer metaphors and had more luck with the ladies. Mike was the coolest brainiac I knew, a real mathlete, but it still probably wasn't a good rule of thumb to rely on the president of the Numbers Club for chick advice.

"Yeah, whatever," I said, bouncing a corner shot off the side of the backboard. If Mike's inflated backside hurt him in hoops, shooting was my ultimate downfall.

We played on, our competitive juices taking over and ending any conversation short of arguing over the score. The evening turned to night, and the night turned to late night before Mike had taken me, four games to two, ass over wheels.

"Gotta go," I said, gathering my stuff.

"Hey, we're still on for Friday, for Monahans, right?"

"Oh, um, we'll see." I hopped the fence that surrounded his backyard and headed for the car.

"Oh, c'moooon Jasp," he moaned. "Don't puss out on me now."

But I was pussing out. The paper, the ballgame, the risk of getting busted, it all weighed against a day of getting drunk in the West Texas desert. I'd have all summer to do that. But Mike could be pretty persuasive, and I'd been suckered by him many times.

See, here was another thing about Mike. Along with being the best American-born student in school, he was also one of the best drinkers. And at Picadilly, that was saying something. Of all the goodies at the Handler house, Mike had tapped into the gold mine a year or so back. Although his folks hardly ever touched a drop, they had a stocked liquor cabinet. Said it was for dinner parties, but I never remembered them having a dinner party.

So every so often, on a Friday morning, well maybe a Thursday, occasionally a Wednesday but rarely a Tuesday, we had breakfast with friends. You know, guys like Jack Daniels, Jim Beam and Jose Cuervo. We'd then refill our buddy with water, or maybe a touch of Apple Juice for added color, and head off to tackle the books.

Tests and quizzes, they were cake to Mike. He would chase down a pack of white donuts with a slug of JD, right from the bottle, and go ace an advanced trig exam. Me, I was lucky to stay out of a snot puddle on my desk. A steady diet of soda and gum and maybe a spoonful of peanut butter to fend off close-talking teachers always seemed to do the trick.

So I was thinking about a zillion things on the six-block drive home from Mike's. I knew the guy would probably squeeze at least a liquid snack out of me on Friday morning. Besides, I could use some relaxing after hanging out so much with Defoe. I had finished the paper earlier that morning, and Mom typed it up in 20 minutes flat while I ate breakfast, not a typo in sight. Crazy fast, like John Henry fast. Plus, with the big game approaching, my nerves were shot. The skipping part would take some work, but I was no rock.

***

As for Mandy, well, my chances looked slim. Corralling her at school was a no go, and she would likely be off the market again after the weekend. I decided there was but one option. I hit the gas, hoping that the girl would be like a dogpile after a fumble; just because you didn't get there first didn't mean you couldn't end up with the ball, or the babe.

Her number wasn't listed, but I had my sources. A friend of a friend of a cousin's friend had gotten me her digits the very first week of school, back before Andy and his parachute pants came into the picture, and I'd kept it stashed. It would be easy, I promised myself. Just seven little numbers, a quick question and a quicker rejection and it would be over. I could officially and permanently return to girls like Amby Zuckerman, who would date a doorstop.

At 10:18, I made it through two numbers before hanging up. At 10:38, I crept to the fourth digit before fading. At 10:56, four minutes from lights out for most girls I called, I petted the seventh button. And mashed it. And cringed.

Busy. At 11:13, past my curfew even, busy. At midnight, when dads usually nabbed the receiver first and started hollering, busy. I swear, a guy put his heart on the line, and all he got was a 'duh,' 'duh' and a 'duh' on the other end.

I gave up and hit the sack, feeling a little better that I'd at least tried and promising myself that tomorrow was another day. Then I got to thinking; of course tomorrow was another day. Why in the heck would that have made me feel better? Some sayings were pretty good, but several of them sucked.

"Gather 'round here, sports fans," Mr. Johnstone barked.

"Gather 'round here now."

Harley Johnstone was my Photography I teacher, which was to say that he knew how to smash the shutter button on a camera. I think drinking and chasing young tail were actually his specialties, because he usually smelled like booze and always hung close to the girls who might be having trouble with, say, developing their pictures. And it was probably no accident that he always gave special attention to the ones who themselves were already developed.

He had supposedly worked at the photo place at J.C. Penney's a thousand years back or so, but he'd come to Picadilly during my sophomore year. I wondered if it was a promotion or just a move to better scenery. Anyway, he meant well, but his class was basically a joke. If you were looking for an 'A,' you looked no farther than Room 131 at Picadilly High.

We had a handful of assignments over the semester, none of them too trying. Take some action shots and develop them, he would suggest. If they turned out, fine. If not, great.

Take a roll of nature shots. If the color panned out, fine. If not, just as well. That was life in Mr.

Johnstone's class, which usually doubled as a field trip over to Dunkle's to score some donuts and chocolate milk.

Amazingly, though, our final project proved to be my big break.

"So here's the plan," Johnstone announced just before the bell. He always rubbed his hands together as he spoke, like what he was saying was good stuff. "I want ya to take a series of shots that tells me a story. I don't give a flip what the story's about, just as long as it tells some kind of story. Five shots or so oughta do the trick. Due Monday. Ya got it?"

A couple of people mumbled something over the swish of shuffling feet, but that was it. Like I said before, teachers had it tough, especially in high school. If we happened to hear anything over the roar of our hormones, it sure wasn't some lecture about the Bay of Pigs. Not that it mattered to Johnstone. If we did the assignment, tremendous. If not, eh. Put some honeys in his class, and the guy was happy as a pig in mud.

But before his spiel was even up, my wheels were already spinning. A story about something. Anything at all. I knew before the next bell rang exactly what I was going to do.

Well, exactly what I was going to try to do, anyway.

Mandy would be my story. I didn't know the plot just yet, but she would be the main character. I just had to figure out a scheme that would convince her to join the cast. I'd pulled off bigger scams before.

My third period was office assistance, a perk of being a senior. During this blow-off class, my third snoozer in four hours, we snatched up roll sheets and passed out memos, but mostly we just roamed the halls and checked out the talent. A guy could do some quality gawking with official school business as a cover. I often wondered how the class would apply to my later life. Of course, I often thought the same thing about Algebra, too. And I didn't need to cheat to pass Office Assistance.

It was simple and really pretty smooth, my grand plan. I scribbled 'Mandy Drake' on the pink slip - sloppy as heck, like a doctor - then checked the 'Report to Office Immediately' box. Peeling away from Oscar Morales, my fellow roll picker upper, I hoofed toward Miss Huggins' government class. I knew, of course, Mandy would be sitting there, third row, second seat, having had almost a full year to memorize such minute details.

Miss Huggins was one of the most popular teachers in school. Not really because of her easy-to-understand lectures about the Constitution or for her easy tests, though she was known and loved for both. See, Miss Huggins owned, in no small terms, incredible hooters. Guys - jocks and geeks, whites and Hispanics and blacks, you name it - always jockeyed to get in her class. Hooters broke down all color barriers.

I snuck a peek at Mandy. Although staring in the direction of Miss Huggins, she was wearing a glassy-eyed look and mindlessly chewing some purple gum. I seriously doubted that she was thinking about hooters, but she definitely wasn't thinking about The Bill of Rights, either.

Before knocking, I considered the risks. Should I chance getting busted of fraud and crossing paths with Mr. Dosh just days before graduation? Was she really worth it? Did I actually think it would all work in the first place?

"Yes hun, can I help you?"

Miss Huggins was turned my way, as was every head in the class. Squirrel-out time had passed.

"Um, yes ma'am, um, I have, um...." I dangled the note in my outstretched hand.

"Oh yes, okay, bring it on in," Miss Huggins said warmly, standing and arching back to expose her, um, frequent topics of discussion. She was wearing a bright, yellow sweater, and though I'd never been lucky enough to take her class, it was easy to see why the guys called her Miss "Give Me A" Huggins. Her chest was like a solar eclipse; you weren't supposed to stare, but you kind of couldn't help it.

She took the paper from my hand with a polite smile and skimmed it over hurriedly. "Mandy Drake, you're wanted at the office right away."

Mandy snapped out of her trance and slid slowly from her desk. She brushed by me without so much as a look and grabbed the thing.

"Can I go?" Mandy asked, shifting the gum in her mouth.

"Of course, dear," Miss Huggins said. "Just get your notes from somebody after class."

Mandy nodded and returned to her desk. The eyes of every guy in the room followed her. She was a girl whose moves demanded attention. Artie Masterson looked like he had that slobbery scurvy disease that pirates always got. I sometimes wondered if girls just sat around and laughed their asses off at us.

See, that was exactly why I'd had to resort to such measures. Every sap in the class would be hustling their lecture notes to her, acting as if they cared if she was up to speed in the lesson, taking up every stinking second of her time. You gave a guy an inch with a Mandy around Picadilly, and they'd take it a country mile (assuming that a country mile was longer than a regular mile).

Anyhow, I needed some of that quality time.

This was it.

***

I waited near the room's entrance, pretending that Mandy required an official escort. Finally, she approached, a red backpack dangling from her left shoulder. I turned to go, figuring it would be instinct and all for her to join me. She walked right past me. A few days earlier, she'd remembered me, but she'd forgotten all over again.

What I didn't understand about girls was a lot.

I had about 10 seconds worth of opportunity. At the end of G-Hall, Mandy would hang a right and then head directly toward the stiffs in the office. There, she would find out that the whole thing was a hoax. Not only was my master plan unraveling, but I had about 30 steps to sabotage the whole thing and avoid Mr. Dosh's chronic halitosis.

I walked behind Mandy for a few seconds, finally breaking into a slow jog as the corner approached. The girl was one of those speed walkers. It never failed; the better the girl, the faster she walked. By the time I caught her, my courage was zilch. Not only could I not say anything, but a strange, bullfrog thing had kicked up in my throat. My left eye, always the left, started to twitch.

"Big" Bradley Kissinger, of all people, bailed me out. Big was a lumpy loner who had a reputation for ducking into the bathroom to eat lunch. Nobody was really sure why, but there were always corn dog sticks and flattened mustard patches in the G-Hall pot after the break. I don't even want to get into the symbolism there. Other than that, well and except for being darn near legally blind, the guy was perfectly normal.

Big turned the corner the same time as us, except headed in the opposite direction. He flat-out leveled Mandy, knocking the backpack from her grasp and sending her multi-colored folders sliding across the floor. Big only wobbled, bumped against my outside shoulder and went on without a word. It was almost lunch time. Figured he had to save a stall.

Mandy was lying on her back, her body sprawled about in a position that you would have expected to see a chalkline drawn around her.

"Are you okay, Mandy?" I gasped. Big's blindness kept him out of sports, but the lug could pack a punch.

"Yeah, I think so," she said, propping herself up onto her elbows and shaking her head. "Who was that?"

"Bradley Kissinger," I replied, hunting down the folders.

"You mean Big, the bathroom guy?"

"Yep," I said, feeling slightly defeated. She knew the farsighted, cornie-in-the-can guy, yet had needed a head-on collision to again acknowledge my existence.

As Mandy composed herself, I dusted off her backpack. There was a faded black University of Georgia sticker on the outside of it. I saw a pint-sized ray of hope.

"So, um, do ya miss Georgia?"

"Huh?"

"Georgia. Do ya miss it?"

"Oh. Yeah, I miss it tons. Every single day."

I kept ahold of her belongings. Figured as long as I had that backpack, I had her attention. It was quite slick, really.

"So whattaya miss about it?"

"Well, um, the summers, my old friends, stuff like that." She rose and leaned against a locker and appeared to be in no rush at all. Sure, it might have been the cobwebs, but I pressed on.

"Yeah, I know how ya feel," I said. "I moved here from Ohio a few years back."

Okay, so it had been like 10 years. What of it?

"Oh really? I didn't know that." She worked her neck around slowly but kept her eyes tuned to me. "So ya know how hard it is to be the new kid in school, to be away from friends and stuff. From really good friends?"

I knew exactly how it felt. But I didn't know people like Mandy Drake found much of anything to be hard. I thought they sort of just flowed effortlessly from one situation to the next. Or got a ride to it.

"So, what, you don't like it here?"

"Oh, I dunno. I guess it's just different, that's all."

Then a crazy thing happened. In the between-class silence of G- Hall, right next to Coach Kirk's Biology class, we had an actual conversation. It wasn't earth shaking or anything, though my legs did a little of that. We talked about moving, about our upcoming exams, about the fact that Coach Kirk sounded exactly like a white Richard Pryor. It was small talk, but it felt pretty big to me.

Finally, after five minutes or so, I noticed Mandy eyeing her backpack, which was still firmly in my clutches.

"Anyway..." she said in that certain tone that, if slowed down, would have translated as "um, ya mind givin' me back my books so I can get the heck out of here?" "Oh, yeah, here." I handed it over.

"Thanks." She half-smiled and pivoted toward the office, toward the Land of Explanations.

I checked the clock. Ten 'til 11. And I still had work to do. She turned to leave. It was now-or-never time.

"Um, Mandy?"

She angled back toward me, raising her eyebrows and pushing the hair out of her eyes.

"Well, this is going to sound kinda weird," I began pretty smoothly. "But see, we have this assignment in my photography class where we hafta tell this story with pictures and, um, I was wonderin' if you could help me out with it and, um, see, the reason ya got called to the office is because

I made up that note so I could ask ya out here and it's due Monday and please don't murder me."

It hadn't turned out so smooth. Instead, I was out of both options and oxygen.

Mandy had listened to my ramble with a blank expression, the same one she wore for the next 15 wordless, eternal seconds. I stood there and wondered if girls always waited on purpose, or if it was all part of their master scheme. Finally, she blew a small bubble and trapped it with her lips.

"So…like, I don't really hafta go to the office?"

"Um, no, um, I mean I'd really a lot appreciate it if ya didn't."

Another painful pause as she stared at the floor.

"Well, so, when?"

I'm not proud; I was stunned to get at least get that far.

"Um, tomorrow before school," I blurted quickly.

"Where?"

I moved over to the locker and leaned next to her. She smelled like that suntan lotion that came in the brown bottles. "Mike Handler's house. He lives at 3000 Derrick Street, in the country club area."

She lifted her eyes to me for the first time in a full minute.

"Well...okay, sounds like fun."

As my mom would say, I was floored.

***

It was a restless night. Truthfully, I didn't know what to do next. It reminded me of the time in grade school that I ordered those Sea Monkeys from the back cover of a comic book. For weeks I waited for them and hurried home each day from school to see if they'd come in the mail yet. Then, when they finally did, I had no idea what to do with them. And plus, I couldn't flush Mandy down the toilet. I lay awake that night with the girl branded to the backs of my eyelids.

I arrived at Mike's place earlier than usual, about 7:15. In fact, I had to wait five minutes for Mrs. Handler to leave for school. Parked down the street in hiding, I watched her pull away in a beat-up Chevy Citation, leaving only Mike's faded, yellow Buick in the sloped driveway. The fun stuff pulled rank on cars in the Handler family.

I let myself in. Mike had The Outfield blaring on the stereo, and my favorite song was playing, the one about Josie and her faraway vacation. I found him in the kitchen, stirring a drink with this finger. It was no doubt a stiffy, because that was all that Mike knew how to pour.

"Hola, mi amigo!" he hollered, looking up and licking his finger. He'd been more than happy to accommodate the morning meeting but had appeared unaffected, and hardly even impressed, when I told him the prettiest girl in school would be joining us.

"Why's she gotta come?" he'd asked.

"Mike, you don't ask why to such things, you just say thank you. Besides, you're the one who told me to take a shot."

Mike only shrugged at that. I knew he didn't care if the Pope showed up at the front door, as long as he brought a quart of brew or something good with him.

He took a long swallow from the cup. "Smooth," he said with a deep, pained voice, a dribble trickling onto his shirt.

Another cup, a faded Dallas Cowboy mug with a galloping Tony Dorsett on each side, was waiting for me. It was filled right to the rim and, upon my taste test, was about as smooth as the stubble on his chin. He was one of those guys who only grew facial hair in spots. A patch here, a patch there. Still, you had to hand it to the guy. Beard or no beard, he was a heck of a host at 7:18 in the morning.

Mike plopped down at the computer while I loaded film into my camera. Well, it wasn't actually mine. It was a school-issued one, stamped with PHS in block letters and appearing almost as old as the art of photography itself. Not that it mattered to me. I was known for decapitating my subjects, anyway.

"So what's the plan?" he asked, giving some body tilt to dodge an alien monster on the computer screen.

"Well, I hafta tell a story about somethin,' so..." Tell you the truth, I hadn't gotten that far. The last time I'd looked at the clock the night before it was 1:42, and I was still drawing a blank. I was tired. Tired and not a little nervous.

"Hey, let's play some quarters," Mike said, throwing aside his joystick. To him, my final project or once-in-a-lifetime shot with Mandy meant squat in comparison to a good game of quarters.

Actually, it wasn't a lousy idea. The ancient drinking game, which I'd first seen my brothers play from practically the high chair, required people to mindlessly bounce a quarter into a waiting glass of beer. You made it, you passed it. You missed it, you drank. I guess it could have loosely been considered an event, a breaking story. In fact, at Picadilly parties at least, it was a major happening.

"Okay, you're on," I said, whipping a shot glass from the cupboard. It wasn't foolproof - I didn't even know if Mandy touched the stuff - but it was all I had.

The doorbell rang at 7:57 a few minutes shy of our agreed-upon meeting time. School began at 9:00, at least for those who weren't ditching. I wasn't quite sure about the whole thing yet, the trip to Monahans on a game day and all, but I'd covered my back with a phone call to the school secretary just in case. I could do this bit where I sounded just like Diane Chambers from *Cheers.*

School obviously wasn't in Mandy's plans. She was wearing shiny red running shorts and a tiny, white tee with the American flag painted across the front. Her hair was pulled back into a tight ponytail, and her silver half-moon earrings were doing a jig. I knew all of this because it took me five full seconds to do anything but give her the up and down.

Anyway, she probably wasn't trying to look incredible, but she kind of couldn't help it. It always amazed me how hard girls worked at looking good, when all it took was a ponytail and maybe a smile. Did they not know how easy we were?

"Um, good morning?'" I finally heard her mutter through the glass storm door.

Feeling pretty happy to be an American, I decided that, yes, it was a good morning. A hell of a good morning.

"Hi, uh, c'mon in," I said. She did, easing around me and heading toward the music. Girls always headed toward the music; guys to the refrigerator.

Mike was already warmed up. His kitchen counter was a natural quarters surface, forgiving and full of spring, and Mike was an all-star in the game. He barely noticed when Mandy and I entered the room, instead honing in on his craft.

I didn't think Mike would end up having a problem with alcohol. School was just too easy for him, so maybe he needed a challenge. And getting past Senor Cordello, our suspenders-wearing Spanish teacher, without getting fingered was a challenge. Plus, Mike's folks put a lot of pressure on him. Mr. Handler was already hounding him to start financially planning for retirement; Mike was an afterschool stocker at Skip's Hardware and Pet Supplies, probably not his stopping point.

"Mike Handler, this is Mandy Drake," I announced.

Without a word, Mike let a quarter roll down his nose.

He was a nose player, a risky-but-deadly style if perfected. It found the center of the half-filled glass. Splash.

"Nice to meet ya," he grunted, pushing the glass toward her.

She smiled and grabbed the gift. "Same here." She wolfed down the beer down in one tilt. Without as much as wiping her chin, she grabbed the opened can, filled the glass to the rim and tossed it down again. She then repeated the process. Twice.

Mandy touched the stuff.

I caught Mike looking. Most girls didn't impress him that much, unless of course they could pound a beer in 30 seconds flat. Mandy finally spread the wealth, using the more conventional counter-top method to drain the coin.

"Your turn," she said to me, filling the glass. I took it and emptied it down my throat, but not without a tilt and a breath. I had a few strengths, chugging beer not being among them.

"So ya got anything stronger?" It was something I'd expect Mike to say, but the pitch of the voice was definitely Mandy's.

You didn't have to ask Mike twice. He whirled to his left, unveiling a liquor lottery of bottom-shelf liquors. Banker's whiskey. Carmelo's tequila. Old South gin. West Bank scotch. We'd about turned Jack and Jose and Jim into apple juice with a little kick.

"Holy hell!" she shouted. "Paradise!"

"Naw, thank my folks," Mike laughed. He flicked his hand toward the cabinet. "So what's your poison?" (Being a big fan of Westerns and especially John Wayne, he liked saying things like that.)

"Oh, I don't care," she said flatly, petting a bottle of bourbon. "I like 'em all. Just as long as it does the trick."

Yep, it was going to be an interesting morning.

***

By ten, we were all a little sloppy. Mike's eyes were thin and glassy, and his hair was still in bedhead condition. He was the decided winner (or loser) of the variety of drinking games we'd played, but being a team player, he usually raised his own glass whether it was his turn or not. His laugh had turned into a cackle, the measuring stick of Mike's turning the corner.

Mandy, all 98 pounds or so of her, was a trouper. She hung tough all morning, drinking when called upon, showcasing a dead-eye shooting touch and even keeping a stiff toddy in reserve. Mike mixed it up special for her, filling a Jordie's Bar-B-Q cup to the brim and even using a spoon to stir it instead of his finger. I still wasn't sure if she was there for business or pleasure; I also didn't give a damn.

Her attitude changed a little over the course of the morning. She was a little stuffy at first, drinking with these two unknowns, but had become the life of the party over the last hour. Along with sporting a stick-on smile, one that made her eyes dance, she'd become very animated, often throwing her hands up in celebration or hopping around to the musical genius of Men at Work.

Most importantly, after hanging between us for the first hour or so, she'd nudged closer to me during the last 20 minutes. It was enough for Mike to get up at one point and give Betsy a ring, a symbolic white flag for sure.

An hour later, I was in the best shape. With the ballgame and the paper in the far corner of my mind, I tried to pace myself, even forcing down a few slugs of non-spiked water. Still, I felt a little queasy, especially after chasing down a cinnamon roll with a rum and root beer. I knew adults would have gagged at the thought of such a concoction, but it really wasn't about the root beer.

"So what's the plan?" Mike asked me in the bathroom. We were crossing swords at the toilet, a childhood ritual that hadn't quite lost its easy appeal. We had to have something on girls.

"I dunno." I shrugged and zipped up. "I mean, I have to get this photography thing done sometime. What time is it?"

He checked his watch, misfiring against the wall.

"11:17."

"Are you drunk?" I asked.

"Shitty."

"What about Mandy?"

"Shitty. Definitely shitty."

And I think she was, too. She was starting to babble a little and sing so loudly and out of tune that Tax, the Handler's arthritic dachshund, was busting a gut.

"Let's go on and get started then."

"Wait," Mike said, clutching my shoulder. "Are ya in for

Millican or not?"

I had been waiting for that question. With five hours left in school and about seven before game time, before trying to baffle the state's third-best team with my not-so baffling stuff, I knew that Millican was out for me. And my face said it all.

"Aw, maaaan," Mike groaned.

"Sorry, bro."

"Well, then can I at least take your car?"

Mike's Buick could barely make it out of his driveway. "Well, okay, as long as you can have it at the fieldhouse by eight tonight."

"No prob."

"So where are my boys?" Mandy cried out from the other room.

Honest, she really said it. Her tone was kind of annoying, and we found her slow dancing with a broom and wearing Mr. Handler's "Trout or Bust" fishing cap when we returned to the kitchen. Gone was the angel I'd worshiped all year, replaced by, well, a drunk teen-age girl, a goof just like us. Only with much nicer legs.

We got my assignment out of the way. It only took a few minutes really. Mike filling the glass. Mike taking and making a shot. Mike sliding the glass to Mandy. Mandy downing the beer. Mandy filling up the glass. Mandy emptying the thing. Mandy opening a beer.

Not exactly Kodak moment stuff.

"Uh, Mandy, I think I got enough pictures," I said. I'd packed away the camera two beers before. Then I figured out that film or no film, the girl was going to keep plowing them down. And she did, too, alternately belting out Duran Duran at the peak of her lungs and swilling from a beer that Mike warned was from the Handler's Super Bowl party of 1980. The Philly Eagles had taken a pounding in that one, causing even Mr. Handler to get sloshed.

"So, I'm going to get goin,'" Mike said as we gathered the empties in the kitchen. We'd done some damage, filing through about a 12-pack of brew and a half bottle of bourbon in four hours or so. Some water and a splash of soda would return the bottle to its previous state, but we'd have to rule it out the next time. "What are y'all going to do?"

Good question. It was still too early to head back to school, so we had an hour or so to kill. I could develop the film during sixth-period study hall, zip by Mrs. Sharp's room to hand in my paper and be suited and sobered up by 4:00. Simple.

But here was something I was learning about girls - things were never all that simple. As Mike slipped out the side door, Mandy slipped in Journey's Escape album. It was the classic make-out record, and people kept it around for just that reason. Mike could pop in anything and still not get squat from Betsy, but still, a guy had to hang on to hope.

"Let's dance," Mandy said. "Wanna?"

It was the classic make-out album, I reminded myself.

"Um, sure. I mean, who doesn't like Journey?"

***

We met in the middle of the living room, right as the song "Open Arms" came on. If Escape was a lineup of makeout songs, "Open Arms" was the clean-up hitter. I gently slid my arms around her waist. She threw her arms around my neck, rocking forward and giving me a mouthful of her hair. After two of Mike's turbo drinks, I figured caution was out the window.

You couldn't really call what we were doing dancing. We just kind of leaned in place, adjusting our feet every so often. I didn't know much different. It was the style I learned all the way back at the church dances in grade school, when the nuns would creep up and nudge us and say to leave some room for the Holy Spirit.

It probably looked like we were trying to get past each other in a hallway more than anything. Really, judging from the weight of her shifts, I was probably just holding her up. Still, it was kind of cool. When you got a chance to be close enough to smell a hottie's breath, even if it smelled like a Pabst Light, well, that's good stuff.

The song ended. Ended way too soon. I wanted to say something suave and sexy, something that would hit her clear down in that tiny triangle that let the air out of you.

But I didn't.

"So," Mandy said. She stopped swaying and lifted her head. For a few seconds, we said nothing and moved not at all. With first kisses, the delivery was crucial. Later on in a relationship or whatever, you could lock lips for a minute and move on to the good stuff. But if you left a girl all slobbery after that first smack, you never got around to the good stuff.

I hated the things, and especially the seconds leading up to them. I mean it; they were right up there with deviled eggs and pea salad on my hate scale. And I couldn't flip that moment over my shoulder or stash it under my plate.

"So," I repeated. More stupid staring. I shrugged. "So, um, so did ya wanna...?"

She did. Mandy reached up and grabbed the back of my head. Before I could even close my eyes, our lips were together. As we jockeyed for position, all I could think of was how glad I was that she'd made the first move. In that situation, I might have stood there through the summer.

Like I said, I had zero experience in the sack, but I at least knew my way to first base. And it helped that Mandy was an amazing, maybe experienced, kisser. We seemed a nice fit, preferring the same pace of things, the same tilt. One girl I'd gone out with, Maggie Champion, went at it like a woodpecker. That alone was grounds for a note to her that started out, "I don't know how to say this...."

The smack went on for a few minutes. One, because it was nice. Real nice. And two, because I didn't know what move to try next. With some girls, you knew you could start wandering around early. With others, you had to feel out the situation to see if you could feel out the situation. In this case, though my lips were good and limbered up, the rest of my body was stiff as the Tin Man.

Tell you the plain truth, I had no clue where it was all going.

Mandy had a good hunch, though. She pulled away from me and unleashed her hair from its ponytail. With a naughty smile, she grabbed my hand and led it to the bottom of her tee, then lifted my hand until the thing was clean off her back.

She did the rest, unbuttoning her bra and letting it fall to the ground. With a quick tug of her shorts, the rest followed, making a small pile of laundry at her feet. As Steve Perry whined the chorus of "Don't Stop Believin,'" Mandy Drake stood in the Handler living room with nothing on but a Trout or Bust cap, socks and a smile.

I couldn't believe it.

"So, is there any place, um, we could go?" She flung the cap over her shoulder with a giggle. Hathead never looked so good.

"Um, sure," I said. My eyes drifted to the nearest room in sight - the master bedroom.

I was running behind. I mean, there she was, all but naked, and all I'd taken off was my Carmex. I fumbled for the most appropriate way to escort the beautiful girl I'd ever seen up-close to my best friend's folks' bed.

Turned out, there wasn't a slick way. We just sort of did it. Hand in hand, right past the big bay window in the dining room, right past Chris Rockafeller's mom picking up the newspaper, we stumbled toward the king-sized bed.

On the way, I realized that Mandy wasn't looking for romance or to be seduced or held or caressed. The girl was looking for sex, for pleasure, and I was supposed to do the pleasuring.

I flipped on the ceiling fan, and things quickly got hot. Within a few seconds, she'd ripped off my clothes, exposing a body that I wasn't all that nuts about. Too skinny for my taste. I mean, for being right in the middle of my formative years, I wasn't doing too much forming. But Mandy seemed to be fine with it. Or at least that's the way I took it, judging from the way she was licking me all over.

I was little paralyzed, if you want to know the truth. It wasn't often that a guy's real life outweighed his wildest dreams. At least not for this guy.

Mandy nuzzled against my neck. "I want you."

I pulled away. "Are ya sure?" I'd been down the same path before, sort of, but never without ramming into a roadblock.

Like I said, I knew only a little about sex. I mean, we had cable, and I'd done the cotton dance with more than a few girls, which was basically like lip synching to music, only with wood. Plus, I busted in on my parents once, though I'd rather not talk about that one. Put it this way: I felt sort of comfortable with the basic calisthenics of it all.

Mandy rolled to her side, facing me. She looked pretty out of it, like the alcohol's effects were taking a turn for the worst. "Yeah, I'm very sure," she said with one eye shut.

I ran my hand through her hair. I knew you couldn't let sexy moments like that go on too long. It was like overheating soup in the microwave - sooner or later, the lid would blow off. A decision had to be made. For once in my life, I had to take charge.

"I gotta go to the bathroom," I said.

At that exact moment, it was the best I could do.

"Um, okaaaaay," she sighed, shrugging and flipping onto her back. I really did have to go, but that wasn't the point. I hoisted myself from the bed, Mandy's eyes tracing my steps, and stumbled into the john.

While I took care of business, I thought about her, all sprawled out in a strange bed waiting for a stranger guy, and about how crazy the whole morning had gotten. And it sort of felt like a bad crazy, too. I'd just wanted to slide into things, maybe weasel my way into a date, just to be seen with her really. You know, the Kevin Petrie Effect. I thought again about Mike telling me to take a shot. Well, I hadn't much counted on it all being a wide-open layup.

Being a guy and all, I hadn't exactly spent much of my boyhood imagining what my first time would be like, but those few times were not a thing like this. I studied myself in the mirror. Looked like hell, all scrawny and naked. Facing the moment that I was about to become a man, or at least less of a kid, I'd never looked more like a dumb punk.

I dropped to the floor and did 14 push-ups, but I knew it was too late. Know how you brush your teeth for two hours and work them into a bloody mess just before you go see the dentist, only to have the guy slowly shake his head and say you have seven cavities? Well, same kind of deal.

I took a deep breath, knowing I had to get back. She must have thought I'd fallen in. Or worse yet, the truth - that I was freaking out.

Actually, I don't think she was thinking about much at all. When I returned, she was asleep. Like really asleep.

Like snoring asleep.

***

"Um, Mandy?" I touched her shoulder lightly. Her hand fell to her side.

I felt a little relieved, if you've got to know. She'd made my decision for me. Or Mike's booze had, anyway. I mulled over my options. One, well, I didn't even want to think about one. Two, I could leave her there and let her sleep it off, give Mr. Handler a nice surprise. Or three, considering that it was past noon and that I badly needed a lift up to school, I could wake her from the dead.

I gave her another nudge. And another. Then a push. And another. Finally, after shaking her like a bottle of salad dressing, Mandy opened her eyes with a start. It took her a minute to zone in, but like one of those coma patients from a soap opera, she was quickly back, just as good as before.

"So is this going to happen or what?" she asked, stretching her arms to the headboard. Let me tell you, it was a heck of a sight, the most perfect I'd ever seen by miles.

Her naked body was highlighted by the sun, which was peeking through the shades, and her legs were spread and a little bent, making a pose I'd only seen in the magazines under my mattress. But something was missing besides her clothes. Her head was turned toward the window, and her eyes were cast down toward the floor. I realized what was missing.

Mandy.

"So...?" she repeated, still looking away. "What, did ya change your mind?"

Above the bed, I noticed a family photo of the Handlers. They looked happier than they really were, the way family shots seemed to go. Trick photography, I figured. I could almost hear Mike whispering for me to go for it. Mr. Handler, in my head anyway, was leaning over and sneaking a nod.

Jimmy, Mike's kid brother, was ready to get on the horn and call over some buds. Lisa, Mike's big sister, was lunging over to slug them all. I looked to Mrs. Handler. Her eyes were burning mad, and she had a big Mom look plastered all over her face. I promised myself, no matter what happened, to not look up.

So there I stood on the carpet, hands folded over my privates like a fig leaf, wondering which of my body parts was going to win out. Amazing how such a small area of a guy's anatomy could have so much pull.

Wait, did I say small?

"What's the matter, don't ya want me?"

For the second time in 24 hours, Mandy Drake made my left eye, always the left, start to twitch.

The ride to school was quiet. I was behind the wheel of her Jeep and feeling a little sick. Mandy was just plain sick. She puked all over the Handler's bathroom while I was making the bed and clearing the evidence. Then, while I was cleaning up that, she heaved in the kitchen. As the Jeep bounced down Parkwood Lane, she made these deep gargling sounds, her head bouncing wildly, her matted hair falling over her face.

It was funny - not really laughing funny, but odd funny - how someone could fall so fast. I made a mental note to swear off alcohol, at least until the summer.

"Are ya going to be okay, Mandy?" It was all I could think of to say.

"Ugh. Awww. Errrr." At the time, it was all she could say. Period.

I knew that her fifth-hour class was on the far end of the school - it's pathetic, sure, but I knew where Mandy's every-hour class was - so I pulled over near its entrance. I eased the car into park and fiddled with the keys. I hadn't noticed it before, but there was a framed picture dangling from the key chain. It was of a guy, a Zeus of a dude wearing a blue-and-orange letter jacket and kneeling next to a football helmet. I didn't recognize him or the uniform, and he obviously wasn't from around Midtex. I was glad, too, probably because he would have wanted to pummel me about then.

I looked at Mandy. She was staring straight ahead, past the football practice field and the baseball diamond and the white, square houses that outlined the school. It was the same faraway look she'd had in the bedroom. If the eyes really were the window to the soul and all that mushy junk, Mandy's were those tinted kind. Anyway, I think she was looking all the way back to Georgia.

"So," I said finally.

Mandy pulled her hair back with one hand and bit her bottom lip.

Her jaw began to shake, forming two dimples on her chin. She blinked, and a tear fell to her cheek and rolled down her neck.

"Thanks," she said, never breaking her stare. One word, that was all.

It was enough, though.

We sat there in silence, a couple of kids trying to grow up too fast, a couple of kids wanting to be accepted for all the wrong reasons. At the same time, though, I'd never felt more like a man. Faced with a moment that had begged and pleaded and kicked and tugged at my pant leg for me to do the wrong thing, I'd done the exact opposite. What do you know, I thought right then and there, Mrs. Sharp was right: there really was an exception to every rule.

So there wouldn't be a Jasper Schitt Effect. So I wouldn't be a hit in the showers. So what? Bunch of naked guys lathering up with the same chunk of soap, it sort of gave me the creeps anyway.

My thoughts drifted to the research paper, and it hit me, hit me hard. Mike had my car. And the paper. In Millican. It was funny - not really laughing funny, but odd funny - how someone could fall so fast.

Being a virgin was one thing. But being an idiot to boot, well, that was extra tough.

Tumbleweed

Someone had tried to make her into somebody she wasn't. And Darla Simpleton never, ever tried to be somebody she wasn't.

She was wearing her favorite sun dress, one of those bright, flowery jobs that hung loosely and fell just below her knees. She wore it on our first date, and she wore it on our second date. I was starting to think she was like Shaggy, wearing the same rags every day and all, but she broke out some Daisy Duke jean shorts and a tank on our third one, so that was nice.

I would have liked her anyhow. Darla and I had kind of known each other since seventh grade, in that we both had classes on the same wings and all, but hadn't really found one another until five days past graduation. One slow, sticky Wednesday, we crossed paths at Swanson's Sandwich Shop in the mall, ended up side by side at the bar and spent the next three hours polishing off our cold-cut combos. Hold the mayo, heavy on the mustard for both of us. The old ladies with the hand weights and rainbow headbands huffed past the shop about 600 times, but we just kept talking and talking.

I swear I would have stayed there until it was time to head off to college, gnawing on the best sandwich I'd ever had with a girl like none I'd ever met. By the last bite, I was pretty much hooked.

Darla wasn't too popular at Picadilly High. She wasn't a cheerleader. She wasn't even a pep girl, and most girls were allowed to be pep girls. She wasn't a student council anything, or an all-conference anything, or the queen or princess or even duchess of anything. She was just Darla Simpleton, take it or leave it. Most guys left it, because I never really saw her with anyone, or at least within slap-ass range of anyone. I think it's because most of us were spinning in circles, and she was just moseying straight ahead. Everybody, including myself, was missing out.

Two things separated her from almost everyone else I knew. One, Darla loved life. I wasn't always that crazy about the thing, and I didn't know many people who were. And two, she loved to smile. And I don't only mean smiling at jokes or farts or funny flicks, but just smiling at stuff. She looked around and pointed things out, even taking time to think and to talk about things. I thought when I had to, like for a test or before crossing the street, but Darla's wheels were always spinning.

She was fearless, too. Once, after we'd been together for only a couple of weeks, Darla invited me to come hear her sing at the mall. It was for one of those area talent shows, the ones where little kids were tossed up on stage by their folks and ordered to tap dance or sing or juggle. She sang "The Greatest Love of All," or at least some form of it, into a crackling Mr. Microphone. It was pretty bad. No, it was really bad, and Whitney Houston would have probably yanked the plug had she been at the Miss Midtex Talent Search Show in June of 1986. Only about four of us made it through the whole thing - me, her mom and two janitors hiding out - but after the cheap stereo system faded, she spread her arms, curtsied and smiled a smile that connected at the back of her head. You would have thought she was performing at the Midtex Coliseum. And she could pull it off for only one reason--unlike myself and most of my buddies, Darla had huge nuts.

"I dunno how ya did that," I said to her later at the ice cream shop. Least I could do was buy her a double scoop.

"Did what?" she asked, turning her spoon upside down and dangling a hunk of Rocky Road before her mouth.

"Stood up there by yourself and just sang away, with nobody even payin' attention. No way I could do that."

"Oh, sure ya could. You've just never tried. Besides, you were payin' attention."

I smiled and nodded and sucked down my malt. Nobody called milkshakes *malts* anymore, but I liked the old-fashioned feel of it. Anyway, it was true. I hadn't stopped paying attention since that first day at Swanson's. We spent the next three months or so together, never missing a single day, and fell in love.

At least it sure felt like love. When we were together, my insides felt all full and content, like I'd just polished off a good meal. And when we were apart, which was pretty much when we slept, I felt hollow and hungry. At first I thought it was the flu or maybe gas, but I couldn't shake it. I knew you probably weren't supposed to use your digestive system as a gauge to your affections, but it was about all I had to go on. Anyway, I know it sounds all mushy, but seeing her was the very best part of my every day, and I had my heart set on her.

We weren't like some couple that tumbled off a romance novel cover, running down the beach in super slow-mo or throwing rose petals all over each other. C'mon, we were still in Midtex. We went to movies and held hands. I even went with her to see a re-release of "The Sound of Music." Couldn't figure out why girls always got so goofy about that flick. Just a family skipping down a mountain, if you asked me.

We drove around and around and back again and listened to tunes. We went swimming and played miniature golf and even went bowling once. When a guy was willing to strap on those clown shoes for someone, he had to be hooked. For once, the goofy stuff didn't seem so goofy.

And we laughed a lot. I even actually started saying some of those funny things I was sometimes thinking. Most of it was self-deprecating stuff, which if translated really meant that I liked to dump on myself, which was really kind of disgusting, but at least I could finally put it all into words. I can't think of any good ones right now, but that's the way it goes.

Plus we didn't drink, which was sort of nice. She didn't, and I didn't feel like I had to. After a couple of weeks the only big difference in one another we found was that I liked Coke and she went with Pepsi. It was a fault in her that I could overlook. Besides, everyone in Texas called everything a Coke anyway. A root beer was a Coke. Big Red was a Coke. Mr. Pibb was a Coke. But our carbonation differences felt like a tiny sacrifice, like when you were willing to get slapped on the chin by some scalding hot cheese from a glorious slice of pizza.

Darla was also a Republican; Dad liked that. Now, I didn't much know a political party from a Tupperware party, but Darla had been on the debate team, and Dad was pretty smart, so Republican sounded good to me.

Didn't know why she couldn't just give Coke a shot, though.

It was a lot of the same stuff I'd always done, only it was more fun with Darla. It was riding around in circles but finally getting somewhere. And best of all, it was so easy. I'd never knew anyone like that, someone who didn't worry about being seen or heard or accepted. I was so glad that high school was over and hoped there wouldn't be as many masks to wear in college.

Best of all, she was pretty sweet on me, too. And you just couldn't overlook that, because I'd gushed over plenty of girls who didn't gush back. And she didn't like the wannabe jock or the guy trying to nudge his nose into the crowd, but just me. She told me so one night at Eastside Park, a place where people went to park or hang out. Mostly park. We were lying on a blanket across the hood of her car and talking about our plans after the summer. Darla was already accepted at Texas Tech, where she was set on getting a nursing degree. She was nuts about kids - called them God's perfect pee-wee angels - and volunteered in the children's wing at the Midtex General Hospital, painting clown faces on pint-sized patients while other girls her age were busy dolling up their own.

I was going to a directional school in a little Texas town called San Marcos, where I was planning on doing something, though I didn't know what. Maybe try and play baseball. Maybe join a fraternity. Maybe transfer to Texas Tech. I really had no clue. It blew me away that some people, girls mainly, had their whole lives mapped out. I wasn't sure what was going to happen from breath to breath. Plus, I'd taken that standardized test that was supposed to tell a guy what he was best-suited to do in life.

Mine said to be a farmer.

I knew we were headed for some tricky times, going to different schools on the opposite sides of our gigantic state. You could probably get away with it in one of those teeny states that could practically be carpeted, but Texas would be tough. I'd heard from a couple of older guys that those sorority girls were harder to turn down than chocolate chips.

And until Darla, I'd never been totally faithful to a girlfriend, and I'd never had one be totally faithful to me. Girlfriends were not much different than Chinese food to me. They were good at the time, but I needed something else pretty quick. Same with them. It was high school.

Mostly, the only reason I dated anyone was so that other girls would be interested. When I was single, I was pretty much an ogre.

Anyhow, we had our work cut out for us.

***

"So Jasp, why didn't you pick me?" Darla asked me that night at Eastside, her head resting against what I called my shoulder.

"Pick you? Whattaya mean?"

"That night at Annie Sedgefield's party, right before sophomore year. When Trapper made that bet, you could have chosen to kiss any girl at that party, and you didn't even consider me."

I hadn't thought about that night in years, but she was right. Darla had been there, right before my eyes yet under the total eclipse of Amber Taylor.

I squirmed. "I did so consider you."

I was lying.

"Oh you most certainly did not," she said, pulling away a bit. "You practically ran right over to Amber."

"Well, I didn't run," (Jogged maybe.)

She wasn't impressed. She turned her shoulders from me, toward Dylan Shipman's green humpmobile.

"Darla, look at me." She did, kinda. I cleared my throat and figured it was time to forget I was a guy.

"Well, see, um, first of all I'm sorry that I didn't pick ya. I am. And I wish more than anything that I had, because maybe we woulda started dating then, and now I woulda been with ya for three years instead of three weeks. I could have been with ya through all the bad homecomings and the bad proms and the bad parties, and I coulda been with ya during all the times that I kinda wondered if there was anyone out there at all. Because that's all that really matters to me anymore, ya know, being with you. That's, well, that's pretty much everything to me."

It might have been the best thing I'd ever said to another human being, at least the best thing that I really meant. See, I'd been talking to girls for years, with mixed results, but with Darla I actually tried to say something.

I waited as she looked off into space. Finally she smiled, though she tried to force it back. Those were the very best kind of smiles.

I seized the opening, put my hand on her cheek and pulled her toward me. Darla wasn't the best-looking girl I'd ever dated, nor had she changed much over the years. She hardly ever wore make-up, and her long, brown hair tended to be all over the place. She was short, about five-foot-three, and her features were on the plain side.

Remember how I described Amber Taylor (who was dating the Picadilly High defensive backs coach) and Allison Rickles (who was marrying The Karate Kid) and Mandy Drake (who had moved back to Georgia about three minutes after graduation)? Well, Darla wasn't in their league. I mean, Darla wasn't even a good-looking name. With Tiffanies and Ashleys and Paiges, it was a given that good looks would follow. But a Darla, well, a Darla could easily be a tanker.

But she had the important stuff down. Her eyes always sparkled and she smelled nice, and she was pretty in all the places that mattered. Put it this way: to me, Darla was the last song you heard before you turned off the car. Even if it wasn't a big hit, it still stuck in your head.

Anyway, I was about to give her a fat kiss, but she laid one on me first.

"I love you Jasper. No matter what happens, no matter where we are, I want ya to know that I love you."

She loved me. Hmm. I stalled by stroking her face and let her words sink in. They felt warm, like a swallow of hot apple cider. I'd never said them to anyone that wasn't at my family reunion the summer before. But I also knew I felt much stronger about Darla than my Uncle Flip. She loved me. She loved me. I took a deep breath and let it fly.

"I love you, too."

And you know what?

It didn't suck.

Cars started to rock on both sides of us, making me more aware that I was well on my way to becoming probably the first college virgin guy in the history of colleges and virgins and guys.

But staring out into the nothingness after the biggest sentence of my life, next to a girl who smelled just like a field of daisies, I decided it could wait. A stab at a quickie in the back seat would have sort of ruined the moment, know what I mean?

It was the prettiest night in Midtex history, and I didn't want it to end.

***

Standing there, numb with disbelief, I couldn't wait for the day to end. Like I said before, Darla was only a few feet away, but she wasn't herself. Not at all. Her hair was bundled up all nice and neat, just like she didn't like it, and her dress was perfectly pressed and spotless, like it was fresh off the rack. If she could have, she would have let her hair loose and shook it out and let a bite of something drip down her dress, just to look lived in. But she couldn't. She couldn't smile or laugh or sing or tell me that the eight-hour drive from San Marcos to Lubbock would be a snap.

She couldn't.

She wouldn't.

She was dead.

Darla was gone.

It was the day before the funeral, and her body was on display like a sleeping puppy in a store window. I thought it was a sick, twisted ritual, a bunch of people shadowing over a lifeless body and pretending to act in a certain way. It was the funeral song and dance, and I recognized it from my grandfather's service. People walked with little steps and smiled politely and spoke softly, then probably left the parlor and thanked God that it wasn't them. I understood the premise behind it all, this final respects thing, but I thought it was a terrible way to remember someone who had been so alive.

"You doin' okay?" It was Kurt, his hand on my shoulder. I hadn't seen much of him over the summer. In fact, I'd drifted apart from most of my buddies. But it was cool. Guys got mad when you blew them off for psycho girls, but they understood when you fell hard for someone cool. It was my first time, so I'd gotten some slack. I knew we'd all drift back together.

"Yeah, I guess," I said. We stepped away from her. A couple of guys in our grade took my place, guys who probably knew her from Biology class or something and were there because they'd heard some chicks were headed over.

We shuffled over to a back wall, and Kurt leaned close to me. "Man, I can't believe it happened," he whispered. "I have no idea what to say except that I'm really sorry."

People kept saying it, that they were really sorry, that they didn't know what to say. It was nice and all, but it didn't help. Nothing had helped for two days, not crying or slugging stuff or driving 90 MPH down FM 80 or even sneaking one of Mom's night-night pills.

I wasn't okay. I just said it to shut Kurt up.

"Hey Kurt, I'll see ya tomorrow, okay?" With that, I brushed past him and sliced sideways through the small crowd. I wasn't much up to polite nods or whispers, and I sure couldn't look at Darla anymore.

I'd gotten the call two days before, at 11:11 a.m., the moment when you're supposed to be allowed to make a wish. I was alone at the house, waiting to hear from her. We had plans to meet at Mike Handler's house, where we were going to kick back in the sun and soak up some of the last hours of summer by his pool. Mike and I would probably end up shooting some hoops, and Darla and Jamie Dunlap, Mike's latest girl, would end up talking about how silly all that competition and rivalry stuff was. They just didn't understand that a good tan was one thing, but a good win was quite another.

Her mom's voice over the phone was so shaky that I couldn't understand a word. "Mrs. Simpleton, you're going to have to slow down," I said. "Just slow down and tell me." I thought she had the hiccups.

"There's...there's....be....en....an...an....ac...ac..."

"Mrs. Simpleton, please." My heart started to sink.

"Ac....ci...accident....Dar.....Dar....Darl....Darla..is....is.... dead."

For some reason, I knew it was coming when I heard her voice. Mrs. Simpleton was a rigid, round woman who wore those half-glasses and seemed to live in the kitchen. Except for the fact that she made great pies, I knew next to nothing about her. Darla said she had a sneaky mean streak. Anyway, there was absolutely no reason for her to call me.

***

After hanging up, I was soon good and drunk. Well, drunk. I scribbled a note to my folks, telling them that Darla was dead and that I would be home later. I knew it wasn't the best way to break the news, that they would worry, but my head was spinning. Besides, I still didn't really know how to talk to them, even when my head wasn't spinning.

True, it wasn't the way that those *ABC Afterschool Specials* dealt with things, but I didn't figure to feel better or to solve the problem after a few commercial breaks. A quart of cheap beer between my legs, I steered through the roads aimlessly, staring straight ahead but seeing little. I passed Half-Moon Pizza, home of Midtex's best deep-dish pies and, last I'd heard, Billy Hamilton. The paint thinner and the needles had gotten the best of the guy, and he'd gotten booted from school for trying to sell hash to an undercover cop disguised as a student. He could probably still get his GED - short for Good Enough Degree - but a dough flipper?

Shoot, I could think of lots of cooler things than that.

After an hour that seemed like a day, I worked up the nerve and just did it. I took a hard swallow and drove to the spot where the guy in the El Camino had ignored the stop sign and killed them both. Broken glass still glittered in the intersection, but other than that, the streets of Midtex were back in business. An El Camino, a piece of crap that couldn't make up its mind if it wanted to be a truck or a car; what a way to go.

I wondered what would have happened if she had brushed her teeth for just a little longer or filled her cereal bowl again for the remaining milk. She always let that mangy mutt of hers have it instead. Or if she had decided to take 18th Street, which was much faster anyhow. Or even if she had washed, rinsed and repeated with the shampoo, like the directions instructed. Naw, I decided, she was no sucker.

Mrs. Simpleton said that Darla died instantly of a broken neck. Merging on to the highway and heading toward Pinwheel, I felt like I was going slowly of something much worse. I took another slug from the bottle. Having learned in

Health class that alcohol was actually a depressant, it seemed pretty appropriate.

It was a metropolis to nearby No Trees, but Pinwheel was little more than a bump in the road. There was an old drag-racing track, a general store, a rusty windmill and a few decaying homes. That was about it. Pinwheel had dried up with the oil, and even the few kids from there who were bussed in called themselves north Midtexans. Here was the deal - when people said they were driving in to Midtex to do some shopping, you knew they were coming from the sticks.

***

But Pinwheel was exactly where Darla and I ended up on our first date. I figured on taking her to a movie, but she had other plans. Better plans.

"C'mon, do ya really wanna go sit in a dark theater for two hours and say nothing?" she asked as we turned into the multiplex that night.

"What, I thought everybody sat in a dark theater for two hours and said nothin' on their first dates," I returned. And I did, too.

"Well, would ya mind if we at least considered doing somethin' else?" "Like what?"

"Well, let's let fate decide," she said. Then she started fumbling around in her little purse. Seemed that girls spent a good part of their lives digging in their purses. Finally, she pulled out a coin. "Okay, heads and we'll go wherever the night takes us. Tails and we'll go see a movie."

"Sounds good."

She flipped the coin. It hung in the air, spiraled in the sunlight and splashed into my Reggie Jackson collector's edition cup of soda in the console. No heads, no tails, only Reggie.

"So what is it?" I laughed.

She squinted and buried her face in the cup. Then she shrugged and smiled, a drop of soda falling from her nose.

"I think it's probably heads."

Darla was always doing off-the-wall stuff like that. For one, she carried around those candy Valentine's Day hearts. Sometimes, when things got quiet, she would reach into her bag and pull one out. She'd read the saying - "Be Mine" or "You're Sweet" or whatever - and plop it into my mouth.

"There, now ya have a little piece of my heart," she'd say. "Chew it up and swallow it, because if ya don't it doesn't work."

They tasted nasty and stale, but I didn't mind much, even when she once spilled a whole box in my car. It scored high on the originality scale.

Anyhow, that first night took us to a wide, empty field in Pinwheel under a bright, starry sky. We hardly moved for the next three hours, but we covered plenty of ground. I'd never tried it much before, the communicating thing. When you weren't trying to figure out how far you were going to get by the end of the night, a guy could actually learn something about somebody. It sure beat *Rocky XX* or whatever.

It came too soon, by the way, the end of the night. And except for a peck on the cheek under her porch light, I got nowhere. As she closed the front door, she said,

"Sure lucky for us that it came up heads."

I agreed. On my way back to the car, I did one of those jumping heel clicks because, well, because I'd always wanted to.

***

I tilted my second quart toward the moon. On the surface, everything was the same. The field was just as empty, the sky just as bright. It was cruel how something meaningless like a dried-up patch of squat just went on and on while the things that mattered most could vanish in a snap. I felt a chill, right there in that steamy August night, and started to cry like a baby for the first time in years.

The day before the funeral, I clipped out her obituary from the *Midtex American*. It was buried at the bottom of page eight, section D, under one for an 88-year-old man named Odie D. Herman IV. I wondered why the family had gotten stuck on Odie. Anyway, someone had stuck in Darla's goofy senior picture above the print. I could almost hear her bickering with the photo guy about how she would never, ever normally lean up against a tree, tilt her head and put her hand on her chin.

But even in black and white, her eyes hopped from the page. The two short paragraphs that followed were straight from some junior funeral director's overworked, unknowing, uncaring fingers. Darla was a beloved daughter. Loved by many. Will be missed by all. Send money or flowers in her name. Blah, blah, blah. I could do much better.

And so I grabbed a pencil, and I did.

Just before the ride to the funeral, I got real sick. More sick than I'd ever been, except for maybe the time I got food poisoning at the Biscuits and Gravy Diner on South 44th. I threw up for three days after that one and turned blue like the girl from *Willy Wonka*. But hanging over the toilet with my parents hollering that it was time to leave for the service, I was pretty sure this wasn't from sour corned beef hash.

The ride to the church was foggy, at least in my head. As the world zoomed past, I tried to stay real still to keep from erupting again. I'd been practicing. For the previous three days, I'd moved little, said little and felt nothing. My blue suit, the one from two Easters before, was one year too small.

Mom wanted to buy me a new one, but I passed. My ugly tie felt like a noose. I didn't know or especially care where my life was headed, but I was almost sure it wouldn't include a suit and a tie. Basically, I just wanted to do something that would keep me out of a clip-on tie or a hair net.

Anything in between would be fine.

I pressed my forehead against the hot window. Midtex hadn't changed much over the years. We had a Wal-Mart and a Luby's and HBO and all, but the place was still pretty Mayberry in its ways. Guys still drove around with their names on their trucks, like "Randy's Air Conditioning" right beside us, and the women still had big hair and small roles around town. Midtex was, and maybe always would be, a blue-collared land full of worker ants.

***

The St. Anthony's parking lot was only half full. I recognized a few of the cars as we pulled in, but most of them had that parent look about them. A few years back, a popular, knockout of a girl named Shelly Hollis had been accidentally shot and killed by a close friend. Her funeral was the social event of the season, and school let out early so that half the student body could pack into Holy Redeemer Methodist on a Thursday afternoon. Some guy was even passing out fliers to a party at that one.

Well, Darla's funeral wasn't the place to be.

And for that, she would have been glad. She would have hated people showing up just to be seen, that she'd had to die before anyone realized that she'd been alive. She hated doing things for show and sometimes joked that she would have hated me if she'd just known me sooner. It was probably the truth. Unlike myself, Darla never wanted to be popular; she just wanted to be.

I didn't know if she'd turned me into a better person. It wasn't like I'd started volunteering at a homeless shelter or even doing nice things for dough. But I knew that I didn't much want to sneak around anymore or lie to the important people or feel the need to be anywhere just to say I was there. I didn't think about myself so much and, more than anything, didn't try so hard to try so hard.

We neared the entrance, and I felt Jesus looking down on me. A statue of the Big Guy, anyway. He was perched high atop the chapel, his arms stretched to the sky. People around town called him Touchdown Jesus. At least nobody had slid a number-one foam finger on Him. My legs were heavy, partly because I'd left what little food I'd eaten over the past 72 hours back home in the sewer. Mostly, though, it was because every step was a little closer to goodbye.

I heard the door slam shut at the back of the chapel. I rotated my shoulders to see a guy with oily hair peeking through the diamond-shaped window. Probably the obituary guy. At the front, an old man with sunken eyes and thin lips stood with his hands behind his back. Figured it was the funeral director, and I couldn't help but wonder if he would get a nice discount when his time came.

After five minutes of coughs and whispers, the old guy motioned to the shadows. An even older and grayer guy in a purple robe appeared and slowly crept to the podium. It was three o'clock on the dot. Funerals apparently weren't like weddings, where they would wait around for the stragglers.

Death. We never talked about it, Darla and me, not once. We were still getting the living part figured out. Death was for people who had milked the most out of life, like the white-haired lady wheezing hard to my left, or for people who wanted to check out, like the three Picadilly sophomores who had shared a cocktail of floor cleaner while listening to Black Sabbath the year before.

Darla was none of those people.

And we sure never talked about marriage. The whole thing seemed like a pretty risky deal, a tire with a slow leak. A bunch of my friends already had moms with these huge, hyphenated names, like Mrs. Runyon-Richards-McGee down the street. For example, Billy Teakwood spent part of the time with his mom and her new husband, part of the time with his dad and his new girlfriend, and even some weekends with his mom's mom and her boyfriend. It all seemed way too confusing, with too many names to remember.

My parents had made it through about 40 years of so of the thing, but even they didn't make it look easy. Plus, Mom was always poking and prodding and plucking at Dad's blackheads and stray hairs. That alone seemed reason enough to stay single.

The whole marriage thing seemed too much like a peach. It could be sweet and all, but a lot of the time it ended up a mess. Still, it would have been nice just to talk about it. Darla and I didn't get to talk about a lot of stuff.

For some reason, right as the priest who didn't know Darla from a can of potted meat started to babble away about what a pity it all was, one of Dad's jokes popped in my head. He'd told me two nights before, just as we were polishing off dinner.

"A guy goes to the doctor," started the joke. Most of Dad's jokes started with a guy going to the doctor.

"Uh huh," I managed.

"And he says, 'Doc, I want to live to be 100 years old, but I'm havin' these terrible chest pains, and I'm scared I'm not going to make it.'"

"So the Doc asks, 'Well, sir, are ya married?' "

"Yep."

"Do ya smoke expensive cigars?"

"Nope."

"Do ya drink fine, expensive wine?"

"Nope."

"Do ya chase after younger women?"

"Oh, noooo sir."

"And so the Doc closes his chart and asks, 'Well, why the heck would ya wanna live to be 100 years old?'"

It wasn't one of his better efforts, but I got the point. It didn't matter how long you were around, but instead what you did while you were. Something like that anyway. Of course, he could have just been fishing for a laugh.

"Darla was a young lady who loved to share and to give her time to good causes," the soft-spoken priest continued. "She loved everyone, and everyone loved her, and she had a pure and innocent heart."

The geezer meant well, putting in overtime for a Wednesday funeral and all, but he hadn't done his homework. If he had, he would have known that Darla didn't love everyone, didn't even especially like everyone. And not everyone loved her, if only because most people didn't even know her. And as for the pure and innocent thing, well, she wasn't all that either. He couldn't have known that, though.

Heck, if not for Harley Hoover, the famous stop-smoking hypnotist, I would have never known either.

***

Might not be the perfect place to tell you, but I didn't end up being the oldest virgin in virgin history after all. Two weeks before to the day, Darla phoned me and asked if I wanted to come over. Her parents were going to be out for a few hours, gone to see this Harley guy. For 300 bucks, Harley promised to be able to get anyone to kick their smoking habit. Her mom, behind her apron and glasses and pies and Peter Pan haircut, was a chimney.

Darla's parents didn't have to be away for me to want to come see her. I always wanted to see her and was beginning to think I would need a hypnotist to ever cure me of her. She was one of my better habits, much better than chewing my fingernails or popping my knuckles, but my folks were going to hate the phone bills at school.

"Pete Rose," I said, locking my fingers behind my head.

"And then who?" Mr. Simpleton asked. We were waiting in the living room for Mrs. Simpleton and Darla. I was also learning that much of a guy's life was spent waiting on girls.

"Garry Maddox."

"And then?"

"Jeez. Playing third and batting clean-up, Mike Schmidt."

"Golleee!"

Mr. Simpleton was a sports nut. He was round and lumpy, like a catcher's mitt, and more inviting than a hunk of apple cobbler. We became tight in a flash, probably because I could recite the starters of almost every major league team on request. Pitching rotations and key reserve players, too. I was telling him the lineup for the 1980 Philadelphia Phillies. I wasn't too wild about the Phils, but any baseball fan worth his stones could name the starting nines to the World Series champs, or at least the ones after wool knickers. It probably wasn't a marketable skill, but it seemed plenty for him.

"So who starts game one?" he asked, rubbing his hands together.

"Hmmm....," I said, pretending to be good and stumped.

"Steve Carlton."

"Man oh man!" he laughed, slapping his thigh. I leaned back in the recliner and grinned. I was pretty sure Steve Carlton was right. Not that it mattered. I could have said Mickey Mouse and he would have bought it.

I owned the guy.

"Samuel James Simpleton, get your hands off my sofa!" Mrs. Simpleton had entered the room, with Darla just behind in the shadows.

"Oh Susan," Mr. Simpleton groaned in a tired voice, like he'd heard it all before. His hands were dirty, but they were stained dirty, branded from working too many hours for not enough cash at Chino's Garage. He did move them, though.

Like I said earlier, when a lady or especially a mom used all three names, she wasn't horsing around. Only thing worse was when they called you 'mister.'

"Thank you, dear," she said warmly.

Mrs. Simpleton was like that, hot and cold. One minute she was cooking up Mr. Simpleton a good meal, the next hounding him to scrub off his plate. Darla said she was going through some major physical changes. Well, I was getting new hairs in weird places almost daily, and I didn't go around hollering at everyone. Anyhow, I couldn't figure the lady out.

"Now kids, we'll be home in two hours or so," Mrs. Simpleton said, throwing what looked like a suitcase around her shoulder. The older girls got, the bigger their purses.

"I dunno why I have to go," Mr. Simpleton muttered, prying himself from the recliner.

"For support, Sam, for support. Don't ya want me to stop smoking so you'll have me around for the next 30 years?"

He paused. Paused too long.

"Sam!"

"Oh, yes dear." I would have struggled with that one, too. Thirty years seemed like an awfully long time.

"Well good, then let's go." She opened the door and waited for him. He moped across the carpet, then whirled back to me and flung out a finger. "Quick, Carlton gets in trouble in the ninth. Who do ya call on?"

"C'mon," I said. "Tug McGraw."

"Geez Louise!" he hooted, slipping out the door. "This kid knows everything!"

Tell you the truth, I didn't know much about anything. I knew sports. I knew how to work dads, though moms were still a weakness. I knew about half of the state capitals and that if I went to the can after I ordered my food in a restaurant that about 93 percent of the time my meal would be there when I got back.

Oh, and I knew there was something different about Darla that night as she slid onto my lap after disappearing back into her room. It wasn't so much in her red dress or in her slow walk or in her soft cuddle up to me, though all were kind of too girlish for her.

It was in her eyes.

"Hello there," she purred, pulling closer.

"Hi there. So did ya..."

For once, she didn't feel like talking. She began to kiss me, a series of short pecks that sounding like smacking food. Then she went to work. She hit the neck and made her way up to my ears, along my cheek and back to my lips. We broke into a long, sloppy one, the kind that made you gasp for air through your nose while you rocked your head a little for effect. Big kisses were hard work.

Then she pulled away, wiped her mouth and looked me dead in the eye. "Jasper, I want you." I waited for the rest.

"I want you," she repeated. With that, she let a strap of her skimpy dress fall from her left shoulder. Like I said, the dress wasn't all that new. The skimpy part was.

I'd heard those words, and only those words, just once before. Just a few months back no less. But Mandy had slurred them. These were clear, and, after letting them register, their meaning was even clearer.

Darla wanted *me*. Period.

I did what any fan of old movies would have done. I picked her up and carried her to the bedroom. By now, you might have guessed that I watched my share of tube. I'm not ashamed to admit it. Okay, it was strange that we sat like eggheads in front of a box and watched all these people living these adventurous, exciting lives, but it sped up the slowness of real life.

I loved black-and-white flicks and especially the Bogart guy. I wanted to be black and white and to sport one of those cool chin dents like Joe DiMaggio. Anyway, I figured if that beanpole Jimmy Stewart could do it, toss a girl up into his arms and all, well, then I could, too.

We didn't stop at her bedroom door, but I will. Out of respect and all. But let me just report that, for a rookie, I wasn't half bad. And knowing all those baseball lineups came in handy, too. I made it through the entire American League West and part of the National League East before my time came. Distractions and all.

There were no candles or bubbles or sexy gowns, just a couple of kids in love. Between the squeaks and the moans and the fumbles, I could hear Hall and Oates singing away in the background. I figured if "Private Eye" was going to be our song, I'd better at least learn who was who.

Afterward, we said nothing for the longest time. Her head rested on my chest, and I twirled her hair and tapped my foot on the headboard to the beat of "Maneater." I wasn't sure what to do next. I knew people were known to smoke after sex, but, considering the circumstances, I thought it would have been inappropriate. For one, neither of us smoked. But more than that, it would have been a slap to Harley Hooper, the great stop-smoking-for-300-bucks hypnotist.

After all, the guy had kind of turned out to be our pimp.

"Jasper Schitt, I hope this lasts forever," she said finally.

I kissed her forehead. It was my way of agreeing.

After that, we didn't go crazy over sex like goats, like my friend Chuck and his girl Maria. They went at it every day and night and sometimes even had each other for breakfast. Once, I crossed paths with them in the school parking lot after lunch.

"So where'd y'all go?" I asked them, already knowing it had been to the nearest side street they could find.

"Oh, ya know." He broke into a wide, shit-eating grin. I didn't have the heart to tell him that his teeth had hair. As in Maria's hair. As in, well, you know. They pulled away, laughing and latching onto each other's belt loops. Sex probably didn't stack up very well on the food pyramid, but it did wonders for their moods.

As for Darla and me, our first time was our only time, and it was the last big first we ever shared.

***

My mom and dad had kicked their smoking habits cold turkey, and Harley might have been worth the dough, but he couldn't beat a family tragedy. Mrs. Simpleton gave up smoking for a week but had started up again. I could smell it in her hair, which was just one row ahead and mostly blocking my view at the priest. She was a mess, and Mr. Simpleton was even worse. Darla was an only child and a daddy's girl at that. Together, they shook and sniffled, not making much noise but clearly hurting real bad inside.

The priest finally closed up shop. "So in conclusion, I believe it's clear to see that Darla is someone who will be dearly missed. Dearly missed indeed." He crinkled his cheat sheets and bowed his head.

"Now, let us pray."

He started up on some prayer. I had all the regular ones memorized, along with the right times to stand and kneel and sit and bow and shake and eat and drink and walk. We Catholics were easily the fittest religious people around.

Anyway, I tuned him out and said my own.

"Amen," he said.

"Amen," returned the crowd.

"Now, would anyone like to say a few words?"

I had more than a few. Most of them were scribbled on notebook paper and wadded in a Dallas Mavericks trash can in my bedroom. But late the night before, I finally jotted them on the back of a Government II test, which was now clenched in my shaking, sweaty hand. I guess it was the Cliff's Notes version of my feelings for Darla.

I raised my left hand and stood up slowly. I could feel every head in the place rotate my way. Immediately, I wanted to plop back down, to say that I was just goofing around. But it wasn't a callbacks type of thing. Besides, I'd let too many things in life pass me by already. If I could keep my legs, this wouldn't be another one.

Like I've told you, except for a grade, I wasn't much for public speaking. And though I'd made speeches about dead people - Lou Gehrig, Babe Ruth, well, several of the dead Yankees from the early century - it was my first about a dead person right in front of me. I felt like puking again, if you want to know the plain truth.

I set the paper on the podium, cleared my throat and almost started telling everyone how some guy named Dewey was president once but really wasn't. Then I turned the test paper over and cleared my throat again.

"Um, I just wanted to say what Darla meant to me," I began, my voice so soft that, even with the mike, I wasn't even sure what I'd said. I took a deep breath and felt a sudden strength, an instant calm. My left eye, always the left, stopped twitching. I could do it. I'd just never tried.

"She was, um, she was a cold-cut special at Swanson's. She was, um, a soft hand in a dark theater. She was a smiling clown and a curious child. She was a teacher. She was a student. She was the last piece in an impossible puzzle. She was....she was...."

I bit my lip. I could do it.

I wanted to do it.

"She was that wildflower you never stopped to smell. She was the diamond that always got passed over. She was everything that is good but nothing that is popular. She was a whisper in my ear and a song inside my head. She was the way things should be. To me, well...to me she was God's perfect little angel."

It didn't rhyme, mostly because I couldn't think of anything decent to rhyme with "popular" or 'puzzle,' and it didn't even make that much sense, except to me. But it was from the heart.

It was my obituary.

I was done, but frozen solid. So I bowed my head and pretended to pray, wondering the whole time how I could pass Darla's coffin without falling apart. I let myself look up a little. In the right corner, just past a blubbering Amy Huckabay, was a chiseled statue of a man holding a container of some sort. I figured it was St. Anthony, seeing as it was his joint and all. Dad said he was the saint in charge of lost stuff, the guy you prayed to when you wanted to find something. Well, I figured asking him for life's answers was a little much, but I did put in a quick request for a little get up and go.

It worked. I made it down the three marble steps without folding and headed toward my seat. On the way, I caught Mr. Simpleton's eye. He nodded. Mrs. Simpleton gave me a tiny smile and leaned her head against her husband's shoulder. It was better than a standing ovation.

"Why thank you, son," the priest said. "Now, Darla will be laid to her final rest at the Maple Tree Cemetery in 30 minutes. For those of you who can't join us, go in peace, to love and to serve the Lord."

And just like that, it was over. Fifteen minutes, give or take. My grandpa's had been much longer, but he was past 80 when he died. He'd earned the unabridged version.

"That was a nice thing, son." It was Dad, his hand on my shoulder. I nodded.

"Just beautiful," Mom whispered. I wasn't really looking for a good review, but it was nice all the same.

"We should get goin,'" Dad said. "Ready?" He was one of those early people. When we had a flight to catch, we always left for the airport like three days before take-off.

I shook my head. I wasn't ready at all.

"But how will you get over to the cemetery?" Mom asked.

I shrugged.

"But you have to..."

"C'mon Katherine, he'll find a way," Dad said.

I sat there as the church emptied out, my chin tucked tight to my chest as the click of shoes and swish of slacks echoed off the walls. A few minutes later, I heard Darla's dad and uncles and cousins struggle past with her coffin. Mr. Simpleton had asked me to be a pallbearer, but I couldn't do it. I just couldn't. And I had no intention of going to that cemetery, either. My last vision of Darla wouldn't be of a guy in a purple robe tossing dirt over her with a little shovel bought from Worthing's Hardware. It just wouldn't.

Besides, I'd already said my goodbyes.

***

The night before, after driving nowhere special for two hours and letting the place clear, I slipped back into the funeral parlor. It was way past visiting hours, or whatever they were called, but the place wasn't exactly Fort Knox.

The door was unlocked, and in the side room Darla's casket was still sitting right there on the marble block, under a yellow light. A few flower arrangements were leaning against the block. Nothing fancy, but they smelled nice.

Just like her.

I tried a couple of different approaches. Standing above her, Darla looked so plastic and, well, so gone. Kneeling beside her, she seemed too close, too real. Her face wasn't bruised or marked up, but it was still too much to deal with. Plus, her photo was staring right at me. So I leaned up against the coffin, grabbed her cold, rubbery hand and just started talking.

Talked to her about I don't know what. About everything and about nothing. It was strange and wonderful and stupid and sad all at the same time, a kid babbling away at the only person he really knew how to talk to, even if it was a dead person.

I ran out of words and crouched down, resting my butt against my heels. A portrait of Jesus was hanging above the coffin. His hands were open and reaching toward the ground, like he was feeding pigeons in a park, and his long hair and beard reminded me of my brother Simon's look back in the seventies.

Sooner or later, all the hairstyles came back around.

I'd thought a lot about God since Darla's wreck. I believed in Him because my parents believed in Him, went to church because my parents went, prayed at dinner because that was just what we did. I figured that my parents did all that because their own parents had. I had a few friends who didn't believe at all and who never went to church for one basic reason - because their folks didn't.

When I was little, I thought that God and Santa Claus were just alike. You couldn't see either one of them, but you still needed to be good, just in case. But even though the whole Santa gig was up - it's a long, tragic story for another book - I'd come to believe that I could see God just by watching my folks.

So religion, at least in my eyes, was one of those hereditary things, like big noses and goofy last names.

Anyway, I was glad they'd set the example. Stuff like teaching kids to wipe their feet at the front door was fine and all, but it didn't exactly help you lead a better life. I didn't understand the deep stuff, didn't speak a lick of Latin and would never be one of those raging lunatics on Sunday morning television, but I tried to follow the big rules and to pray a little every day. It didn't always work out that way, just like a guy couldn't be expected to floss every single day, but I still hoped to get a ticket up.

As for Darla, I knew she was already leaning back on her elbows in her flowery dress, chewing on a piece of grass and wondering where in the heck she could get a good sub sandwich. Plus, she could sing all she wanted to up there; those sweet-sounding angels would help drown her out.

Still, I couldn't help but be a little pissed at Him. I mean, I knew He had a plan for everyone, but I thought He'd gotten careless when He'd penciled in Darla's. Know how you started off a letter all nice and neat and ended up with chicken scratch by the end? Well, that kind of thing. Only instead of ending it with "sorry so sloppy," He had just snapped her away. Later. Adios.

I turned away from the portrait. It was tough thinking bad thoughts about someone who could read your mind and zap you in a second. I knew nothing could last forever, I did. I mean, even David Lee Roth was leaving Van Halen. I knew that life wasn't permanent, but I'd hoped for a longer temporary for Darla and me, or at least more than two months and 27 days.

Before I left the funeral home, I slid my senior ring onto Darla's finger. I knew I wouldn't need it anymore because, except for the junior college leeches that prowled the Picadilly parking lot after the seventh-hour bell, senior rings pretty much went out of style the day after graduation. I wasn't sure what I wanted the gesture to mean.

I was 18 years old. It didn't have to mean anything. It just felt like the right thing to do.

***

“Been eight years ago to the day since I lost my sweet Charlotte." An old man had taken a knee beside me in the St. Anthony's back chapel. It was probably an hour after the service. I'd been too busy hurting to notice.

"Um, oh, excuse me?" I scooted over, out of politeness and all. Plus, the guy reeked.

The man tilted his head toward me slightly but continued to look straight into the burning candles before us. He held a brown hat in his left hand, the kind they wore on the old detective shows, and he smelled like a combination of Brut and Budweiser. "I said eight years ago to the day, I lost my wife."

"Oh…I'm sorry to hear that, sir," I said.

"Oh don't be sorry, son." He turned toward me. His white whiskers glistened in the crooked sunlight that angled through the stained glass, and his skin was red and rough. His outfit – a ragged green-and-yellow checkered sports coat, white T-shirt and brown jeans – was straight out of a Goodwill catalog. "She died all right, died right in my arms, but she didn't leave, not really."

"Excuse me? I said. Oh no, I thought, here we go.

"See son, she's right here." He thumped his chest twice.

I peeked over with one eye. His shaky hand was covered with those old people spots, and his fingers were spread clear across his heart.

"See, whenever I need her, son, she's right here." He thumped again. "I get dressed up and come here every August 21, because this here is the very spot where we got hitched in nineteen and forty-four. Prettiest bride you ever saw, too. But I don't need a church, and I don't need a cemetery. My sweet Charlotte is with me wherever I go, whenever I need her."

I angled a bit toward him. "But it's still not the same."

"Nope, reckon it ain't the same. But the way I figure, I'm darn lucky to've known the girl at all."

He winked. Then he did something real strange. He put both hands on my shoulders and pulled me real close. And I let him. He leaned toward my right ear and whispered,

"Darn lucky to have known the girl at all."

With that, he hoisted himself off the kneeler, using my shoulder as a crutch, and pulled on his hat. He tipped it, waddled to the double doors and leaned against them, vanishing behind a burst of sunlight and a rush of hot air.

I wasn't sure if I believed in miracles. I wasn't sure that I didn't either. But I felt better, like I'd, well, just finished a good meal. I said a quick apology to God. Strange as it sounds, even though the Big Guy had a heck of a lot of ground to cover, I sort of believed He'd taken a minute to stop on by. Then, on the way out, I lit three candles - one for Darla, one for Charlotte and one for Saint Budweiser.

***

I had about a two-mile hike ahead of me, but I felt like walking. It seemed a good way to see Midtex up close one last time. I was leaving for school in three days, leaving and except for holiday breaks probably never coming back, not for keeps anyway. Some people grew up and grew old in Midtex, but I wouldn't be one of them. If I was going to be young and poor and confused, I intended to do it someplace with a lot better view.

Down the street from the church, in the playground for St. Anthony's Catholic School, three girls were playing hopscotch. The two older ones skipped through the course with ease; the younger one, a white-haired, bow-legged girl, did not. She would hop a couple of times, get crossed up or lose her balance and have to start all over again.

Three straight times, she loused it up. Finally, on her fourth try, she slowed down and got it right.

The next morning, I was about ready to roll. The clothes were packed, the posters rolled, the books stacked. Seemed funny that my life could be whittled down to six boxes, a set of golf clubs and a garbage sack full of shoes, or that 18 years could fit into a hatchback.

But except for a bunch of old trophies and some outdated clothes that were headed for the attic, that was about it. I plucked a pair of acid wash jeans and a jacket from the discard pile. A guy could never have too much acid wash, but the Members Only jacket had seen its day.

"Sure you don't need any help?" It was Mom, who over the past two days had asked me that very question at least 37 times. It was okay. I knew I'd miss her the very first time my clothes hamper was full. Maybe even before then, for reasons that had nothing to do with racing stripes and underwear.

"Naw, I'm fine, Mom," I returned. She shrugged, took a quick peek around the room and left. Just itching to roll in her sewing machine and make a shoal.

I plopped on my old bed, which was bare to the mattress. It had seen its share of sheets, from the American Bicentennial jobs to the NFL ones to the cowboy theme to the soft white ones that were stuffed in the 'DORM ROOM' box. I knew the bed would be blanketed with girlie sheets, probably tulips or violets, by the time I came home for Thanksgiving. It wasn't my decision, not anymore. Come to think of it, though, none of them had been. Sheets were a mom thing, no matter when, no matter what.

I wondered what would happen to my folks. Because I'd been such a late comer, they'd had kids ripping through and roaming around the house for like 30 straight years. Four boys at that, none of them especially cut out for the choir. John, Matt and Simon had all been altar boys at one point or another, but they got booted for drinking holy wine in the dressing room. If you want to get all symbolic, they were chugging down the blood of Christ, which was really pretty nasty. Still, I didn't see why it was such a big deal. From what I knew of the Bible, Jesus seemed like a pretty big wino.

My brothers, by the way, had changed in my eyes over the years. When I was real little, I just used them for a few laughs. Free tickles and piggyback rides and stuff. They were my personal clowns. Then they figured out it could work both ways, and they started bossing me around to go fetch their smokes and fix them sandwiches and junk. Tried to make a game out of it, but I knew what was up. I was their slave. Then for the longest time, after we moved down to Texas, the guys were just crackly voices over the phone a couple of times a month. Strangers.

But the past few times we'd all gotten together had been, well, different. They talked to me instead of talking at me, asked me questions instead of just telling me stuff. And Simon, who had finally moved his girlfriend Jan down and gotten hitched and started his own pack by stewing up a couple of girls, sometimes even showed up on goulash or pepper steak nights. I was their kid brother, sure, always would be, but that didn't mean we couldn't be friends.

As for my folks, I figured things wouldn't change that much around the house. Most of the time, I just came home from school or practice and disappeared into my room to yap on the phone anyhow. Mom always said I was going to grow cauliflower out of my ears or something, whatever the heck that meant. At least at college when we talked we'd have something to talk about.

Dad was set to retire in a few years, and he could devote his time to golf and woodwork. In other words, to hacking away in one way or another. Mom would stay busy with cooking and cleaning and sewing and shopping and worrying. Those were just some of her many jobs, and she would never retire.

***

San Marcos was about a six-hour drive, but I was in no big hurry. I wasn't sure why I'd even decided to go there in the first place, except that I heard that the town was pretty and the girls were prettier. At the time, it seemed like enough. But I still doubted if any of them smelled like a field of flowers without even trying.

It had only been three days since the funeral. Three days wasn't enough to feel much better. Falling in love with Darla had been a snap, but falling out of love with her was going to be tricky. I was eating and sleeping again, but I knew it would take more than some slices of pizza and a few decent nights of rest to feel human again. It would take time, so they said. I was never really sure who 'they' were, but 'they' sure pretended to know it all.

I didn't quite feel like leaving. Under my elbow, in the box marked 'BOOKS & CRAP,' was my 1986 Picadilly High School annual. It had a montage of pictures on the cover, including one of Mike sticking his tongue out at the camera at one of the pep rallies. I wondered if anyone else knew that our salutatorian - he finished a close second to a tall girl I had never seen - was maybe the only guy in town that could tell you the abbreviations of every element on the periodic chart while doing a handstand on a keg. Both would probably come in handy in college.

The chemistry stuff would make him rich someday; the keg thing would get him laid.

I began to flip through the thing, just for old time's sake and all. The first few pages were filled with signatures, mostly from people I would never see or talk to again. "I can't believe we finally made it!" wrote Tamara. "It was fun having ya in science, and I hope to see ya lots and lots this summer!" I couldn't remember ever knowing a Tamara, but I was pretty sure I hadn't seen her all summer, and I was positive she hadn't helped me one bit in science.

"Let's hang out before we bolt for school! Later!" That was Kurt's scratch. I'd known him for six years, and that's all he came up with. Kurt was always more of talker than a writer anyway. He was heading off to a small college in a week or so and was going to try and play football. I wondered if Angelo Tech had room for a 170-pound linebacker. Bingham had, and so had Picadilly. If they didn't watch it, he'd talk his way into the mix there, too. I also wondered for his sake if they offered a BS in BS.

Danny left another scribbled, almost unreadable, two-sentence guy message. We'd stayed tight over the years, Danny and me. He still had a year of high school left, but he'd grown much bigger and faster and stronger than me, and colleges were already hounding him to come play ball for them. We never hung out much during the school years, seeing as a senior couldn't much run around with a bunch of juniors without hearing about it, but the summers always brought us back together.

No matter the season, he was still like a brother to me, always would be. And it would get better over time, like an old mitt. I didn't have to see him or even talk to him much to know that.

And so it went, all the signatures of my friends and nonfriends jammed into five pages or so. Girls were especially crazy about signing. One girl I dated my junior year, Jamie Ann Blanks, practically tackled me in the parking lot so we could swap annuals. Triple-name girls were always ones to watch out for. I didn't know what to write. I thought about going with, "Remember that time when we were goin' out and you disappeared out at Ponderosa and I found ya blowin' Coop Littleton in the back seat of my car? That was a blast! See ya this summer!" But I settled on, "Good luck at Tech. Bye, Jasper."

Shelby Warren had signed her name and little else. I went to Senior Prom with Shelby, a last-minute thing with a girl I barely knew. Rented a tux, washed my car, opened the door for her, the works. But I couldn't get dinner reservations for any place that used real silverware, so we ended up eating at Roscoe's Wing and Things over on the west side. Here's a free tip - never take a girl in a white prom dress to a barbecue joint.

Anyway, I thought the whole signing thing was bizarre.

Then again, so was high school.

I turned to our grade. Seniors got the big color photos, but we also got the trees. Seemed like every photographer in town went nuts over the things. There was Ben Binford, leaning against a tree. And Angie Aimley, hugging a tree. And Mark Cameron, hanging upside down from a tree. No joke, in his tux jacket and jeans and cowboy boots and everything. And yep, there was me, spiked hair and all, making good with a tree. Some people went with the bookshelf thing, but overall you would have thought we were a bunch of lumberjacks.

I flipped through my class. Margaret Blanton, a pale brunette with a flat nose, was going to Princeton. Allison Craig, a sizzling blonde with a toothpaste commercial smile, was headed to beautician school at Midtex Junior College. Marty Colletti, a guy who hadn't spoken in years, was going to Stanford with high honors. Mike Dobbins, a face guy who never shut up, was going to welding school with a reportedly runaway case of herpes. I sensed a pattern. The stuff we had believed to be important was about to become very unimportant.

I found the index. You could judge someone's popularity by the amount of page numbers beside their name. Amber Brennan, our homecoming queen, needed three extra lines. She was probably still seeing spots from all the pictures she'd taken. I had a couple of numbers that led to my baseball and basketball team photos. I hoped my tube sock days were over.

Darla was on page 119, down at the lower right. One picture, that was all. No clubs, no crowns, no "Most Likely To Do or Be or Start or Make" anything. Just her and the same dumb tree. I swear I saw her roll her eyes. I laughed a little and set the annual back, stuffing a decade or so of friends and memories, good and bad, into an old popcorn popper box.

Of the 2,000 kids at Picadilly, many of whom I'd practically grown up with, I didn't know any of them better than Darla Simpleton.

It was one of those quality over quantity things.

I took down my Honor Society certificate, which was stuffed in a cheap frame and hanging crooked above my bed. Somehow, with a lot of memorizing, a little learning, plenty of cramming and the occasional-but-ever-tricky test swap, I managed to sneak into the top 10 percent of our class of 700. Then again, a trained animal, or at least a chimp actor or maybe Flipper, could have landed in the top half. Picadilly was a good place full of teachers who cared and maybe even cared if we cared, but it was no think tank.

I promised my parents that I would write and gave them both a hug. Mom started bawling and pulled me close, getting lipstick all over my neck. I didn't mind. Shoot, it was a bargain for 18 years of service. Dad and I did the basic back-patting bit that guys did when they hugged. But we didn't clobber each other or anything, just a few light raps. That was the thing with guys and hugs; the softer you slugged, the more you cared.

Side by side, they stood in the shadow of the garage as I climbed in the car. I knew that no matter how old I got, or how old they got, they'd always be waiting there for me, if only in the shadows. I hit reverse, stopped to wave and pulled away from 4616 Ridgewood Road, from the only house and bed and life I could really remember anymore.

I wound around Loop 337 and passed the city limit sign. Even though I would never again live in Midtex, I also hoped to never call one of those traffic jam cities home. Big cities, they were too much like playing Frogger. I watched the miniature skyline fade in my rear view mirror. Sometimes I still saw those guys in suits hustling around in the shadows of the taller buildings. Still had absolutely no idea what they did.

I felt a lump in my throat. I loved that I was leaving but hated to go.

***

I didn't make it through two songs before realizing that the directions to San Marcos were still on the kitchen table, right next to the 40 bucks my parents had given me for the trip. I got one of those sharp pains in my stomach, like I'd swallowed a brick.

On my own for five miles and already lost and busted.

Thought I'd just wing it. Bad thought. It took me less than a half hour to lose my way. I made it just fine to Gordon City, about 20 miles from Midtex, before hitting a fork in the road. I knew San Marcos was east, but two of the four road signs were pointing off to the east. They would both send me in the right general direction, but you didn't want to get lost in Texas. One wrong turn could land you in a day's worth of cow dung. A double-wide truck with six fat tires honked behind me. I pulled over, cussing both my memory and trucks with training wheels.

There was a service station to the left, but the two guys in uniform were flipping washers by the side of the garage. There were a few flat-out rules to live by in Texas, and one was to never bust up a game of washers in a one-stoplight town. I remembered seeing a map under my seat. I dug for it and came up with about three years of stuff, the product of too many nights out and not enough vacuuming. There was a ticket stub from a football game and an empty beer can from halftime of the same game. A baseball that had been rolling around for months. About four toothpicks, 70 cents worth of change and one tennis shoe. So that's where it went, I thought as I took another stab.

I found the map and opened it. Some more coins dropped, along with a faded receipt from Burrito Barn. So did my stomach when three candy hearts fell out. They were faded, two yellows and a pink. The yellows each said "True Love." The pink one was cracked in half. In white letters, it said only "Bye."

It gave me a chill, like I wasn't alone in the car. And chills were in short supply in Midtex on an August afternoon. And for whatever reason, I got this feeling that Highway 111, the sign on the left, was the one to follow. No kidding. "Let's let fate decide," I heard Darla's voice echo in my mind. What do you know, I thought, she's leading my way.

Still, I checked the map, fate not knowing or caring that I had to check into my dorm by no later than seven o'clock.

We were wrong. Unless I wanted to go to Mexico, Highway 87, the sign on the right, was the one to obey. Having squeaked through two semesters of Spanish by the skin of my *dientes*, I turned up the radio and steered right. About a mile or so later, the truck bounced into the left lane, hit the gas and sped around me. A black sports car with those bubbly tinted windows did the same. I knew there would always be faster cars and fatter tires, plus plenty of forks and curves and crossroads.

But slowly, maybe even surely, I hoped to find my way.

I rolled the hearts in my hand like dice. Okay, so they weren't magic. All the same, I tucked them in my pocket, knowing they'd be there whenever I needed them.

A few miles later, I got stuck behind this rusty pick-up truck. The guy driving had a straw cowboy hat that was sitting crooked on his head, which meant big trouble. Anytime you got behind an old guy in an old pick-up with a crooked cowboy hat on a two-lane road in Texas, you'd better have some time to burn. Only thing slower was getting wedged behind a house on wheels, one of those wide-load jobs that needed a baby truck with flashing lights behind it so you wouldn't go driving through its living room.

So I eased the seat back a tad and lived with 50 an hour for a while. I looked in the mirror and, maybe for the first time ever, wasn't so put out by the reflection looking back. And he didn't remind me of anyone. Just me, Jasper, Jasper Schitt. I was kind of looking forward to getting to know the guy.

Alongside me, a tumbleweed made its way through the yellow pasture. The prickly things had gotten a little smaller as I'd gotten bigger, but they still had the run of the place. It blew to the right, straightened out, then drifted left and whipped sideways toward my car. All of a sudden, it hopped up, spun across the hood and disappeared, off to the next thing.

A guy just never knew about those damn tumbleweeds.

ABOUT THE AUTHOR

Jeff Mudd is a Texas-based author known for writing character-driven stories that blend humor, nostalgia, and heart. A West Texas native now living outside of Austin, he draws from everyday moments, familiar places, and the people who make them matter. His work often centers on simple lives that aren't so simple when you take the time to look a little closer.

Before becoming a full-time storyteller, Jeff spent over two decades as a personal trainer and several years as a sportswriter, experiences that continue to shape the rhythm and perspective of his writing. He has published multiple books across a range of styles, all grounded in a distinct voice that values honesty, observation, and a well-timed line that sounds like something someone might actually say.

Jeff is the proud father of three—McKenzie, McCoy, and Mitch—who continue to inspire much of what he writes. His books are available on Amazon and at MuddBooks.com, where readers can find his full catalog and follow along as he continues telling stories from Texas and beyond.

www.ingramcontent.com/pod-product-compliance
Lightning Source LLC
LaVergne TN
LVHW010557100826
845148LV00014B/2745
9780967918402